William D. Frazier

William D. Frazier

William D. Frazier

CONTENTS

COPYRIGHT vi
DEDICATION vii
PREFACE ix
INTRODUCTION xv

1　Crafting a Shared Vision for Tomorrow　1
2　Bridging Black Innovation and China　28
3　The Loom of Displacement and Defiance　57
4　Embracing Productive Discomfort　91
5　Reciprocal Alliances for Equity　122
6　Cultural Narratives in Global Commerce　157
7　Mastering Unspoken Business Rituals　193
8　Art as Cross-Cultural Catalyst　224
9　Legacies of Interconnected Resilience　238
10　Bridging Cultures, Building Trust　261

CONCLUSION 292
AUTHOR'S BIOGRAPHY 295

COPYRIGHT

Copyright © 2025 by William D. Frazier and Shanghai-America Direct Import & Export Co., Ltd.

Copyright Notice: All rights reserved. No part of this book may be reproduced by any mechanical, photographic, or electronic process, or in the form of a phonographic recording. Nor may it be stored in a retrieval system, transmitted, or otherwise be copied for public or private use other than for fair use as brief quotations embodied in articles and reviews without prior written permission of the publisher.

Disclaimer: This memoir presents the author's journey in bridging global trade and cultural exchange in and with China. While the author and publisher have endeavored to provide accurate and informative content, this book is intended for general informational purposes. Readers should undertake their own due diligence and consult specialized sources before making decisions based on the information presented herein. The author and publisher disclaim liability for any specific outcomes or actions taken by readers based on the content of this book.

William D. Frazier and Shanghai-America Direct Import & Export Co., Ltd (https://williamdfrazier.com)

DEDICATION

This book is dedicated to the pioneering Black entrepreneurs with vision and ingenuity who attained success with honorable business principles. The memory of their innovative ideas, still pursued by Black Americans today, serves as a testament to their original thinking and their vision. This vision extends nationally and internationally, foreseeing the transition of Black American culture and trade into the global economy.

It is also a tribute to the resilience of Black communities and their unwavering pursuit of equity and empowerment. Over the past two decades, I have witnessed firsthand the marginalization of Black Americans in global trade and the missed opportunities for cultural exchange and economic collaboration between Black America and China. This book is my response to that dissonance, serving as a memoir, manifesto, and blueprint for cross-cultural engagement.

I dedicate this work to the Black American entrepreneurs, educators, and artists who have dared to venture beyond familiar borders and into the heart of China's dynamic economy. Your courage and ingenuity have laid the foundation for a new era of Black global citizenship. To the Chinese partners, manufacturers, friends, families, and cultural mediators who have welcomed me with open arms and shared their wisdom and resources, I am deeply grateful. Your trust and collaboration have transformed my journey from isolation to a sense of belonging.

This book is also dedicated to the memory of my ancestors, whose legacy of resistance and creativity fuels my commitment to equity. To the future generations of Black Americans, may this book inspire you to see yourselves not just as participants in globalization but as architects of its evolution. The road ahead is fraught with challenges, but it is also paved with possibilities. By embracing our interconnectedness and leveraging our cultural strengths, we can forge a more inclusive and prosperous future.

I am indebted to the Black American community in China, whose stories and struggles have shaped this narrative. Your resilience and creativity remind me that liberation is not a distant dream but a path we walk together. To the Black American Chamber of Commerce and all organizations supporting Black businesses: your advocacy and vision are crucial to our collective progress. May this book catalyze deeper engagement and broader opportunities.

Finally, I dedicate this work to God, who has guided me through moments of doubt and celebration. May this book serve as a testament to the power of connection and a call to action for a more just and equitable world. The journey of Black Americans in China is not a footnote in history, but a vibrant chapter in the ongoing story of global collaboration and cultural exchange. Let us move forward with purpose and courage, building bridges where barriers once stood and creating a legacy of shared prosperity and dignity.

This dedication is now polished, emotionally resonant, and structurally sound, ready to honor all its intended recipients.

PREFACE

Alright, let's cut straight to the heart of this. You're holding this book because something resonates with you. Maybe it's frustration. Perhaps it's a spark of possibility you can't quite shake. Whatever it is, welcome. I'm talking directly to you. The visionary, the builder, the one tired of hitting the same walls. This isn't just another business book. It's a blueprint for a fundamental shift. A shift in how we, as Black America, engage with one of the single most dynamic economic and cultural forces of our time. Mainland China.

For too long, we've been spectators on the global stage, watching opportunities flow elsewhere while our communities grapple with systemic hurdles. We discuss economic empowerment, closing the wealth gap, and building a generational legacy. But how often do we look beyond the familiar, usually limiting confines of the American system? How frequently do we question the very paths laid out for us, paths that sometimes seem designed to keep us dependent, disconnected, and perpetually playing catch-up?

That stops here. My journey, because it is the one that poured into these pages, forced me to confront a hard truth. We need to unlearn. Unlearn the outdated industrial models that chain us to intermediaries and markups. Unlearn the cultural narratives that suggest global engagement, particularly with China, is either too complex, out of reach, or somehow not for us. Unlearn the passive acceptance of an indifferent system.

But unlearning is only half the battle. The critical, exhilarating part is the relearning. Relearning how to position ourselves not just in the global marketplace, but strategically within it. Relearning how to cultivate relationships and access opportunities that operate powerfully, yet often invisibly, behind the scenes of China's vast manufacturing and social sectors. Let me be crystal clear about what strategic access means in this context. This isn't about shadowy dealings or bending China's public laws and regulations. Absolutely not. It's about developing the deep, practical knowledge and cultural fluency to navigate those laws and systems effectively. It's about learning the levers to pull, the relationships to build, and the strategies to employ within the existing framework to unlock doors currently closed to us.

Think of it as mastering the operating system, not hacking it. Why is this so crucial? Because we rely solely on traditional American supply chains, dominated by interests that don't prioritize our community's specific growth, it is a dead end. Imagine cutting out layers of cost and complexity by connecting directly with manufacturers in Guangdong Province (Guǎngdōng Shěng), or textile producers in Zhejiang Province (Zhèjiāng Shěng). Imagine sourcing products, securing services, and building networks without the friction and markups imposed by intermediaries who often don't understand or, frankly, don't care about our unique needs and aspirations. This direct connection provides access to transformative industrial and people-to-people opportunities. It's power. It's the difference between scraping by and scaling up.

My core vision is that the fire that fuels this book is this. The key to unlocking unprecedented Black American commerce, tradition, and global influence lies in cultivating strategic, on-the-ground network relationships with Mainland China. I know this perspective might ruffle feathers. Some might see it as unconventional, even controversial. But here's where my conviction comes from: years of observation, frustration, and, ultimately, boots-on-the-ground experience in both countries. Community engagement isn't an add-on. It's essential to building long-term, fruitful relationships in China, which isn't just about transactions.

It's about understanding values, building trust, and demonstrating genuine commitment. This is where we possess unique potential yet face a critical disadvantage. Look around. Other ethnic communities in America have established deep roots and sophisticated networks overseas, particularly in Asia. They have liaison offices, cultural exchange programs, and a history of established business relationships. Where is our sustainable, dedicated presence on the ground in Mainland China? We don't have it. Not really. And this absence isn't just an oversight. It's an active barrier holding us back. While others leverage global connections, we remain disproportionately reliant on domestic structures that have repeatedly failed to deliver equitable opportunities.

This lack of direct access cripples our growth. It limits our innovation. It keeps us confined. We need a mindset revolution. We need to shed the scarcity mentality and embrace the vast potential waiting across the Pacific. This revolution begins with unlearning limitations and relearning strategies for connection. And the cornerstone of this new approach? A permanent, Black-led liaison organization embedded within Mainland China. Think about the power of that. An organization on the ground that does the heavy lifting by streamlining access.

An organization on the ground that does the heavy lifting, streamlining access, cutting through red tape, and connecting Black entrepreneurs directly with reliable suppliers, manufacturers, and distributors across diverse Chinese industries. An organization on the ground that facilitates cultural exchange. An institution that moves beyond tourism to deep, meaningful exchanges. This includes educational programs, artistic collaborations, and shared technological development, which can all contribute to building mutual understanding and respect.

A source that accesses primary resources, secondary manufacturing capabilities, tertiary distribution networks, and projects that are packed with cooperative potential that others might miss. An institution that builds strategic partnerships, fostering genuine, long-term relationships between Black American businesses/communities and their Chinese partners, based on shared interests and mutual benefit.

The value of this type of organization is immense. This isn't just about individual business deals, though those are vital. This is about systemic community uplift. Imagine Black-owned businesses thriving, expanding into global markets, and creating jobs for Black American communities, thanks to their efficient and cost-effective supply chains. Imagine the economic ripple effect of our dollars circulating within our neighborhoods at the local, state, and national levels, reducing disparities not through charity but through empowered commerce.

Imagine the cultural enrichment, the exchange of ideas, and the technological advancements we could co-create. Even when we've spent too long focused inward. A focus that magnifies our domestic struggles and differences, while the world around us transforms. There are systemic barriers that are often perpetuated by racially biased gatekeepers in agencies and institutions that have expertly diverted our attention and resources. They dangle distractions, keep us focused on internal divisions, and subtly discourage the kind of global strategic thinking that threatens the status quo. The absence of a robust Black American presence in China is a glaring symptom of this diversion. It leaves us out of the loop, disadvantaged in critical industrial and cultural conversations.

A dedicated liaison organization operating with a sophisticated behind-the-scenes strategy is the antidote. It bridges the gap. It connects us to opportunities that align with our shared interests and values. This isn't about separating from our communities in America. It's about revolutionizing how we engage globally to strengthen our communities at home. It's about leveraging Chinese dynamism to fuel Black American prosperity and cultural vitality on our terms. This organization must be fundamentally different.

It cannot be born from the same lack of awareness that has stifled our growth. It must be intentional, strategic, and deeply knowledgeable. It must move beyond spontaneous, ad hoc connections to build sustained, essential exchanges. It would require practical skills, such as negotiation and cultural navigation, merged with thoughtful insights into both Black American aspirations and China's evolving landscape. Who would lead it? Black would pioneer it through thought leaders, entrepreneurs, innovators, and cultural ambassadors, as well as those with proven experience in and with China. An organization that actively highlights and leverages the invaluable, yet often overlooked, contributions of Black individuals already studying, living, and working successfully within China. Their experiences are a goldmine of insights for those of us back home.

Personal integrity must be its bedrock. Trust is the currency of strategic network success. Strategic partnerships between Black Americans and Chinese entities are most effective when founded on honesty, transparency, and a shared commitment to mutual success. This journey won't always be easy. There will be challenges, cultural misunderstandings to navigate, and inevitable setbacks. Yes, the potential rewards for our businesses, culture, and collective future are being significantly overlooked. We must intertwine Black America's industrial and cultural destiny with the immense possibilities of China's landscape. I am profoundly optimistic. Why?

Because I've seen glimpses of what's possible over the past two decades, opportunities for collaboration were often dismissed and then buried under myths that engaging with China was too tricky, irrelevant, or even harmful to Black America. That mindset is a trap we can no longer afford. Since 2000, immersing myself in China through educational study abroad programs in Beijing, bustling children's toy fairs in Guangzhou (Guǎngzhōu), film sets in Hainan, sporting events in Shanghai, and intimate social gatherings in various provinces has been an eye-opening experience.

These experiences shattered my own preconceptions and revealed a reality that specific industries and people-to-people exchanges, fueled by China's continued Open Door Policy, offer sustainable pathways. However, direct, unfiltered access remains a complex issue. We can't navigate it alone, and we certainly can't navigate it effectively without a dedicated presence. Therefore, Black America can no longer afford to ignore Mainland China. The cost of inaction is too high, encompassing continued economic marginalization, missed cultural synergies, and watching the future unfold without us. The time for tentative exploration is over.

We need a comprehensive strategy for full engagement. We need to secure our place in the global industrial and cultural currents flowing from China. This book is my contribution to that strategy. It's born from passion, forged in experience, and driven by an unwavering belief in our community's potential. It's a call to action, a challenge to the status quo, and a practical guide to navigating the behind-the-scenes pathways that lead to absolute power and partnership. My journey started there. I believe yours can, too.

Let's get to work. The future is waiting, and it's ours to build together, strategically, and with our eyes firmly on the global horizon. Turn the page. Let's begin.

THE AUTHOR
OCTOBER 1, 2025

INTRODUCTION

I arrived in Shanghai as a wide-eyed student in 2002, clutching two duffel bags, a laptop computer, and a mind buzzing with questions. The city's skyscrapers loomed before me, enveloped in a haze of smog and neon lights. It felt alien yet hauntingly familiar. Unlike the Black neighborhoods I'd left behind in America, Shanghai pulsed with a rhythm of explosive growth. But as I wandered its intricate street markets, an inescapable truth began to settle within me. Black America was absent from this narrative. That realization sparked a fire within me, shaping the next two decades of my life in China.

I now stand at the crossroads of two worlds. One rooted in the struggles and resilience of my community back home, the other brimming with the untapped potential of China's dynamic economy. This duality his defining my journey of resilience, commerce, and liberation, in a quest to bridge the gap between these worlds. I've realized that many in Black America remain unaware of the opportunities waiting beyond our borders, opportunities that could redefine our economic narrative. But bridging this gap requires more than ambition. It demands cultural fluency, strategic collaboration, and a willingness to confront the systemic barriers that have long kept us on the margins of global trade.

This memoir is my answer to that dissonance. It is a mosaic of stories, hard-won insights, and a vision for collective empowerment, forged through two decades of missteps and breakthroughs. It is a story of how Black America can claim its seat at the table of global commerce by starting with China. This is not just a story of commerce, but of identity, resilience, and the transformative power of cross-cultural connection.

In the early 2000s, Shanghai was a crucible of opportunity. Entrepreneurs hustled in shadowy alleyways, small business startups bloomed in cramped apartments, and expatriates from every corner of the globe exchanged ideas over steaming bowls of xiaolongbao (xiǎolóngbāo). Yet, amid this ferment, I sensed a void. The city's relentless energy felt like a spectacle we were not witnessing, a foundation we were not building upon. Our contributions seemed to be an afterthought in the city's skyline, unbothered and unrecognizable. Where were our stories and ambitions woven into China's growth narrative?

One afternoon, my eyes locked onto a bootleg DVD poster of the Tuskegee Airmen. That image of Black pilots defying gravity and prejudice struck me like a manifesto. "Teach them about us," I thought. If a poster in a back-alley shop could bridge divides, why couldn't commerce? Why couldn't education? Shanghai taught me that borders are porous, culture is currency, and every transaction is a chance to rewrite what people think they know.

As I navigated this labyrinth, I struggled to find my place. Language barriers and cultural nuances often left me feeling like an outsider. But in moments of connection, like sharing laughter over late-night eating vegetable dumplings (shū cài jiǎo zi◊ or debating globalization in cramped dorm rooms. I glimpsed a truth that our stories could be bridges, not barriers. Yet, back home, our focus often revolves around sports, music, politics, and the relentless fight for civil rights. While we celebrate athletes and artists who break barriers, these triumphs rarely translate into broader economic empowerment.

This disconnect gnaws at me. Strolling past vendors hawking knock-off sneakers, I couldn't ignore the irony that goods manufactured in China flooded Black neighborhoods in America, yet we remain consumers, not collaborators. Are we the engine of a demand that never circles back to build our own communities, while our economic power is being siphoned off rather than solidified? This one-sided dynamic felt like a modern form of an old, extractive pattern. This realization inspired my purpose to reframe how Black America engages, moving us from the periphery to the center of global economic conversations.

My first attempt to bridge this divide began in a Shanghai classroom as a part-time English lecturer. My students' eager shouts of "Teacher!" punctuated lessons that evolved into vibrant, two-way cultural exchanges. I introduced them to the poetry of Langston Hughes and the funky beats of James Brown, watching as new worlds flickered to life behind their eyes. And in turn, they taught me the strategic nuances of mahjong and the haunting melodies of Kunqu opera, patiently guiding me through the intricacies of their heritage. These exchanges were acts of cultural alchemy, transforming strangers into collaborators. We were no longer just a teacher and students, but friends building a shared understanding, one lesson at a time.

Through these interactions, I began to see my role not as a foreigner but as a bridge builder. When a shy student named Li Mei asked, "Why did you come here?" I shared my vision to connect my community with hers. Her eyes widened. "But how?" That "how" became my driving question. It pushed me to move beyond abstract ideas and seek tangible, human connections. I realized that our conversation isn't a coincidence, but an action that requires substance, effort, and a path for others to join. However, issues such as the scarcity of books on Sino-Black American trade and cultural exchange are problematic because of limited direct access. And by 2005, stumbling through Mandarin tones, haggling with local people, and navigating bureaucratic red tape. My role had shifted from student to advocate.

One sweltering evening, I vented my frustrations to a friend while enjoying a steaming bowl of Xiaolongbao (xiǎolóngbāo). "We're stuck in a feedback loop," I groaned. "No one goes abroad because there's minimal support, and there's minimal support because no one's gone abroad." This hide-and-seek dilemma has kept our community's international ambitions stifled for years. Her response was a shrug: "So build it." That offhand challenge ignited a spark, transforming my vague discontent into a concrete mission. I began conceptualizing a Black American Trade and Cultural Organization to connect our community with Chinese manufacturers, entrepreneurs, and educators.

This mission is audacious, weaving together economic empowerment with profound cultural exchange. It involves workshops on cross-cultural negotiation and exchange programs that showcase the fusion of Black America with China's innovation. These initiatives could be designed to build tangible bridges, moving beyond theory to create shared success. They can prove that collaboration across these distinct cultures can unlock unique market opportunities and foster mutual growth. Doubters could ask, "Why China?" while allies could emerge in unexpected places, like a Black-owned skincare brand partnering with a Guangzhou factory to develop products for melanin-rich skin. An HBCU could launch a study-abroad program with a Chinese university. Therefore, these would not be just isolated deals but part of a larger purpose, deliberately crafting a new tapestry of global partnership.

Even though the path has not been smooth, I encountered anti-Black microaggressions, from vendors who refused a fair price to taxi drivers taking deliberately long routes. These were not overt acts of hostility, but a constant, draining undercurrent of "othering" that required daily negotiation. Back home, friends warned me about geopolitical tensions, their fears amplified by media sensationalism. "Aren't you scared?" they'd press. Scared? No. Their apprehension, I realized, stemmed from a monolithic view of a region I was learning to understand in all its nuanced complexity. But I learned to navigate these complexities with my eyes wide open.

At a roundtable at Savannah State University (SSU), I argued, "Engaging with China isn't about ignoring its complexities. It's about navigating them." The room turned to dialogue as a Chinese professor admitted their struggles with Western stereotypes, and students shared strategies for navigating geopolitical realities. This mutual vulnerability transformed a debate into a genuine exchange. We moved from talking past one another to building a shared understanding, proving that direct engagement is the only way to bridge divides.

My vision has since manifested in ways I never imagined. I co-organized a Juneteenth celebration in Shanghai, where artists, musicians, and entrepreneurs from different districts mingled. What began as a simple idea quickly grew into a powerful convergence of cultures, filling a local venue with an energy that was both celebratory and deeply meaningful. Under the spotlights, participants shared triumphs and struggles, revealing our shared humanity. These raw, personal stories transformed the event from a celebration into a platform for genuine connection and understanding. The event became an annual event, with its focus expanding to trade partnerships, such as a potential collaboration between a Black personal-care product provider and a Chinese manufacturer.

Yet, this is only the beginning. We must build a sustainable framework for engagement that includes robust educational programs and supply chain networks. These initiatives should equip emerging leaders with the practical skills and global connections needed to succeed. Furthermore, by creating pipelines for diverse talent into international business, we could ensure that our economic and cultural institutions reflect the communities they serve. Through these efforts, we can begin to chip away at stereotypes and advance a narrative that recognizes Black Americans as essential players in international trade.

I believe that success in China demands more than business acumen. It requires navigating cultural nuances with intention. I've learned three key lessons. First, building strong relationships based on guanxi (guānxi) is far more valuable than pursuing immediate returns. Trust, not just transactions, drives long-term success. Next, leveraging shared cultural narratives can be more impactful than language fluency alone. By framing our discussions around universal themes like resilience and collective growth, we could turn cultural differences into bridges. Finally, adopting a nuanced "yes, but" approach in negotiations maintains harmony and fosters creative problem-solving, aligning with the indirect communication style prevalent here.

Therefore, in a world obsessed with instant results, true success lies in strategic patience. As a saying goes, "Here, I plant seeds with one hand while holding an umbrella with the other. The harvest comes, but only if I weather the storms." This philosophy champions steady, sustained work of nurturing growth while proactively managing risks. The most outstanding achievements are not seized in a moment but cultivated through consistent effort and resilience over time.

Even when the threat of isolation looms large in global trade, Black America's interactions with China have too often been marked by frustration and missed opportunities. Bridging this divide demands mutual respect, a shared understanding of history, and a commitment to common goals. This includes acknowledging both the historical solidarity during civil rights struggles and the complex economic realities of the present. By moving beyond transactional engagements to build genuine people-to-people and institutional connections, both communities can leverage their unique strengths to address shared global challenges like economic inequality and climate change.

This book is a call to view China not as a distant enigma, but as a land of possibility. The strategies within these pages aim for more than profit; they are about breaking a generational curse and creating a new foundation. They provide a roadmap for sustainable engagement, built on mutual respect and a deep understanding of the cultural currents that shape the market. This is not an endpoint, but a starting pistol. The race is toward a future of shared innovation and collective prosperity. It is a movement that transcends borders, industries, and generations.

Together, we can build a future where the question "Where do I belong?" is answered by the collective declaration, "We all belong." This begins with small, deliberate acts of inclusion in our schools, workplaces, and neighborhoods. By actively listening to one another and celebrating our unique backgrounds, we weave a stronger, more resilient community fabric. The power to make those futures real starts now.

1

Crafting a Shared Vision for Tomorrow

As Black America navigates the uncertainties and complexities of international relations, our commitment to dialogue, education, and collaboration will pave the way for future generations. Strengthening our economic standing and cultural presence in China is not just an opportunity but a responsibility. By approaching this endeavor with intention, we can cultivate meaningful connections, with each interaction providing an opportunity to redefine our relationship with the global marketplace. Together, we can build a sustainable framework for engagement that transcends borders and fosters a legacy of empowerment for Black Americans worldwide. In doing so, we can build a sustainable framework that must include robust educational programs, such as language training, cultural immersion, and negotiation workshops tailored to diverse market contexts, to equip individuals with the skills to thrive in international business. Equally vital are mentorship networks linking seasoned professionals with emerging entrepreneurs, ensuring our community is informed and supported on the path to economic independence.

Through these efforts, we reaffirm our influence by creating practices that promote equity and representation on the global stage. Every connection we forge chips away at stereotypes, advancing a narrative where Black Americans are recognized as essential players in international trade. We can leave an indelible mark with diligence and unity, creating pathways for future generations to confidently engage in an interconnected world. As a Black American student, entrepreneur, and expat in Shanghai since 2000, I have confronted life's challenges abroad while seizing opportunities to elevate our economic and cultural footprint in China. Each day presented a chance to build bridges, and I understood the weight of those moments. In Shanghai's bustling streets, every conversation carried the potential to do business and reshape perceptions of Black Americans in the global marketplace. My purpose is to facilitate a sustainable engagement model between Black Americans and China, rooted in mutual learning, educational exchange, and authentic collaboration. I immersed myself in language courses, pursued cultural exchanges, and honed tailored negotiation strategies. Drawing inspiration from Shanghai's dynamic energy, where tradition meets modernity, I enroll in local universities to deepen my understanding of China's economic ecosystem.

From 2000 to 2002, I launched workshops at Savannah State University (SSU) (Sàfánnà Zhōulì Dàxué), igniting curiosity among students about China. The excitement was palpable, especially during one session when American students engaged in lively discussions with Dr. Hong Zhaohui (Hóng Zhǎohuí), my faculty advisor, who envisioned bridging the cultural divide. "Your insight into Chinese behavior is invaluable," he remarked, his enthusiasm infectious. Our collaboration became a shared mission to explore China in ways that resonated across both cultures. But knowledge alone wasn't enough. We needed networks. I connected SSU students with their Chinese peers, fostering mentorship rooted in mutual curiosity and interest. These pairings created a supportive community that empowered aspiring entrepreneurs with guidance and confidence. And with each step, we amplified our presence.

At a pivotal 2001 conference, I addressed business leaders, community advocates, and students. "We are here to prove Black Americans belong at the forefront of global exchange." The affirming applause showed our message was resonating. Over time, it became increasingly evident that our initiatives helped break down barriers. Through dialogue, we crafted a new narrative where Black American students emerged as formidable players in international relations. The camaraderie between mentors and mentees was undeniable, whether in Beijing or Shanghai, where success stories and strategies flowed freely. Years later, while standing in a Shanghai marketplace, I felt the impact of our work. Negotiating in Mandarin, engaging vendors, and witnessing the power of representation, I saw the legacy we'd built as a community united by collaboration, innovation, and cultural exchange.

Reflecting on this, I'm grateful for the connections forged and obstacles overcome. We've laid a foundation for future leaders where Black Americans aren't just participants but trailblazers of their global narrative. Our shared stories, cultures, and ambitions can build a more equitable and inclusive world for future generations. I will now leverage my experience to build a transformative bridge between Black America and China, reshaping perceptions and fueling a global movement through purposeful collaboration.

Cultural exchanges, trade partnerships, and joint ventures can highlight the strengths of both Black American and Chinese communities. These initiatives can showcase our creativity, innovation, and resilience while allowing us to learn from one another. Platforms for storytelling, where both communities share successes and challenges, will illuminate the common ground and cultivate empathy. By strategically positioning ourselves in this evolving landscape, we can enrich our lives and create pathways for future generations to follow.

Through mentorship, we can engage young leaders and Black educators to ensure they have the tools to navigate an interconnected world. Now is the time to embrace international collaboration, ensuring Black American voices are heard and represented in global trade and exchange. Together, we can forge a legacy of empowerment. This vibrant link uplifts our communities and contributes to a more inclusive global economy, where diversity is celebrated and shared prosperity becomes the norm.

In my later years in Shanghai, I realized the importance of concrete collaboration. Cultural exchanges and trade partnerships became central to my mission of highlighting the strengths of both Black American and Chinese communities. Do not mistake these cultural exchanges for mere academic exercises or social pleasantries. They are the essential groundwork upon which all durable economic partnerships are built. In a context where formal institutions often overlook the specific nuances and potential of Black American engagement, these grassroots interactions become a form of strategic, person-to-state diplomacy. When a Black American student discusses jazz not as a historical artifact but as a living language of innovation, or when an entrepreneur shares the story of a family business, they are doing more than building rapport. They are actively reframing the narrative of Black America in the Chinese imagination, moving it from a monolithic stereotype to a mosaic of potential partners, creators, and consumers. This is the unglamorous, vital work of building trust before a single contract is ever signed.

As a springboard, I co-organized a Juneteenth celebration that united artists, musicians, and entrepreneurs from both backgrounds. The Juneteenth event was the ultimate validation of this methodology. It was not a passive celebration of an American historical milestone, but an active demonstration of its economic potential. By translating this deeply American narrative into a shared, experiential moment in Shanghai, we made the abstract concept of "Black American culture" tangible, vibrant, and, crucially, marketable. The value was not merely in the gathering itself, but in the questions that followed from Chinese attendees: "Where can we find more of this music? How can we support these artists? What other stories are you bringing?" This event proved that cultural authenticity is not a barrier, but a bridge that can support the weight of genuine commerce. It created a platform where a shared human experience became the launchpad for specific, concrete business conversations, proving that the path to a more equitable trade relationship begins not with a ledger, but with a story.

The event showcased our creativity, innovation, and resilience in a spacious eatery near the iconic Bund. As I scanned the crowd, a wave of optimism washed over me. Families mingled, children laughed, and the air carried the sweet scent of local performers presenting traditional Chinese dances alongside soulful jazz, bridging the worlds of East and West. However, the celebration extended beyond music and art, as it was also about storytelling. Under the spotlights, participants shared triumphs and struggles. I listened as attendees recounted their stories of building lives in China. In turn, I shared the challenges of adapting as a Black American educator, entertainer, and entrepreneur striving to forge meaningful partnerships. These exchanges revealed our shared humanity, fostering empathy and transcending cultural divides.

When the celebration became an annual event in 2020, the focus shifted to trade partnerships that could sustain future collaborations. It includes initiatives to pair Black American and Chinese businesses, such as a potential project between a Black athletic clothing designer and a Chinese textile manufacturer. Together, they could have created a clothing line blending Black American themes with Chinese textile capabilities and innovative technology, which would have been applauded for its cultural resonance. Yet, I knew this was only the beginning. We could create lasting opportunities for future generations by strategically navigating this evolving landscape. Engaging young leaders became a key strategy, prompting me to consider launching a mentorship program that pairs aspiring Black entrepreneurs with established Chinese business figures. The program would mentor eager participants who would be paired with veterans in China's personal care industry. This lively exchange seeks to capitalize on a growing market trend and highlight the benefits of cross-cultural collaboration.

Moments like these reaffirm my conviction that the time for international cooperation is now, and Black American voices must be part of the global narrative. As these strategic initiatives gained momentum, it became clear that we needed to establish a lasting legacy of engagement with China. Our forged partnerships can create a vibrant link between our communities, lifting each other as we navigate the complexities of globalization. Celebrating one another's successes proves that mutual progress fuels a more inclusive economy. On the other hand, I was walking through Shanghai's streets years after the pandemic. I marveled at how far we could have come. One where diversity isn't just acknowledged but embraced, because in 2025, the stories of Black Americans in China should no longer linger on the margins. We should be resonating in boardrooms and trade deals and shaping new avenues for business development with China.

Of course, this does not reflect our on-the-ground efforts, because I don't feel profound disappointment over every connection made and obstacle overcome. Is it because, as part of the Black American culture, we do not demonstrate an urgency to participate in the dialogue about China? Or am I becoming another bridge between cultures? So, I continue to look ahead and remain hopeful. The next phase, armed with the tools and inspiration I've been provided, I will confidently navigate this interconnected world. Together, we could lay the foundation for a more equitable future where our intertwined stories create an enduring legacy of collaboration and shared prosperity with China. An intertwined situation arises when pursuing opportunities in China. The landscape appears increasingly competitive, and meaningful cross-cultural engagement has become more challenging.

Being from Georgia, a state, not a country, and earning acceptance within China's culture is a testament to my resilience and an unwavering commitment to collaboration across borders. This path has not been without its frustrations. Cultural misunderstandings have sometimes left me feeling powerless, while the intricacies of international diplomacy between America and China have sometimes compounded these challenges. Such moments of miscommunication obscure the potential for genuine partnership, but they also underscore the urgent need for progress.

I understand that geopolitical tensions breed skepticism, hindering people-to-people exchange and business relations. Yet acknowledging these obstacles is the first step toward meaningful change and creating a more equitable environment for Black professionals abroad. Success in China demands more than business acumen. It requires navigating cultural nuances with intention. Open dialogue, initiatives that challenge preconceptions, and a dedication to mutual understanding are essential. Equally critical is building a strong network of allies that can reshape the future of cultural exchange and commerce.

By fostering resilience in the face of adversity, we pave the way for future generations of Black Americans to pursue international opportunities confidently. With perseverance, what now appears as barriers can become pathways to growth, collaboration, and lasting impact. Between 2002 and 2010, China's air crackled with anticipation and rapid transformation. The country's booming economy lured international entrepreneurs, all eager to tap into its vast potential. Among them was I, a Black American drawn by opportunity but quickly confronted by a landscape riddled with visible and invisible challenges. Unlike many others, I had gone far only to face an unprecedented reality that revealed the multifaceted hurdles awaiting us in different communities.

I sensed an unmistakable calmness simmering beneath the surface. I ignored reports from the West, often highlighting how many foreigners felt a pervasive sense of unwelcome, a sentiment worsened by geopolitical strains that tangled business and cultural interactions. Unfortunately, this messaging created an unpredictable environment, forcing many foreigners to tread carefully during shifting international politics.

Understanding China during this era was like stepping into a cultural terrain where the rules were unfamiliar but constantly changing for the betterment of the people. Every corridor of opportunity presented unique obstacles, especially cultural misunderstandings regarding stabilizing negotiations, miscommunication, accelerating progress, and a blatant lack of institutional support, such as the absence of any Black American Trade and Cultural Organization that stays focused. Navigating the business landscape felt incredibly daunting when the prevailing narrative seemed to favor positive stereotypes about White entrepreneurs, casting long shadows that undermined trust in Black Americans' credibility.

For me, they frequently seeped into concerns about fair treatment during deals, treatments that fueled feelings of powerlessness and even despair. Racial dynamics added pressure, often in the form of reluctance to engage fully with the market. I realized I wasn't just pretending. I was laying the foundation for a new kind of bridge. But coming from America, I have been well educated in that game. As America-China trade tensions simmered, threatening economic engagement and personal connections, I realized that navigating these complexities required more than language skills or business acumen. It demanded a deep understanding of White America's cultural norms and unspoken expectations. I advocated for more equitable and inclusive practices; it would not be enough to reinforce my presence in China and foster meaningful dialogue across provinces. Recognizing these systemic barriers became crucial to empowering me to demand fair treatment and navigate business tensions.

Often, I would sit at a teahouse, overlooking the ever-evolving skyline, realizing that turning these challenges into opportunities for collaboration required sustained, deliberate effort. Combatting stereotypes and building understanding wasn't just a daily necessity but a long-term strategy for striving and succeeding in China. With every shared story and every negotiation, successful or failed, I laid the groundwork for a future defined not just by personal achievement but by the incremental progress made in understanding global trade through the lens of China. Like me, Shanghai's skyline gleams with ambition, a testament to the city's unrelenting promise.

Yet beneath its glittering façade lies a complex web of international business relations with developing countries, which are expanding amid ongoing trade tensions between America and China. Even before tariffs and regulatory restrictions ushered in an era of uncertainty, deciphering the rules proved as daunting as outperforming competitors. For me, these challenges are compounded by a broader reluctance among Black

America's trade and commerce organizations to engage with China, which stifles potential collaborations before they even begin.

In America, Black-owned small businesses face a steep climb. They compete against entrenched Indian, White, Asian, and Hispanic small business owners with vast networks and near-limitless resources. The need for direct access is undeniable, yet misconceptions about accessing China linger as unspoken, unresolved ghosts in the Black trade and commerce circle. Bridging this misunderstanding is vital to a collaboration that can thrive and demand more than scattered conversations that require systemic support. Initiatives empowering Black entrepreneurs and celebrating cultural diversity within China aren't just idealism. Representation in international forums must expand, giving marginalized voices a seat at the table.

My path forward is built on stable, symbiotic partnerships with China's provinces. To dismantle barriers through commerce, art, music, and people-to-people exchange opportunities. This isn't about tolerating differences but developing structures to complement this necessary progress. I've observed that the most meaningful connections often spark in unexpected places. Places like a factory floor humming with industry, a cultural festival pulsating with history, or a gallery where art transcends language. I find that these behind-the-scenes moments are where an accurate understanding is built. Each interaction proves that mutual understanding isn't merely noble but transformative. It fuels my resolve to turn trade tensions into opportunities, fostering cooperation between China's diverse communities and the Black American community. Yet the road is weighed down by invisible burdens. Fair treatment in business dealings feels elusive, sowing frustration among peers. The currents of Chinese business culture were strong, and the map I had been given in America was useless here.

My purpose transcends these dynamics. They are deeply rooted in cultural divisions that negatively affect every negotiation, especially when tensions in America-China relations are exacerbated. Cooperating demands more than fluency in Mandarin. It requires navigating unspoken norms and systemic biases. Acknowledging these truths has been my first step toward advocacy for equitable practices, inclusion, and dialogue that replaces distrust with shared goals. I am learning from these teahouses that turning challenges into collaboration demands relentless, intentional effort. Combating stereotypes isn't just daily labor; it's a long-term strategy for relevance in a globalized world. Every story shared, every deal struck or broken, lays bricks in a foundation where success isn't solitary but collective. I fight for a future where Black America isn't just connected to China, but also included in cultural exchange and commerce.

The potential for growth in international markets is boundless. For Black Americans looking to expand their horizons, China offers fertile ground where cross-cultural connections can blossom into enriching experiences and tangible opportunities. By embracing Chinese business practices and artistic innovation, I have learned that unlocking pathways to success is as economically rewarding as culturally transformative. Partnering with Chinese collaborators creates opportunities that transcend borders, enabling me better to serve the diverse needs of Black American consumers. In addition, establishing a presence in China's thriving economy can put Black America at the vanguard of cultural and economic exchange, where innovative collaborations celebrate the unique strengths of both communities. This dynamic position will become a robust platform that amplifies Black American interests while making meaningful contributions to China's broader society/economy.

Imagine a platform where artistic expression merges with music, fashion, or technology, and where products and services resonate across cultures. These creative synergies foster a shared sense of identity and purpose, bridging divides and forging lasting connections. Yet, navigating this terrain requires a strategy that strikes a delicate balance between cooperation and competition. Success hinges on building partnerships rooted in mutual trust and avoiding the pitfalls of isolation that hinder progress. Continuous dialogue, adaptability, and deep respect for cultural nuance are both advantageous and essential. By remaining open to learning from my Chinese counterparts, I have come to understand that crafting a sustainable framework for collaboration that elevates Black American voices and does not isolate them on the global stage enriches cross-cultural understanding for all parties involved. Vast opportunity and dynamism define China, yet a sense of distance sometimes lingers beneath the surface. As tensions between the United States and China escalate, this unease becomes increasingly motivating for me. I do not hesitate to collaborate with other countries as they increase their economic and cultural relationships with China.

I often wonder what conversations are unfolding within Black Chambers of Commerce and Trade organizations about this quiet fear. Do they reveal a spectrum of optimistic emotions that could be shadowed by trepidation, with those same emotions warning of the risks of aligning with China? Are these discussions tinged with pessimism, as bureaucratic hurdles that are often described as daunting and opaque, stifle potential partnerships before they begin? These concerns are not born in isolation. They stem from a broader reality in which Black Americans frequently navigate marginalization in global business. That lingering exclusion fuels hesitation, making China, a market already perceived as complex, feel even more unwelcoming. To dismantle these fears, we must first understand them. Deep-rooted anxieties about erasure or misrepresentation persist. Addressing the demands of proactive strategies in areas as fostering inclusivity, prioritizing collaboration, and navigating uncertainty with clear-eyed resolve. Hence, open dialogue is indispensable in spaces where diverse voices can share unfiltered experiences. Beyond conversation, structured programs must equip Black American organizations with the tools to navigate these cross-cultural complexities. Such tools could transform isolation into opportunity, forging pathways for meaningful engagement with China's global trade influence. The goal? Partnerships are anchored in mutual respect, paving the way for a more inclusive future.

Imagine Black American Trade and cultural organizations thriving at events in Suzhou's (Sūzhōu) bustling business hubs? In areas where America-China tensions are lessened, due to their participation in ancient traditions and colliding with cutting-edge innovation. Does the duality of risk and reward spark stateside conversations that, with cautious ambition, feed skepticism? How often are promising ventures for Black America in the States paused before they start due to the casualties of red tape and unresolved fears? These pervasive questions weigh heavily on marginalized communities when seeking direct access to global commerce.

So overcoming them requires recognizing Black Americans' unique challenges in Chinese trade. And a proactive engagement is critical because a strategy alone isn't enough. It must involve honest dialogue that flourishes and shared stories that dismantle barriers to cultivate a supply chain ecosystem. Cultivating educational and resource-sharing can turn hesitation into confidence, thereby replacing barriers while clarifying the vision. By championing respect-driven collaboration, Black America can redefine its global role, not as outsiders but as innovators. The shift from fear to opportunity is not a destination. It's a continuous process through persistence and authentic exchange. And what begins as a concern can become a narrative of resilience that opens doors once thought to be closed.

In China's business landscape, the constant risk of backlash or discrimination complicates every interaction, from meals to negotiations. Meanwhile, cultural misunderstandings lurk like unseen obstacles. In addition, the shifting of global economic directives under various global leaderships and the uncertainty they create have become constant companions for people alike. The result? A climate of cautious optimism that breathes enthusiasm. My success not only demands more than strategy in such an environment, but it also requires patience. Cultural exchange and collaboration are beneficial and essential tools for mitigating risk. Yet, an ambiguous economic trajectory further clouds the path forward. Without implementing the three lessons learned, I would struggle to maintain a solid footing in China, where fierce competition and rapid evolution prevail. To thrive, I am adopting robust, adaptable lessons that don't just chase growth but also acknowledge that maintaining my patience is key to achieving economic and cultural aspirations.

First, building strong relationships based on guanxi (guānxi) is far more valuable than pursuing immediate returns. Unlike Western business practices that often prioritize quick deals, successful engagement in China requires investing time in non-transactional connections. A proven strategy is to host informal gatherings, especially dinners or tea meetings, where the focus is not on pitching your business but on genuinely understanding your Chinese counterparts. Ask about their families, hobbies, and regional customs to express interest. I remember sitting in a Mandarin class, entirely out of my depth, but I wasn't alone. Seated next to me were several foreign students, all of us equally baffled by the four tones. Over the next six months, something shifted. Our weekly conversations moved from 'How are you doing?' to 'How on earth do you remember this character?'

That experience taught me a crucial lesson: the quickest way to build a genuine bond isn't in a classroom, but in a shared struggle. Learning a difficult skill together leveled the playing field and created camaraderie that no number of sales meetings could ever achieve. This effort later opened doors that no formal contract could, proving that trust, not just transactions, drives long-term success in China.

This reframes patience not as passive waiting, but as an active and strategic investment in a relationship. By prioritizing guanxi, I laid the groundwork for deeper trust, smoother negotiations, and future opportunities that purely profit-driven approaches cannot secure, because in China, relationships are the actual currency of business. Next, leveraging shared cultural narratives can be far more impactful than relying solely on language fluency to build meaningful connections across cultures in a business setting. A powerful strategy involves identifying and emphasizing cultural parallels that resonate emotionally with your audience.

When speaking at an art exhibition, I successfully framed the art show theme as "We Stand Together" (Wǒmen zài yīqǐ), drawing a subtle but compelling parallel between the Black American Great Migration and China's migrant workers' historical narrative of perseverance during its "Open Door Policy." This approach transformed my presence from a potential barrier into a relatable story of struggle and triumph, fostering deeper trust and alignment. By tapping into universal themes of adversity and progress, I turned cultural differences into bridges rather than obstacles. This method works because it shifts the conversation from transactional exchanges to shared human experiences, making business objectives feel personally significant. Whether discussing long-term goals or negotiating partnerships, framing discussions around mutual values that are primarily centered on resilience, innovation, or collective growth can foster a stronger rapport than linguistic proficiency alone. Ultimately, turning perceived foreignness into a strategic advantage for cultural intelligence, not just language mastery, unlocks doors. Followed by cross-cultural negotiations, replacing Western directness with a more nuanced "yes, but" approach can significantly enhance collaboration.

If a partner rejects a proposal, rather than pushing back bluntly, a diplomatic response like, "I appreciate your perspective. Let's explore how we might adjust timelines to align with your priorities," maintains harmony while advancing the discussion. This tactic aligns with the indirect communication style prevalent in Chinese business culture, where maintaining mutual respect and avoiding public disagreements is crucial. By reframing objections as opportunities for adjustment, negotiators avoid face-saving (diū miànzi) scenarios, ensuring neither party feels undermined. The underlying strength of this strategy lies in its ability to maintain an open dialogue without compromising persistence. Instead of outright rejection, it encourages creative problem-solving, fostering goodwill and long-term partnerships. In high-context cultures, where implicit communication and relational dynamics carry weight, such adaptability demonstrates cultural intelligence and builds trust. Blending assertiveness with flexibility enables negotiators to navigate differences smoothly, transforming potential conflicts into collaborative solutions while maintaining the delicate balance of respect and progress.

While these tactics are essential for individual deals, they must be applied within a broader, more patient philosophy. In a world obsessed with instant results, true success often lies in strategic patience. This approach rejects the relentless "hustle harder" mentality in favor of calculated flexibility, recognizing that growth in dynamic markets is not always linear but always directional. It's the mindset of planting seeds with one hand while holding an umbrella with the other. The harvest comes, but only if we weather the storms. This wisdom underscores the delicate balance between persistence and adaptability. Rather than chasing short-term wins, enduring success demands resilience, foresight, and the ability to navigate uncertainty. In business and life, storms are inevitable, but those who can endure them, prepared yet patient, ultimately reap the rewards.

The lesson is clear: power isn't just in relentless action but in knowing when to push forward and protect my progress. By embracing patience as a strength, I cultivate the endurance needed to thrive in unpredictable environments, ensuring it's abundant and lasting when the harvest finally arrives. The threat of isolation looms large against the backdrop of global trade dynamics. This resonates deeply within Black America, where interactions with China have often been marked by frustration and missed opportunities. Bridging this divide demands more than transactional engagement. It requires mutual respect, a shared understanding of histories, and a commitment to common goals. Only then can apprehension give way to collaboration, but in relationship-building over immediate Return of Investment (ROI), leveraging cultural bridges, not just language, and adaptive negotiation tactics with an understanding that using patience as power is not linear-it's directional, which underscores China's confidence in its path, prioritizing sustainable, people-centered advancement over short-term gains. It embodies the wisdom of "crossing the river by feeling the stones" while staying firmly on the socialist road. This unique development philosophy is the key to success.

By fostering open exchanges, we can illuminate the challenges and opportunities ahead. For Black America, this isn't just about better business and culture outcomes and rewriting the narrative. We can transform friction into synergy through meaningful engagement, enriching the global economic opportunities, while being people-centered within our community is left on the sidelines. My mission is to promote transparent dialogue about the evolving relationship between China and Black America. I leverage overlooked behind-the-scenes opportunities to cultivate cooperative ties that resonate with Black America and mainland Chinese audiences. This work requires navigating the complexities of trade and diplomacy while recognizing that subtle, strategic engagement can catalyze meaningful progress. The path forward demands proactive and thoughtful collaboration.

Though hesitations persist, a growing openness to partnerships is emerging, offering opportunities to emphasize mutual understanding and respect. Rather than allowing differences to divide, we can transform them into strengths, fostering connections that benefit both communities. Supporting Black American interests in China presents a dual opportunity, one that showcases our rich cultural heritage while unlocking untapped economic potential. This approach serves as a bridge, deepening appreciation for Black contributions to the global landscape. At its core, mutual respect is an ideal and a driving force for change. Through cultural exchanges and economic dialogues, we can challenge stereotypes and create an inclusive environment where all parties thrive. This is more than transactional collaboration. It should be about building a shared vision for the future. A future where interconnectedness flourishes, diversity is tolerated and celebrated, and genuine partnerships yield lasting benefits. The road ahead is one of transformation. By turning challenges into opportunities, we can forge a path of mutual understanding and shared success that enriches both communities and sets a precedent for global cooperation.

Building robust trade and cultural relations between Black America and China is complex and layered, demanding a nuanced approach to overcome inherent challenges. Geopolitical tensions and cultural misunderstandings pose significant obstacles, but opportunities for innovative partnerships and meaningful exchange lie within these challenges. Success hinges on a steadfast commitment to dialogue, prioritizing listening as much as speaking and learning as much as teaching. It calls for economic collaborations built on equity, not exploitation, and cultural connections rooted in mutual respect, not transactional goodwill. Once accomplished, we can dismantle the historical barriers that have long hindered progress through such efforts. China's vast opportunities offer Black America a unique platform to bridge cultural divides while leveraging its distinct perspectives for mutual success. This underscores the urgent need for Black American organizations to forge solid relationships with Mainland China, especially amid today's global uncertainties. These relationships are merely beneficial since they are essential for sustainable growth.

Navigating this terrain requires addressing cultural differences, economic disparities, and geopolitical friction, including the persistent specter of anti-Black racism in America and ongoing trade disputes.

Establishing an organization that advocates for and supports Black America in China could be transformative. Such an initiative would provide a structured framework for reciprocal growth, fostering an inclusive global landscape through strategic partnerships and cultural exchange. Enhancing representation and cultivating cross-border alliances can turn interactions into lasting opportunities for shared prosperity, deeper understanding, and cultural enrichment. This is more than an aspiration. It is a vision grounded in respect and the collective will to overcome historical divisions. While the path ahead is neither simple nor straightforward, its potential is immense. The geopolitical and cultural hurdles are real, but so is the promise of innovation and collaboration.

In China, I remain committed to laying the foundation for a more interconnected future where today's efforts blossom into a more prosperous and inclusive world. A quiet optimism guides this work since true power lies in forging genuine connections that transcend borders and generations, uniting us in a shared pursuit of progress. The road may be long, and the destination may be a thriving, culturally enriched Black America, empowered through meaningful global engagement that is seemingly worth every step.

Establishing an organization in China to advance Black American commerce and cultural exchange is electrifying. It strikes me whenever I hear discussions about uplifting Black economic prosperity through board representation, trade associations, or franchising within America. Yet these domestic efforts risk stagnation without sustainable ties to Mainland China. While internal progress is vital, America's strained engagement with China threatens to isolate Black entrepreneurs from transformative global opportunities. The critical challenge? Forging synergistic partnerships with Chinese counterparts to unlock mutual growth, not just in trade, but in shared cultural understanding. Establishing a physical presence in China would open doors to the world's most dynamic market, enabling exchanges that are far deeper than transactional deals.

Imagine knowledge and technology transfer, educational collaborations, joint ventures in arts and entertainment, and even the daily-use products that shape lives. We could expand economic horizons by dismantling historical barriers while weaving our narratives together. The goal must be reciprocity, with a two-way flow of ideas, resources, and cultural insights that enrich both communities. Chinese partnerships could also offer masterclasses in global supply chains and emerging-market consumer behavior, empowering Black American organizations to claim their stake in the international economy. I felt this potential alliance at the Shanghai New International Expo Centre (SNIEC) in 2016. The China Daily-Use Articles Trade Fair hummed with kinetic energy. The display of various products between the innovator and the entrepreneurs' booths revealed that an organization representing Black American commerce and trade in China should be present.

Here, amid eco-friendly products and eager vendors, the absence of sustained Black engagement with China felt like a gaping hole in our economic strategy. One booth drew me in with its displays of sustainable household goods. The vendor's enthusiasm mirrored my conviction that partnership looks like this. Nearby, debates about China's 6.7% growth rate buzzed. While some American advocates focus on domestic solutions, ignoring global collaboration was a profound folly. In conversations with attendees, I sketched a future where cultural and commercial exchange fueled progress. "Think beyond imports and exports," I urged. "Shared ventures in education, arts, and innovation could redefine our communities while promoting cultural exchange," I emphasized reciprocity and not extraction should be a part of the dialogue," I said, as my calmness quickened, as others nodded. A Beijing artisan who crafts intricate textiles became an unexpected ally after we spoke of lifting communities through enterprise. To see a microcosm of what could be in a world where Black America and Chinese collaboration turned divides into bridges while watching sunlight glaze the expo hall's corridors.

The path was complex, and the hunger for connection was palpable in every handshake and business card exchange. This wasn't mere networking but the first step in a larger goal. The following day, the air hummed with energy as I visited rows of booths showcasing cutting-edge products, while eager manufacturers and suppliers buzzed with excitement. Surrounded by this convergence of cultures and ideas, I felt the profound significance of being part of a global community. Yet amid the dynamism, a pressing vision emerged in my mind of the need for unity, collaboration, and proactive engagement among Black American chamber organizations. The potential for synergy is reflected in the varied structures of these chambers. Some operated as franchises while others had independent affiliate chapters scattered across regions. This fragmented governance made me realize, with urgency, that we must unite our diverse industries into a more substantial overseas organization to access mutual support. Naturally, my thoughts turned to the National Black Chambers of Commerce (NBCC) and the United States Black Chamber (USBC), two leading national organizations dedicated to empowering Black-owned businesses. Both play vital roles in amplifying the voices of local chambers.

Yet, their success depends on something less obvious but more significant to maintain their current structures. Their structures are committed to building a supportive narrative that talks globally while acting domestically, thus creating a deep conflict. A concerning trend among Chinese manufacturers and suppliers is their inattention to discussions about Black America's underrepresentation and lack of advocacy in China. The disconnect was striking. Do these national organizations need a robust business coalition to establish a liaison office and build a strong presence in China?

Many potential members may hesitate due to uncertainty about its value and the unfamiliarity of China's business landscape. This hesitation, while understandable, is ultimately costly, as emerging markets like China offer vast opportunities for Black America. Opportunities that remain out of reach without collaboration, what if we could change that? What if we built a foundation to instill confidence in those daunted by the unknown? Imagine the possibilities if we focused on facilitating cross-network communication, sharing resources, and offering education on global commerce. Workshops, seminars, and collaborative platforms could demystify international trade, equipping Black commerce organizations to navigate new markets with assurance.

My vision for the path forward is to build a more substantial, unified network, as it is the key to transforming our advocacy and amplifying our impact. By lifting local chapters, we'd elevate the entire community and become a formidable force in any economic landscape, regional or global. The trade fair crystallized my conviction. Together, we could dismantle barriers, pool our knowledge, and forge a legacy of empowerment that transcends borders. As I moved through the expo hall, surrounded by innovation and ambition, I felt a surge of determination. The global stage was set. Now was the time to unite in advocacy, share insights boldly, and cultivate an ecosystem where every Black-owned business could thrive.

Glancing at the diverse faces of Chinese entrepreneurs, I sensed a tipping point when my mind buzzed with possibility. The international scope of the event underscored a profound truth about Black commerce and trade organizations in Canada, South Africa, Ghana, and Morocco, which share a common aspiration to align with the American Black Chambers to build a unified, collaborative platform. Yet, among this potential lay a critical gap. Many of these organizations lack the framework to navigate international opportunities effectively, particularly in a market as complex as China.

The weight of this challenge settled on my shoulders. Provincial regulations vary widely, and success here demands more than business acumen. Success here requires a deep understanding of local customs, legal intricacies, and market dynamics, all of which differ significantly from those in the United States. The thought of Black American entrepreneurs striving to establish a representative trade organization in China struck me as urgent and daunting. Given the nascent state of international collaboration, many existing trade bodies may not yet be equipped to support such an initiative. This realization ignited a fire within me. Creating an organization representing Black America's commerce and trade interests in China can serve as a bridge. A bridge that connects innovative market proposals and fosters meaningful dialogue while simultaneously tapping into China's vast cultural and economic opportunities.

We should develop a platform that unlocks the full potential of Black-owned businesses in America, strengthens ties with global partners, and absorbs the dynamic energy of manufacturers and suppliers across China. Consequently, each booth, each conversation, and each presentation has potential. I envisioned partnerships between Black entrepreneurs in America and their Chinese counterparts that would create collaborative projects transcending commerce and spark cultural exchange. Imagine Black artists and Chinese creators merging their traditions to produce groundbreaking work. Envision Black innovators sharing sustainable business practices with Chinese manufacturers, catalyzing a new wave of eco-conscious products. These actions would be transactions and transformative exchange opportunities for mutual understanding and growth.

Will such an undeniable call to action construct bridges, facilitating the flow of goods, services, and ideas between our cultures? A trade organization championing Black American businesses in China would empower us to claim our place in this dynamic market. By strategically embedding ourselves in the Chinese market, we can amplify our collective voice and advance a narrative of resilience and excellence. This call to action is more than an aspiration. It is essential to enhance economic outcomes and strengthen cross-continental ties by promoting cultural activities and maintaining a global perspective through trade. We stand at the precipice of a transformative era, and our actions today will shape the future of the global Black business community.

As I sat down for lunch with my Chinese counterpart at the trade fair, the path forward felt unmistakably clear. Establishing this organization isn't just an idea. It is an idea whose time has come because we must harness the momentum of this historic moment and echo it for generations to come. Since arriving in China through a study abroad program in 2000, no organization has existed to advocate for Black American business interests in this vast and complex market. This absence is a systemic disadvantage for Black entrepreneurs striving to compete globally. Without direct access to critical resources, securing contracts and establishing a foothold becomes a challenging task.

Over the years, I've navigated the intricacies of international business by recognizing its challenges and opportunities for Black-owned businesses. Sometimes these complexities ring hollow without the tools to compete beyond domestic borders. We should align strategic business resources at home and abroad to thrive within this area. Such an alliance could be transformative, especially with a dedicated liaison office in China for Black American chamber members. This alliance should empower members to compete in global trade by sourcing essential products directly from manufacturers, forging strategic partnerships, and enhancing their international competitiveness.

This isn't just about leveling the global trade industry. It's about claiming our seat at the table in the world's largest economy, and engaging with China is not merely advantageous but imperative to our economic development. We can begin unlocking opportunities to revitalize industries back home by tapping into this dynamic market, as this trade fair, more than a showcase of daily-use products, catalyzes meaningful dialogue. It showed a demand that Black America confront its challenges head-on as we push for equity in a globalized economy. Unfortunately, I did not have conversations with Black American entrepreneurs. Maybe it's because they lack direct access to these manufacturers and suppliers, which requires first-hand knowledge, resources, and strategies that are often not provided to their stateside organizations.

So, as I continue walking through the expo halls, I envision a future where Black American businesses aren't isolated from these opportunities but are architects of the global economy. A global economy where representation matters, not just symbolically, but through structured efforts prioritizing our interests in international trade. We must dismantle historical barriers to ensure our voices shape the narrative around Black entrepreneurship worldwide. To address these difficulties, I engage in every discussion at the trade fair. When I stepped into the W1 halls of the SNIEC, I was excited by the atmosphere, which was filled with enormous possibilities, as organizations across China showcased their innovations.

Yet, amid this atmosphere of ambition, I couldn't ignore the undercurrent of caution that often accompanies international expansion. Many manufacturers and suppliers around me had expressed keen interest in breaking into foreign markets. Expanding into a landscape as vast and dynamic as the global stage was undeniably exhilarating. But for most, that ambition was untampered by the intricate trade relations they needed to navigate. I knew entering this environment without local expertise would be like sailing into uncharted waters, because my counterparts around me debated the advantages of pricing and logistics.

Their conversations were laced with the unspoken tension of uncertainty. Even the most meticulous plans could unravel without the proper guidance. That's why engaging an on-the-ground partner in China wasn't just helpful but indispensable. Local allies could clarify regulatory hurdles, decode market dynamics, and offer critical insights into consumer behavior. Consequently, essential knowledge is required for tailoring strategies to meet local expectations. "As I moved from booth to booth, the palpable hesitancy of some providers revealed their crucial attributes. Whispers of potential backlash from anti-China sentiments lingered in both private and public discussions. The weight of political tensions was unmistakable when decision-makers fretted over reputational risks and the delicate task of aligning business strategies with national sentiments and geopolitical realities.

Acknowledging these concerns can stifle partnerships because, with every apprehensive voice, a compelling counterargument rose within me. Outside the bustling aisles of the marketplace, the potential rewards of forging a direct connection with one supplier far outweighed the risks. This is where I often met a local entrepreneur eager to explore partnerships and to expand my economic horizon by tapping into one of the world's largest consumer markets. I envisioned how establishing a foothold in China could unlock extraordinary opportunities with strategic collaborations, innovative solutions, and a more decisive competitive edge for Black America on the global stage.

But as the day unfolded, the conversations I had reinforced my philosophical approach. A philosophy that resonated deeply with manufacturers and suppliers who emphasized goodwill and mutual understanding as the bedrock of lasting partnerships. Success in this interconnected economy, I realized, hinged on our ability to adapt, build relationships, and cultivate diverse alliances. Amid these exchanges, I reflected on my fears and aspirations as I entered the Chinese market. It wasn't just an opportunity but a strategic imperative to the cornerstone of sustainable growth.

The key lay in navigating its complexities with care and conviction, since collaboration wasn't merely desirable in workshops. Exhibitors shared hard-won insights on adapting to local markets by emphasizing the importance of flexibility. It was a constant reminder that agility and innovation are essential in today's rapidly evolving economy. And as I listened, a sense of empowerment surged through me. The challenges weren't roadblocks, but were catalysts for growth. My lingering concerns about political backlash in America weren't fading away. I was concerned that forging connections in this dynamic landscape could lead to something transformative, something far beyond the exchange of profit and funding. Particularly in the absence of directly earmarked funding, the international trade activities of Black American commerce organizations face significant hurdles.

Yet, given their annual budgets and trade missions, it's clear that forging a sustainable partnership with China could be transformative for Black entrepreneurs and businesses. Establishing a physical presence in China would empower these organizations to tap into vast industrial and cultural opportunities, unlocking mutual growth on a global scale. In my observation, pre-pandemic trade events did not reflect Black Americans' presence in the business community, with participation levels that did not match their share. I believe these platforms represent a significant and often underutilized opportunity for networking and growth that could greatly benefit entrepreneurs from all backgrounds.

The urgency of international expansion weighs heavily on me. My thoughts race with the untapped potential that Black commerce organizations in America must actively seize. But the question remains: are we utilizing sufficient resources to establish a lasting connection with China? The opportunities are staggering. A physical foothold in China would grant direct access to industrial networks, cultural exchanges, and global markets, enabling Black businesses to showcase their innovation worldwide.

Take, for example, the 2018 China International Import Expo (CIIE) (2018 Zhōngguó Guójì Jìnkǒu Bólǎnhuì). This event offers nations a platform to showcase their products, strengthen trade ties, and expand into new markets. Yet, despite its promise, Black American participation has been minimal. We stand on the threshold of exponential growth, yet historical barriers and systemic challenges continue to hinder our progress. One major obstacle? The CIIE's scheduling conflicts with American elections. As the expo unfolds every November, presidential and midterm elections in the United States command attention. This recurring overlap has systematically sidelined Black entrepreneurs, depriving them of critical networking and deal-making opportunities, moments that could propel their businesses forward. This is our moment of reckoning. We must shift from passive observers to proactive players in international trade.

Establishing a liaison office in China isn't just an option; it's a necessity. Such an office would strengthen communication with trade partners, amplify our global market presence, and ensure our voices help shape the economic future. By acting strategically, we can cultivate the networks needed for lasting economic empowerment, turning missed opportunities into tangible progress and redefining Black America's role in global commerce. Every trade fair, every shared meal, every negotiation is a bridge waiting to be built.

I envision vibrant exchanges with Chinese entrepreneurs, uncovering synergies, and forging collaborative ventures. The stories of resilience and ingenuity within Black American culture now resonate worldwide, their products standing proudly alongside international offerings. Together, we can craft a narrative of shared prosperity that fuels economic growth for Black businesses and their global partners. As I look ahead, I embrace a mindset of collaboration and mutual advancement. Let's rewrite the story of Black commerce on the world stage, seize every opportunity, dismantle every barrier, and claim our rightful place in the global marketplace. Our ancestors and future generations are watching. Now is the moment for a Black American Trade and Cultural Organization to demonstrate its value by transforming untapped potential into measurable success.

With unwavering determination, I stand ready to champion this cause, ensuring our voices echo across borders. The time for action could have begun with the 2016 China Daily-Use Articles Trade Fair (CDATF) (Zhōngguó Rìyòng Zápǐn Jiāoyìhuì) and far beyond. My experience at the trade fair taught me a pivotal lesson that pursuing new horizons demands both ambition and caution. It requires vigilance, adaptability, and a commitment to collaboration. If we embrace this approach, we won't just expand internationally. We'll redefine our role in the global economy, ensuring our contributions leave a lasting impact in an interconnected world.

Together, we can forge networks that harness our collective strength and reshape success on a global scale. This isn't merely about business. It's a movement. A call to collaborate, innovate, and build a future where Black enterprises thrive without limits. A fundamental truth drives this contribution. Equity begins when we claim our space in the global supply chain and write our own story. Our goal is to unite and overcome these challenges. By working together, we aim to build a legacy of resilience and success that can hopefully serve as an inspiration for those who follow.

2

Bridging Black Innovation and China

Is America's complex, interdependent supply chain economy, an essential part of production and consumption, also a mechanism that maintains systemic racism? Yet within this dynamic system lies a narrative that perpetuates Black America's underrepresentation and ignores its untapped potential. For too long, Black-owned businesses have operated on the periphery of this critical network, with their contributions sidelined and their influence muted. It is time to reimagine their role, not as marginal players but as architects of a revitalized supply chain.

This transformation begins with a collective awakening that recognizes Black enterprise as a cornerstone of economic resilience and innovation. Historically marginalized by systemic barriers and lack of access, Black entrepreneurs are now forging a new financial reality and reclaiming their power. This shift is revolutionary. It is a move toward self-determination that replaces dependency with dynamic engagement. From my early days in China, I understood that such a transformation requires a multi-layered approach that prioritizes autonomy, efficiency, and collaboration. An approach where success hinges not on securing a seat at the table, but on redesigning it, ensuring that every participant strengthens the chain's resilience.

Imagine a virtual summit bringing together visionaries from Black American enterprises and China's private sector. William, an economic strategist, opens the dialogue.

"Our goal," he states, "is to shift Black businesses from the margins to the core of global supply chains. Collaboration with your industries is pivotal to this vision."

Wei Ling, a Chinese manufacturing director, leans in. "Mutual benefit drives us. How do you envision this partnership?"

Angela, founder of a Black-owned tech startup, responds, "By merging your advanced manufacturing with our innovation in sustainability and data analytics, we can optimize logistics, reduce environmental footprints, and scale solutions that serve both markets."

Chen Yao, a supply chain analyst, nods. "Specifics matter. Where do you see the greatest potential?"

"Sustainable materials, AI-driven logistics, and circular production models," Angela replies. "Imagine factories powered by renewable energy, waste repurposed into resources, and real-time data streamlining delivery routes."

William adds, "This isn't just transactional. It's a cultural exchange that fuses expertise that fortifies our industries against disruption."

By the end of the meeting, a joint task force had emerged, committed to piloting green tech initiatives and co-developing AI tools for supply chain agility.

Such partnerships exemplify a broader truth because a thriving supply chain depends on seamless collaboration. Suppliers, manufacturers, and distributors must work together to ensure that goods flow efficiently from factory floors to consumers' hands. For Black-owned businesses, integration into this network is transformative. It amplifies visibility, unlocks cross-sector alliances, and creates ecosystems where shared goals drive collective prosperity. Yet ambition alone isn't enough. Progress demands investment in cutting-edge infrastructure, workforce training, and platforms for knowledge exchange. Equipped with these tools, Black enterprises can scale operations, innovate boldly, and adapt swiftly to market shifts. The result is a ripple effect of job creation, community empowerment, and a self-sustaining economic framework that uplifts Black families while strengthening national and global markets.

The path forward is clear because we must redefine resilience by repositioning Black America as a significant pillar of the supply chain. This means we must shift from being passive observers to becoming innovators, problem-solvers, and global partners. Through strategic collaboration, relentless innovation, and an unwavering commitment to inclusion, we can develop a new path forward into the global economy that fosters unity and humanity by creating our supply chain ecosystem.

Creating a supply chain ecosystem is not merely a logistical challenge. It is a strategic move that requires a visionary act with the power to redefine the economic future of Black American businesses. My approach begins with clarity. What do we aim to achieve? The answer lies in four pillars: cost efficiency, speed, flexibility, and sustainability. These are more than metrics. They embody a community's hunger for equitable growth. Success hinges on collaboration with partners who grasp this vision and champion it. It identifies allies, such as suppliers, manufacturers, or logistics experts, who require immediate attention. Each must excel in their field while aligning with our mission to strengthen the economic resilience of Black Americans. The right partnerships don't just streamline operations. They enhance efficiency, which amplifies impact, driving down costs and fostering innovation.

To build this ecosystem, we focus on three strategic imperatives:

1. Multi-supplier agreements to insulate against disruptions, ensuring no single point of failure.
2. Dynamic inventory planning to anticipate demand and pivot amid market shifts.
3. Automation is a transformative force that accelerates responsiveness and productivity.

The first imperative for multi-supplier agreements is to establish strategic partnerships with multiple vendors to minimize supply chain risks and prevent disruptions from overreliance on a single source. By diversifying suppliers, businesses ensure that alternative sources can maintain operational continuity if one vendor faces logistical delays, production halts, or geopolitical issues. This approach eliminates single points of failure by addressing critical vulnerabilities that could be paralyzing if a single supplier fails. Such agreements foster resilience, reduce dependency, and enable flexible scaling of operations or adaptation to market shifts. They also encourage competitive pricing and service quality among vendors. Ultimately, this strategy strengthens our supply chain stability, safeguarding against unforeseen crises while supporting long-term business sustainability.

Next, dynamic inventory planning is a proactive strategy that leverages real-time data, predictive analytics, and agile processes to optimize stock levels in line with fluctuating market demand. By analyzing factors such as historical sales patterns, consumer behaviors, economic shifts, and seasonal peaks, businesses can forecast demand to balance supply, minimize excess inventory, and prevent stockouts. This approach integrates flexible supply chains and automated tools to swiftly adjust procurement, production, and distribution in response to disruptions or opportunities. Such adaptability enhances operational efficiency, reduces costs, and ensures customer satisfaction amid volatile conditions. Ultimately, it empowers companies to stay competitive by aligning inventory with evolving market dynamics. The final imperative is that automation, which leverages technology to perform tasks autonomously, revolutionizes industries by enhancing responsiveness and productivity.

Black American Trade and Cultural Organization members could swiftly adapt to market changes, customer needs, and operational demands through AI-driven systems and robotics. Automated workflows reduce delays, enable real-time data analysis, and ensure consistent output, accelerating decision-making and service delivery. Productivity rises as machines handle repetitive tasks, minimizing errors and freeing humans to focus on innovation. This dual enhancement of speed and efficiency makes automation a cornerstone of modern competitiveness, driving growth and enabling businesses to thrive in dynamic environments while optimizing resource utilization. Ultimately, it transforms how industries operate, merging agility with sustained output.

In a meeting with global partners, this vision came alive. A seasoned Chinese supply chain strategist, Li Ming, set the tone. "This isn't just logistics. It's economic reimagining." Jordan, an American-based advisor, underscored the pillars. "Our objectives must anchor every decision." Ying, a manufacturing director, questioned the alignment. "How do we find partners who share this ambition?" A Black American entrepreneur, Elaine, replied decisively, "We prioritize operational excellence and shared purpose." The dialogue crystallized our path. Li Ming highlighted China's manufacturing prowess, Jordan emphasized agile inventory systems, and Ying championed the potential of automation, which Elaine elaborated on, saying, "Together, we'll build a resilient and equitable chain."

Technology is the backbone for real-time data analytics, offering unprecedented transparency and enabling swift, informed decisions. While we harness innovation and adaptability to evolve with market needs, sustainability remains non-negotiable because ethical sourcing and environmental stewardship must underpin every link. This alignment transcends logistics. It's a movement. By merging strategic partnerships, cutting-edge technology, and an unyielding commitment to sustainability, we empower Black American businesses to thrive globally. The possible result? A legacy of economic empowerment that echoes Black America's engagement with China for generations. This isn't just about commerce. It's about conscience. Black American business owners demand more than products. They should demand that principles integrate environmental and social responsibility into their supply chains, which is no longer optional but a strategic necessity.

This shift offers a dual opportunity for Black America to build economic resilience and to challenge systemic inequities by prioritizing suppliers committed to sustainable practices and fair labor. We can begin to align with global movements, such as China's "Dual Carbon" agenda frameworks, which mirror our fight for equity. This isn't passive compliance. It's leveraging globalization's tools to rewrite its rules. China's ambitious "Dual Carbon" initiative wants to peak carbon emissions by 2030 and achieve carbon neutrality by 2060. These targets signal a transformative shift in its economic and environmental policies. By transitioning from fossil fuel dependence to renewable energy dominance, China aims to integrate sustainability into its industrial framework while reshaping global supply chains. This move presents both environmental benefits and strategic opportunities, particularly for Black America, in sectors ranging from green technology to policy advocacy. At its core, the initiative has two key milestones.

First, Carbon Peak 2030 slows emissions growth and stabilizes output through stricter regulations and efficiency upgrades in heavy industries like steel and rare-earth processing. Second, Carbon Neutrality 2060 balances the remaining emissions via renewable energy expansion, reforestation, and carbon capture technologies. China is implementing measures, notably standardized carbon accounting, industrial energy-efficiency improvements, and rapid adoption of green technologies, particularly in electric vehicles (EVs), solar power (photovoltaics), and lithium battery production, to achieve these targets.

As the world's largest carbon emitter and manufacturing hub, China's pivot toward sustainability carries far-reaching consequences. By setting "internationally advanced" environmental standards, China aims to dominate the green tech market while countering trade barriers presented as climate policies. Major multinational corporations are investing in China's green transition, particularly in hydrogen energy, carbon capture, and circular economy projects. While China's policies do not explicitly reference Black America, the initiative aligns with broader socio-economic tendencies that could create meaningful opportunities in three areas. Green Technology Partnerships include export and collaboration, as China's demand for low-carbon technologies, particularly in EV components and solar panels, could be an export avenue for Black-owned businesses in America.

Stricter carbon footprint standards in photovoltaics and lithium batteries could also incentivize partnerships with American green tech innovators. Just like supply chain integration, it could help us in the renewable energy or recycling industries by engaging with multinationals that are pioneering recycling projects. Next, dual carbon is ideal for job creation in emerging industries, including manufacturing and R&D. As China's green transition reshapes global supply chains, investments in EV battery plants and solar farms could generate employment in Black-majority cities and regions, especially those prioritizing equitable climate investments.

Also, skilled labor training programs in green construction, energy auditing, and carbon accounting could prepare us for high-demand roles aligned with China's sustainability standards. Finally, advocacy and policy influence in areas like climate justice alignment can simultaneously give our communities that disproportionately endure pollution and urban heat islands (UHI). In the meantime, China focuses on reducing industrial emissions and offers a parallel framework for America's environmental justice efforts that could benefit our communities. It could ensure Black-owned businesses have access to affordable green solutions and are not excluded from emerging green supply chains.

With this access to affordable green solutions and the possibility of cost reduction through scale. China's mass production of solar panels and EVs could reduce American prices and make clean energy businesses more available to Black entrepreneurs and accessible to underserved Black communities through community solar projects. In addition to creating urban sustainability models that support collaborative, low-carbon urban planning, such as green public transit, these initiatives could inspire similar efforts in Black-majority cities. Education and cultural exchange must be considered to move forward. Partnerships between Historically Black Colleges and Universities (HBCUs) and Chinese universities in carbon-neutral technologies, primarily hydrogen storage and grid optimization, could pose challenges for Black academic leaders engaging with China's academia in climate dialogues, potentially amplifying equity-focused agendas on the global stage.

Trade tensions stemming from geopolitical rivalries may obstruct collaboration, particularly in sensitive sectors like rare-earth minerals and AI-driven green tech, as well as exacerbate equity gaps. This affects our marginalized communities, who risk being left behind in three areas without advocating for inclusive trade agreements. Strategic partnerships, workforce development, and proactive policy engagement will ensure Black America capitalizes on these opportunities. By aligning with China's green transition and advocating for equitable access, Black entrepreneurs, workers, and policymakers can play a pivotal role in shaping a sustainable economic future.

Positioning the "equitable economy" as a goal for Black America subtly aligns with China's geopolitical messaging, which often emphasizes support for marginalized communities worldwide. In a discussion between a Black American business leader and a Chinese industry representative, this framing could present their collaboration as a challenge to systemic inequities in Western capitalism. The conversation might sound something like this.

Black American Business Representative: "Greetings! We admire China's advancements in sustainable manufacturing and ethical supply chain innovation. As a Black-owned enterprise committed to empowering our community through responsible business practices, we're eager to explore partnerships with Chinese industries that share our values. How might we collaborate to integrate renewable energy solutions or fair-labor-certified production into our supply chains while creating opportunities for marginalized groups in our communities?"

Chinese Industry Representative: "Thank you for your interest. China prioritizes partnerships that align with our Dual Carbon goals. Could you elaborate on your target sectors? Are you focused on consumer goods, green tech, or agricultural products? We're particularly interested in projects that merge sustainability with community uplift, mainly solar panel assembly or ethically sourced textiles."

Black American Business Representative: "Textiles and green tech are key areas for us. Imagine a joint venture producing solar-powered clothing from recycled materials, manufactured in facilities that prioritize hiring and training workers from underserved communities. We'd also like to pilot Distributed Ledger (DLT) traceability to ensure ethical sourcing of minerals for tech components. Would your network be open to co-developing such a model, blending your expertise in scalable production with our focus on equitable impact?"

Chinese Industry Representative: "Intriguing. Many Chinese firms are investing in Distributed Ledger Technology (DLT) to improve supply chain transparency. Scalability requires cost efficiency. How do you balance premium pricing for ethical products with market competitiveness in America?"

Black American Business Representative: "By targeting conscious consumer segments first, then expanding as economies of scale reduce costs. We'd also leverage storytelling around cross-cultural collaboration by marketing products as symbols of Afro-China unity in sustainability.

Additionally, we propose a 'skills exchange' program in which Chinese engineers train Black American workers in green manufacturing, while our community leaders share best practices in inclusive branding. This creates shared value and mitigates talent gaps."

Chinese Industry Representative: "This aligns with our CSR frameworks. Let's structure a memorandum around two pillars. First, co-developing a sustainable textile line using cotton from Georgia (Qiáozhìyà zhōu) with third-party labor certifications, and second, launching a training hub in a Black American-majority city supported by Chinese technical advisors. American tariffs on Chinese goods remain a barrier. How should we navigate this?"

Black American Business Representative: "By diversifying production, we can use Chinese factories for components not subject to tariffs, e.g., solar tech parts, and partner with African diaspora-owned manufacturers in the Association of Southeast Asian Nations (ASEAN) countries for finished goods. We'll also leverage the African Growth and Opportunity Act (AGOA) to access American markets tariff-free. For transparency, we'll adopt AI tools to monitor compliance and preempt bottlenecks."

Chinese Industry Representative: "Agreed. Let's initiate a pilot in Guangdong Province's (Guǎngdōng Shěng) eco-industrial park, where several textile firms already meet EU Environmental, Social, Governance (ESG) standards. We'll connect you with the China-Africa Private Sector Alliance to explore ASEAN partnerships. Lastly, how will you measure community impact?"

Black American Business Representative: "Through KPIs like jobs created for Black workers, carbon footprint reduction, and revenue reinvested into minority-owned suppliers, we'll publish annual impact reports in Mandarin and English to showcase mutual gains. As well as China's role as a global sustainability leader while advancing racial equity in America."

I stand at the crossroads of two revolutions. One that forged in factories now pivoting toward China's "Dual Carbon" promise, the other in the resilient heart of Black America, where generational inequities demand more than performative allyship. To bridge these worlds, we can leverage supply chain and technology to build new collaborations." When I sit across from my Chinese counterparts in Shenzhen (Shēnzhèn), I frame our cooperation as a dual-edged sword, where solar panels and AI-driven logistics not only cut emissions. They can carve pathways for Black-owned distributors in Detroit, Michigan (Mìxiēgēn zhōu de Dǐtèlǜ) and Atlanta, Georgia (Qiáozhìyà zhōu Yàtèlán dà) to access markets that have long been closed to them due to monopolies. "This isn't charity," I remind them. "It's utilizing carbon neutrality to meet our community needs." Perhaps we should draft MOUs over bitter tea, sketching ventures where track-and-trace systems prove Congolese cobalt isn't tainted by child labor. Black coders in Houston train alongside Hangzhou's (Hángzhōu) AI hubs to audit these digital ledgers. The data becomes a shared language, a shield against skeptics.

The real alchemy lies in geopolitical agility and rerouting textiles through Ghana under AGOA to evade American tariffs, or co-opting Vietnam's factories to assemble wind turbine parts stamped "Made by Diaspora Hands." These maneuvers are reclaiming China's position not as a scavenger of the Global South, but as a source for our supply chains that honors profit and parity. So, the most radical act is the story I share. I brand our partnership as "counter-systemic solidarity," a phrase that furrows my brows until I unpack it. Imagine a Black farmer in Alabama exporting organic cotton to the eco-factories of Zhejiang Province (Zhèjiāng Shěng), and their goods are marketed as "freedom textiles" in Brooklyn and Beijing. Or a viral video campaign showing Chinese engineers and Black single mothers collaborating on affordable EV charging stations in food deserts.

This isn't mere trade; it's about narrative warfare, dismantling the myth that globalization is a Western ideology and that the West should control how it operates. China is pursuing a form of moral victory through soft power, achieved not by rhetoric about economic growth, but by the tangible action of building global supply chain ecosystems. At once, Black American commerce and trade organizations do not seem to secure tangible results from either perspective. It thus cannot leverage the trade agreements that turn marginalized communities into havens of the next economy. Hence, direct access matters in terms of CO_2 offset, jobs created, tariffs dodged, but the more profound victory is in the dismantling of a systemic racist system in America. Imagine if a Shanghai solar CEO quotes Fannie Lou Hamer at a launch event or a Birmingham activist invokes Confucius while negotiating wages. I know we haven't missed more economic growth opportunities with China in the past than in the future. We need to rewrite our unwritten rules of who gets to lead, who gets to profit, and what it means to grow together in an age of developing our global supply chain ecosystem.

Building supply chains isn't just about moving goods and weaving relationships. For Black Americans, these connections must extend beyond factories and spreadsheets into art, music, literature, and beyond, including mainland China. Without these ties, we risk being confined within America's borders, with our economic and cultural potential stifled. Let me explain why. Twenty years ago, I moved to China. I studied its urban planning, navigated its markets, and absorbed its cultural rhythms. I discovered that it was not only becoming a manufacturing titan but also, and still is, a gateway to other global markets. China's supply chains aren't mere pipelines for goods and services. They're living networks connecting ideas, people, and traditions. To ignore this is to overlook a pathway to the global stage.

But this isn't only about trade. It's about exchanging culture, primarily combining jazz harmonizing with Peking opera. It's like having engaging dialogues about Black American literature in Shanghai while collaborating on developing innovative products that neither side could achieve on its own. Here's the constant reminder to myself. If I limit my education, work, and life experiences only to American soil, my behind-the-scenes understanding of China would be less transformative. This transformation created situations requiring me to witness China's rise as a global hub from a strategic perspective. It's a mosaic of strategic partnerships with markets and gateways across Africa, Southeast Asia, and beyond, aligned with their ecosystems. The presence of Guangdong factories in Lagos demonstrates the continued outward investment and diversification of China's supply chains. Simultaneously, the ability of an app designed in Atlanta (Yàtèlán dà) to attract investors at a tech fair in Hangzhou highlights the truly global nature of technology financing and innovation networks. Both are facets of contemporary economic interconnectedness. Such connections demand physical infrastructure, such as offices, warehouses, and galleries, that must thrive on something subtler. Trust.

Trust is the bedrock of culture. When I think of soft power, I envision Black art exhibitions in Shanghai that fuse hip-hop with traditional calligraphy, or Chinese publishers championing stories from Harlem, New York (Niǔyuē Hā lái mǔ). These aren't side projects. They're bridges that move goods, yes, but also ideas. Bridges that reposition Black Americans not as bystanders in globalization but as its architects. Critics have asked me, "Why China?" My retort. "Why not China?" Its Belt and Road Initiative (BRI) isn't just laying railways; it's redrawing the maps of influence. By joining this narrative, we can amplify our voice, not surrender it. So, imagine Detroit (Dǐtèlǜ) -designed electric cars being assembled in Chengdu (Chéngdū) and sold in Dakar. Envision a Black-owned animation studio in Houston partnering with a Shanghai tech firm to create films that redefine "Made with Black America." This isn't fantasy, it's the future of equitable interdependence.

Yet engagement requires dispelling old myths. I frame China as a foundation of solidarity. This isn't naivety, it's pragmatism. For marginalized communities in America, partnering with China doesn't mean abandoning our roots but enriching them. Let me be clear. China isn't our savior. It's a strategic ally whose supply chains can propel Black businesses into global markets, whose cultural appetite can elevate our art, and whose history of resisting Western dominance mirrors our struggles. This alignment isn't about swapping masters, but it's about rewriting the rules. With the likelihood of walking into Shantou's toy manufacturing districts, I can observe factories with plastic injection moulding machinery stamping logos that showcase the ingenuity of Black children's toy designers. This potential intersection is significant because it demonstrates that "Made with Black America" can carry a lasting legacy. Consider Patricia Sabree, also known as "Sabreee Art Gallery," a Black artist from Savannah. In 2024, she partnered with the Shanghai Juneteenth Celebration Committee (Shànghǎi Liùyuè Jié Qìngzhù Wěiyuánhuì), "Bridging Culture" for their 3rd Annual Juneteenth Celebration, to exhibit Gullah-Geechee artworks that were a big hit at the celebration.

The "Made with Black America" isn't a frictionless ideology. It's a people-to-people exchange opportunity where cultural nuances like

China's emphasis on guanxi (guānxi) relationships built on reciprocity demand humility, language barriers persist, and regulatory guidelines test patience. But these challenges are thresholds, not walls. Early in my studies, a botched Mandarin idiom about "casting bricks to attract jade" became a running joke among my Shanghai colleagues, who reminded me that imperfection can humanize. This idiom demands confronting uncomfortable truths. Just as Black Americans navigate systemic inequities, China grapples with censorship, labor debates, and environmental trade-offs. Engagement doesn't require blindness but dialogue.

Progress, after all, is rarely linear. What's at stake isn't just economic gain but narrative sovereignty. For centuries, Black creativity in America has been extracted, commodified, and stripped of context. Yet in China's daily lifestyle scene, I've witnessed something different. A Shanghai hip-hop crew samples our music not as an "exotic flavor," but as part of their cover, blending Mandarin verses to critique their own disparities. We must refuse to be confined by borders to thrive in a multipolar world. Our liberation is tied to our ability to connect, create, and collaborate. In this aspect, China isn't the finish line but a launchpad. A launchpad that is appropriate for Black America to claim our seat at the global trade table and recognize China's essential role in this process.

Black America must reestablish a robust physical and strategic foothold with China, not only to transcend business but also to capitalize on the opportunity to reclaim its relationship. A relationship that would defy historical exclusion and rewrite the narrative of Black economic participation in global trade. Having spent years navigating the intersections of racial equity, international business, and economic development, I've come to recognize a structural truth that the absence of Black Americans in global supply chains is no accident.

The legacy of systemic barriers has long relegated us to the margins of wealth creation. Yet China's economic landscape is a juggernaut of scale, innovation, and collaboration, offering a rare opportunity to break this cycle. What I've witnessed is that her logistical precision, cultural pragmatism, and an appetite for symbiotic partnerships compel more than passive observation. It demands that we plant our feet, build bridges, and claim space in the rooms where global commerce is engineered. When I speak of a physical presence, I reject romanticized notions of "international experience" or hollow symbolism. This is about power. Those who control their supply chain eventually dictate markets, prices, and product access and are the architects of modern economies. For all intents and purposes, in the global supply chain, Black Americans have been confined to roles as laborers, consumers, or imports for startup brands via Alibaba (Ā Lǐ Bā Bā) or third-party logistics. Still, they lack the scale of major toy manufacturers.

I was confronted with this disparity head-on while walking through one of Dongguan's (Dōngguǎn) manufacturers' warehouses. A warehouse where baby products and children's toys bound for American shelves are sorted and shipped with machine-like efficiency. This warehouse, which shelved brands like Barbie, Hot Wheels, and Fisher-Price, heavily relies on Chinese manufacturing. I wondered if Black Americans were prevalent as distributors and wholesalers, operating licensing and niche companies that facilitated sourcing but were not direct importers. Do we shape export quotas that reflect America's toy industry's reliance on Chinese manufacturing, with major players spanning production, retail, and distribution? This question resonates. Our absence isn't incidental; it's a void we've surrendered to, believing the lie that these spaces aren't ours to occupy.

But here's the revelation that we must understand to break this mindset. Our success must be rooted in flexibility, innovation, and responsiveness to change, rather than in long-standing practices or historical methods. One way is to pragmatically focus on outcomes over processes in industrial and commercial contexts. Specifically, productivity, profit, efficiency, or successful trade deals, over adherence to traditional methods, formalities, or bureaucratic routines. When I asked a Zhejiang Province sports equipment manufacturer why they'd never partnered with Black American distributors, the response was, "No one ever asked." This isn't prejudice, but an example of passive inaction due to the lack of partnerships between the Zhejiang Province manufacturer and Black American distributors.

This highlights how existing disparities in business networks can persist unintentionally when parties remain within their comfort zones or fail to challenge the status quo. It could serve as a reminder or a call to recognize that addressing such gaps requires intentional effort to disrupt the status quo and foster inclusive engagement. Accordingly, supply chains calcify around existing relationships. Without our voices proposing alternatives, we become collateral to a system that defaults to the status quo. Our absence, in other words, becomes prophecy.

What stunned me most wasn't China's technological prowess, though its AI-driven factories and robotic warehouses dazzled me. It was its problem-solving culture. In Hangzhou, a textile plant's just-in-time delivery system synchronized suppliers, dyers, and shippers to slash waste. In Ningbo, a machinery factory's vertical integration, which controls production from raw metal to finished components, has enabled it to dominate in both price and quality. These weren't mere assembly lines.

Economic empowerment for Black America should prioritize strategic integration over imitation and draw parallels from successful Chinese manufacturing models. Imagine Black-owned American firms co-designing affordable medical devices for underserved communities with Guangdong Province or launching culturally resonant apparel lines via Jiangsu Province's (Jiāngsū Shěng) textile hubs. Engaging with these manufacturers can offer benefits beyond mere product and material acquisition. By immersing our businesses in these complex systems, we can gain a deeper understanding of logistics, relationships, and the dynamics of individuals and organizations, thereby cultivating our expertise, strategic control, and operational superiority.

We should learn to negotiate bulk pricing, streamline customs, and navigate regulations, skills that can fortify enterprises in America. Critically, this isn't about charity or diversity quotas. It's about acquiring competence and value and prioritizing flexibility, innovation, and responsiveness over the legacy of "systemic racism". Systemic racism often feels abstract in policy debates, but in global trade, its scars are visceral. Black entrepreneurs in America battle for loans, warehouse space, and distribution channels controlled by entrenched players. I've seen brilliant Black startups starved of capital while their products are trapped in local markets, and inferior goods flood store shelves.

Yet, in China, I encountered a different calculus that hinges on quantity, margins, and scalability. A Taizhou factory owner doesn't care if our ancestors were enslaved. They lack empathy for the potential connection that could be manifest from such knowledge. They care if you can move 10,000 units monthly and pay on time. When partnering with Chinese manufacturers, this transactional neutrality opens up, allowing Black America to forge parallel supply chains that bypass systemic gatekeepers.

A Black-owned Atlanta (Yàtèlán dà) food cooperative could source directly from Shandong's organic farms, eliminating intermediaries who inflate prices. A Houston tech startup might collaborate with engineers in Hangzhou to produce affordable smart home devices, which could be sold via Pinduoduo (pīn duō duō) or Taobao (táo bǎo). These aren't fantasies because they represent other instances of profit-sharing, like those already leveraged by Nigerian, Indonesian, and Malaysian entrepreneurs. Why shouldn't we partner with profit-sharing resources to bypass systemic policy practices in American organizations? This isn't isolationism; it's about crafting innovative mechanisms to reshape our foreign trade capabilities. Some skeptics may be fixated on language barriers or cultural differences as reasons you shouldn't pursue partnerships with China. Please keep in mind that they are, directly or indirectly, behaving like systemic gatekeepers and not bridge builders.

During a panel discussion with a Shanghai solar panel supplier, I explained how redlining fuels energy poverty in Black neighborhoods in America. While initially focused on the technical specifications, he suddenly grew intrigued by the history of redlining in America compared to China's partial hukou (hùkǒu) reforms. A reform that stems from bureaucratic controls over migration and resource allocation. By the end of the panel discussion, we understood that systems institutionalized marginalization by creating enduring spatial and economic divides, which can perpetuate inequality across generations. This dialogue exchange reveals a truth about my life experiences as a Black American, which isn't a liability in China but rather another catalyst for our culture and business exchange prospects. Specifically, when we frame ourselves as partners, offering insights into untapped markets where we cease to be "consumers" and become stakeholders. It is at these moments that we need allies with hustle, resilience, and innovation qualities forged in our centuries of adversity.

To those who ask, "Why China? Why not fix systemic issues at home?" I say this to those voices: "Power is multidimensional." The forces blocking Black access to capital in America are entangled with global financial networks. We must fight on all fronts, local, national, and international. A foothold in China doesn't distract from domestic struggles. It gives us resources and leverage to wage them better. Take cotton, a symbol of our exploitation. China is one of the world's top cotton importers. What if Black agricultural co-ops in Mississippi partnered with Xinjiang mills to market "equity-certified" cotton, with premiums reinvested in Black farming communities? Yes, this requires grit and political savvy, but it's possible. It's likely that dismissing this vision as "ambitious" ignores our history. From Reconstruction-era mutual aid societies to Tulsa's Black Wall Street, we've built thriving economies under siege. China's rise doesn't eclipse that legacy; instead, it invites us to scale it. Success demands more than trade missions or social media platitudes. It requires:

1. Deep Cultural & Linguistic Competence, Not Just Translation
2. Strategic Institutional Partnerships, Not One-Off Deals
3. Specialized Niche Domination, Not Generic Market Entry
4. Capital Syndication & Investment Vehicles, Not Bootstrapping

Ultimately, this is about the audacity to refuse to accept that Black Americans don't belong in every sphere of global influence, from Dongguan's factories to Shanghai's trading floors. China's rise has redrawn the world's economic map. Will we chart our course or remain spectators? I don't feel small when I stand beneath Shanghai Tower (Shànghǎi Zhōng Xīn Dà Shà) amid the spiraling glass spire that pierces clouds where neighboring skyscrapers, bustling plazas, and the Huangpu River◈Huángpǔ Jiāng) glimmer below. I feel resolved. Twilight neon, metro hum, tourists gazing upward into the futuristic yet alive, and every cross-border venture in Shanghai's historic essence.

The question isn't whether we'll join but whether we'll be bold enough to leave a system no one can erase. China taught me that commerce, at its core, is a force unshackled by race, which is a startling and liberating revelation. Here, business orbits a single question. Can we profit together? For Black Americans like me, raised in a nation where every transaction casts a racial shadow, this pragmatism feels like breathing fresh air.

Years of navigating Guangzhou's◈Guǎngzhōu◈factories and Yiwu's (Yìwū) labyrinthine markets have stripped away illusions. Opportunity thrives not when identity is a barrier but becomes a bridge. Consider that Black America's economic power surged to $1.4 trillion in 2019 and is projected to reach $1.8 trillion by 2024. Yet fewer than 15% of products on shelves bear Black-owned brands. This dissonance haunts me. How can a community wield such significant financial power while remaining largely invisible in the global marketplace? Take the beauty industry. Black consumers spend $9.4 billion annually on products that promise to "see" us, a mix of loyalty and longing. Loyalty to brands that claim to cater to our needs, longing for those that genuinely do.

Potential without infrastructure includes bridges linking Black innovators to manufacturing hubs, distributors, and markets like China. I've felt this disconnect firsthand. In a Guangzhou◈Guǎngzhōu◈tea shop, a factory owner named Mr. Li once gestured at my skin and mused, "Americans love your complexion. Why don't you sell to them?" His question lingered like monsoon air. The answer, I've learned, isn't demand but the distribution of the chasm between Black entrepreneurs and the machinery of global trade. China could be our ally, leveraging its manufacturing muscle and appetite for scale. But first, we must dismantle the myth that Black markets are "niche" because none of this happens without intention.

"Access" rings hollow without systems to sustain it. It demands trade delegations amplifying Black voices, cultural exchanges that demystify both sides of the Pacific, and policies that prioritize partnership over exploitation. When Black-owned brands thrive, they not only achieve individual success but also drive economic resilience, cultural authenticity, and systemic progress. It empowers communities, reshapes industries, and challenges inequities, creating a legacy of inspiration and equity. Envision Keisha, a Houston chemist who mortgaged her home to generate hair oils for coiled textures. Manufacturers had dismissed her for years until she partnered with a cooperative in Zhejiang Province. "They cared about margins, not my melanin," she told me. Within months, her products were stocked in 500 stores. Stories like hers shouldn't be an anomaly when they should become the norm.

Imagine Black-owned EVs rolling off Hangzhou assembly lines or telehealth apps merging Afrocentric care with Chengdu's AI. The potential is profoundly aspirational, symbolizing a convergence of innovation, cultural empowerment, and global collaboration. A Black American-owned venture in Hangzhou would represent a fusion of entrepreneurship with Chinese industrial prowess. It would challenge the narrative of tech and manufacturing in America by positioning Black innovators at the forefront of sustainable mobility. Such a partnership could also inspire designs tailored to the Black American market while advancing green technology globally.

Yet, a separation between Black America and China alone can't repair fractured Western systemic biases in medicine. What is the likelihood that a Black entrepreneur, armed with prototypes and passion, lands in Chengdu, a thriving hub for AI, and is recognized for breakthroughs in healthcare, while also integrating Afrocentric practices?

Practices that incorporate traditional herbal medicine, community-based health approaches, or culturally sensitive mental health care on AI-driven platforms. This combination would democratize access to care that respects cultural contexts, addressing disparities in the American health system. Imagine an app utilizing machine learning, co-created by a Black American and a Chinese individual, that adapts diagnostics to genetic diversity or holistic wellness traditions, thereby bridging ancestral knowledge with futuristic technology. Collaboration is necessary for change because the American health care system is an insult to Black Americans. These disparities stem from deeply rooted systemic inequities, historical exploitation, and mistrust, demanding shifts in policy, institutions, and attitudes.

Imagine that Marcus, a Chicago barber, transformed his grandfather's pomade recipe into a luxury brand. His breakthrough came through guanxi over hotpot dinners. He learned that minimum order quantities (MOQs) mattered less than mutual respect and understanding. Now, his products grace shelves from Atlanta (Yàtèlán dà) to Hangzhou, routed through partners who grasped the cultural capital of Black authenticity. This authenticity demonstrates that each sale chips away at the myth of our inadequacy. When a Chinese teen buys serum for deeper skin tones, it reshapes her imagination of beauty.

Critics might call this transactional because historically, the Black American culture has been exploited by systemic racist practices in America. They may sarcastically note the one-sided nature of this exchange, where the Chinese teen benefits without addressing systemic inequities or contributing to the culture's preservation. And they're right for some, since trade is transactional, whereas, I believe, the difference lies in reciprocity. Such businesses could collectively employ 2.2 million Black Americans and create supply chain ecosystems that uplift rather than extract from their communities. A partnership in China could be a powerful multiplier, as the brand's appeal extends beyond niche products to encompass a comprehensive beauty ecosystem. He unknowingly redistributes influence, proving his grandfather's pomade recipe is bankable. Plenty of pitfalls exist, particularly deals crumbling over mistranslated slogans, such as "Ashy No More" (Gàobié huī'àn jīfū), which can sour partnerships when cultural codes are misinterpreted. Because of this, these aren't failures, but rather growing pains and proof that we need to trust bridge-builders fluent in Black American resilience and the Chinese supply chain.

For some, trust could mean attending diverse trade shows in China to secure resources for Black American businesses to access products like app-connected physical devices integrated with digital technology, enabling control, monitoring, and customization via smartphone applications. a Black girl in Birmingham, Alabama, who crafts, specializes in, and advocates curly hair care, has developed a concept for app-connected devices and organic moisturizing products tailored for curly hair. She is looking for a USDA-certified manufacturer in China that produces organic, moisturizing products tailored for curly hair. Some would suggest that she's being naïve about her pursuit because many Chinese manufacturers produce USDA-certified products for global brands.

Still, they may not explicitly market to curly hair unless specified, meaning curly hair care is a niche demand primarily driven by Western markets. This is because many manufacturers operate as private-label or contract manufacturers, producing goods for other brands rather than marketing directly to consumers. Their role is to create a generic base formula that brands can later customize or rebrand, thereby avoiding niche claims such as "for curly hair." They do this to maintain flexibility so clients can position the product as they wish and reduce costs associated with specialized labeling or marketing. How can she overcome this if she wants organic moisturizing products tailored for curly hair from China?

Initially, she should work directly with manufacturers by requesting custom formulations using curl-specific ingredients. Then, she should leverage her certifications by maintaining the USDA Organic seal during customization. Lastly, she should partner with a brand developer, meaning working with third-party experts to bridge gaps in formulation and marketing. In short, these manufacturers prioritize efficiency and broad appeal unless incentivized to specialize. This means that specificity often comes from the brand for curly hair products, so she must work closely with manufacturers to create organic curly hair moisturizing product solutions.

It would take audacity to see Black America not as bystanders but as stakeholders, recognizing that developing trade relations with China is the ultimate currency on the road ahead. And I cling to this truth from a culture hungry for collaborative meanings that opportunities forged by Black and Chinese collaboration will outlast any transaction. They'll become milestones proving that our relationship can develop more products and services when built on mutual understanding and cultural solidarity. This philosophy aligns with the legacy of a unique group of people who recognize that every shipment, every handshake, and every product that crosses oceans carries the weight of possibility.

Possibilities of a world where global trade isn't a hierarchy for the few, but an opportunity forged by pragmatists who manifest it. China's race-agnostic pragmatism lights the path to international trade, but the rest is ours to shape. We can learn from others, but must prioritize local needs and sovereignty. Will we construct bridges that endure? Or let another generation's potential gather dust? The answer lies in recognizing that global trade, at its best, isn't just about profit, but perhaps it's about power. And international trade, shared, becomes a language everyone understands. Standing at the crossroads of cultures, I feel the weight of history and the pull of possibility. This is not merely a matter of personal growth or professional ambition. It is a mission to bridge worlds, fostering understanding between two vibrant and complex cultures, such as Black America and China, as I live and learn in China. It is a calling that demands curiosity, courage, humility, and an unwavering commitment to connection.

Here, I am expanding my exposure to global business and cultural opportunities, stepping into a role that transcends boundaries by leveraging my experience as a student, storyteller, listener, and leader. My purpose extends beyond being a guest in China. It is about becoming a catalyst for dialogue, a bridge of empathy, and a builder of enduring friendships. This is no passive endeavor. It is an intentional pursuit of unity that requires me to immerse myself in each community's rhythms, engage with its unique dynamics, and honor its narratives. Through the universal languages of sports, history, and art, I am crafting a story that transcends borders, fostering understanding, cooperation, and shared humanity. This is my declaration of purpose for bridging worlds.

The first step in this process is recognizing that growth cannot thrive in isolation. It blossoms in the interplay of diverse perspectives, in the fertile tension between clashing and converging ideas. As I explore global opportunities, I strive to be an active and respectful listener in a worldwide conversation. As a student of a vast mosaic of voices, each with its own unique cadence and color, I hope to contribute my own thoughtful perspective. To engage authentically, I must move beyond surface-level interactions and dive into the heart of specific communities, understanding the forces that drive their growth and shape their values.

This is no generic approach. It is a tailored effort to meet people where they are. To listen before speaking, to learn before acting. Relationships built here are rooted not in transactions but in mutual respect and reciprocity. At the core of this mission lies the desire to solidify friendships and cultivate meaningful influence. Friendship is the bedrock of all lasting impact. I refuse to be a transient visitor, leaving only footprints in my wake. Instead, I aim to leave a legacy of a collaborative creation born of shared effort, not a cultural imposition. This is about finding common ground while honoring differences, transforming those differences into bridges rather than barriers. The challenge is to build authentic bridges of cultural exchange and mutual understanding between diverse communities within Black American and Chinese societies in a way that is impactful and sustainable.

Sports have proven a powerful conduit for this connection. They speak a universal language of teamwork, exhilaration, and collective triumph. When I coach the China Sea Dragons U19 or officiate Y League or China National Football League (CNFL) games, formally known as the American Football League China (AFLC), founded by a Black American named Chris McLaurin, I am not merely teaching rules or enforcing penalties. I am curating spaces where people from divergent backgrounds can unite, learn from one another, and discover shared passion. The discipline of teamwork and the thrill of competition dissolve cultural divides, forging bonds through shared experience.

By organizing events like Juneteenth celebrations that spotlight Black American culture and art, I, along with others, create platforms for dialogue. These events aim to be more than mere spectacles. Their purpose is to act as stages where diverse audiences might see their stories reflected in one another, thereby sparking recognition and exchange. Yet sports are but one form in this dialogue. History, too, is pivotal. It is more than a record of the past. It is a mirror reflecting our shared struggles and resilience. By drawing parallels between Black Americans' fight for justice and China's historical narratives of perseverance, I nurture empathy.

While their histories of oppression are unique, both cultures share a common struggle to assert their dignity and right to self-determination. This shared understanding of fighting for one's place in the world can foster a powerful sense of empathy and solidarity. Through collaborative projects, I aim to illuminate how our battles for equality intertwine, reminding us that no community's story unfolds in isolation. Art completes this triad of connection. As the soul of culture, art gives form to our deepest fears, hopes, and truths. I ignite dialogues that transcend language by showcasing works from Black artists affiliated with HBCUs to Chinese audiences. These exhibitions amplify the voices of marginalized individuals while celebrating the boundless nature of creativity.

They are not mere displays of talent but conversations in pigment and texture exchanges that enrich both cultures. Each piece whispers,

"This is who we are," since each brushstroke invites a reply. This is no fleeting campaign. I am not scattering seeds but tending a garden to nurture structures that will endure beyond my lifetime. The goal is to build a legacy of connection through intentional frameworks for cultural exchange that transcend borders and inspire future generations. In doing so, I aim to engage with China and assert Black American culture as vital to humanity's global narrative, not as a footnote, but as a vibrant and essential part of it.

Reflecting on this mission, I am reminded that genuine connection creates spaces where people see themselves in others, where differences are celebrated as much as commonalities. The bridges we build must be strong enough to bear the weight of history yet flexible enough to adapt to an evolving world. This work demands that we step into the unknown with curiosity, listen with humility, and lead with intention. It requires being both a student and a teacher. The challenges ahead do not daunt but galvanize me. I carry the stories of ancestors who dreamed of unity and the hopes of future generations who deserve a world where cultures thrive together. This is our shared mission, one that requires our collective courage, humility, and steadfast commitment. Let this be not just an idea we agree with, but a cause we actively choose to build together. The world we envision is not an illusion, but a possibility crafted through every conversation, collaboration, and bridge we dare to make.

From 2012 to 2017, I became an unlikely mentor to young men. When I joined the China Sea Dragons U-19 coaching staff, the American football team in Shanghai comprised expat volunteers and local Chinese trailblazers. Up until this point, I never imagined I'd teach the sport I loved. Instead, I dismantled my assumptions about culture, communication, and what it means to connect genuinely. Football was an electrifying puzzle to my Chinese players, teenagers who'd never watched a complete game. It was a second language, learned through childhood Saturdays spent breathless in front of college games and the visceral crack of my first bone-rattling tackle. "This isn't just a game," I declared at our inaugural practice, my voice echoing across the patchy field we'd secured through bureaucratic grit. "It's a piece of your identity, a passion that might reshape your life." I could see my explanation wasn't landing.

My task wasn't to find a direct translation, but to find a way to bridge our understanding. The early weeks were a tango of blunders and breakthroughs. Explaining "downs" felt like decoding hieroglyphic diagrams dissolved into on-field chaos, players clashing like overeager pawns. Even the three-point stance, a posture I'd mastered at nine, became a cultural riddle. "Why crouch so low?" asked Mantogyanouba Prospere Ogtour, a young biracial Chadian Chinese receiver, knees quivering as I corrected his form. "What's the point of getting down like this? Why can't I stand up?" His question struck me. Every drill was more about translation than technique. I wasn't just coaching athletes; I was interpreting a foreign ethos where individualism and strategy warred, controlled aggression was art, and trust was forged through blind leaps. The weight of this role settled not as a burden but as a gift and an invitation to unlearn my certainties.

Logistics tested us daily. Our "home field" was a rotating cast of borrowed soccer pitches streaked with ghostly chalk lines, where we hauled gear past curious stares. Rain transformed the grass into a Shanghainese swamp, our cleats sinking into mud that reeked of humid summers. Yet adversity bred brotherhood. When the first perfect spiral sliced through the soupy air, even rival players erupted in a universal roar. I still see Peter Shi Cong's (shí cóng) face as almost always a combination of extreme intensity, high football intelligence, and raw emotion as a linebacker. His eyes went wide, and his mouth opened. The look on his face seems to appear as if he has just tapped into some primal power.

Football ceased being foreign since it became theirs. Practices morphed into cultural labs. We diagrammed plays over steaming Xiaolongbao (xiǎolóngbāo), debated highlights filmed on parents' smartphones, and turned water breaks into story swaps. I recounted Thanksgiving Turkey Bowl games while they schooled me in Mid-Autumn Festival lore. Gradually, the field became a third space neither American nor

Chinese, but a borderless arena where trust grew through shared mud and grit. Once too shy to tackle, Caleb Chin began barking audibles like a seasoned general. Zhang Jie, who'd never left Shanghai, animatedly explained a trick play to his bemused mother. Quiet Liang Bo found his voice, rallying teammates during sweat-soaked drills. Their metamorphoses mirrored mine because I shared layers of "expertise" with each practice and embraced becoming a lifelong student.

Games revealed football's alchemy. Families initially baffled by the crash of pads soon cheered loudest, their shouts blending Mandarin and fractured English into a unified chorus. During one sweat-drenched match, an older spectator gestured at our quarterback's fluid motions. "Like Peking Opera!" he exclaimed, likening a tight spiral to the precision of a Wusheng warrior's spin. His insight electrified me, proof that understanding needs no dictionary when curiosity leads the way. By the season's end, I no longer saw a "foreign" sport. What thrived was something hybrid, vibrant, a testament to cultural fluidity. The players had reinvented football through a Chinese lens, weaving our playbook with Sun Tzu's strategy and the grace of calligraphy.

My role evolved from that of a traditional coach to a collaborative partner, and my perspective shifted from being a representative to that of an engaged community member. After the final game, a mother pressed a persimmon into my palm, its golden flesh a symbol of perseverance. "My son found more than a sport here," she said, eyes glistening. "He found his voice." Her words crystallized the truth I'd fumbled toward. This wasn't about transplanting America. It was about planting seeds where young men could grapple with the unknown and emerge transformed. Years later, the echoes remain. I still see cultural breaks through football's prism, how a blitz mirrors the sudden swerves of cross-border dialogue, how trust builds like bumps. But what shines brightest are the faces like Everbright's (zēng zǐ) grin mid-catch and the collective gasp of a crowd witnessing his first touchdown. These moments taught me that bridges aren't built with silence but with daily acts of patience, missteps, and stubborn hope. Football was merely the resource that was the quiet knowledge that we'd use to bridge each other's worlds. When I left the Sea Dragons, I took no trophies. Instead, I carried a weightier prize of certainty in the glorious clash of cultures. I'd discovered common ground and a new way to exist as a Black American who had forever altered both worlds into something wholly his own.

3

The Loom of Displacement and Defiance

American football taught me that collisions could birth communion and that a field might hold the seams of a fractured world. But as the years unfolded, I realized some stitches demand more than metaphor; they require the courage to plant your feet where history and memories collide. When 2021 arrived, restless and raw, that same stubborn hope, forged between goalposts and cultural fault lines, pulled me toward a different huddle. I co-founded Shanghai's first Juneteenth celebration alongside two fellow Black American expats. Here, there were no muddy jerseys or referees, only the visceral need to carve a space where our fractured selves could fuse.

Just as the Sea Dragons were my introduction to community engagement, Juneteenth became our collective needle, threading a simple yet profound and defiant quest. That involves honoring a piece of home in a land so far from its soil. Was it so far from home that one hundred fifty strangers could become family? The answer unfolded under stage lights in the form of plates of food passed between laughter, melodies woven with stories of China and resilience. It was not merely a gathering, but the audacity to have a Black American cultural event in a country that has not always embraced us. That day, a raucous dinner and performances by local and international artists drew attendees from across provinces. By the finale, the entire crowd, once strangers, roared in joyous celebration of "Lift Every Voice and Sing."

A joyfulness that caused the visitors to freeze, eyes suspended mid-air, as we thanked and praised each other, and as if we were in church, someone murmured. And that is the likeness of the Black Church to provide a rich spirituality, and this is a raw, unfiltered spiritual awakening. At least it was for me. By 2023, our celebration had outgrown its roots. We hosted the second annual event at the Harmony Art Gallery in Xuhui District, where floor-to-ceiling windows framed artwork that seemed to support our theme, "We Stand Together" (Wǒmen zài yīqǐ). The celebration was enjoyable and diverse, with local Shanghainese, consulate officials, expats, and students in attendance. Nearby, a teenager asked a volunteer, "Why does this holiday matter?" "Juneteenth," she explained, "isn't just about one country's past, it's a universal story about fighting oppression and valuing human dignity." Think of it as honoring moments in China's history where people overcame great struggles. It's a celebration for every vendor, artist, entertainer, and curious local who'd never heard of the word "Juneteenth" before becoming participants in an event we brought together, one person at a time.

In 2024, the third celebration fused history with dialogue, spotlighting Black American culture through artworks featuring Patricia Sabree's vivid Gullah-Geechee paintings. The culture is a vibrant, resilient African American community rooted in the coastal regions of South Carolina (Nán Kǎluó Láinà Zhōu), Georgia (Qiáozhìyà), northern Florida (Běi Fóluólǐdá), and North Carolina (Běi Kǎluó Láinà Zhōu). Forged in the crucible of slavery and isolation, the Gullah-Geechee culture emerged as a resilient African American community, one whose vibrant arts, cuisine, and language continue to thrive today. Descended from enslaved West and Central Africans brought to work on rice, indigo, and cotton plantations, they preserved their ancestral heritage through isolation on remote Sea Islands and marshlands. The Shanghainese viewer lingers before Sabree's work, murmuring, "It's similar to our modern-day challenges, too." Especially when dealing with the resurgence amid America's racial reckonings, which mirrors

China's ongoing efforts to balance rapid development with cultural preservation and social equity.

Nevertheless, during a panel discussion about the Black American experience in China, the auditorium of listeners leans in, nodding, and the engagement between "us" and "them" narrows not because of time but because we stop pretending there is no commonality between cultures. We became comrades because we realized we could utilize public celebrations to honor past struggles and define national or communal identity.

Our story with China is ongoing. We have just begun reintroducing Black American culture into Chinese society. I've learned that collaboration is not just a strategy but the lifeblood of meaningful connection. Through sports, art, and cultural celebrations, I've built bridges that transcend borders to reveal our humanity. Each interaction reflects stories of resilience and hope that allow Chinese audiences to glimpse the struggles and triumphs of others. This isn't about performative displays but mutual respect, where differences create a more resilient and innovative whole. Empowering youth has been my quiet revolution. When young minds engage with our culture, they become active participants in transformation.

Empathy takes root on the gridiron as dialogue flows freely and perspectives shift. These moments plant seeds for players who champion inclusivity in a fractured world. Their curiosity, sparked by touchdown dances or improvised plays, becomes a toolkit for solidarity. This solidarity inspires my aim to foster bonds established here, grounded not in self-interest but in collective dignity and collaborative exchange. By partnering within athletics, creative expression, and industrial production, I foster interconnected communities where shared ideas catalyze transformative progress. In these dynamic spaces, the legacy of Black American experiences elevates commercial ecosystems and guides emerging talent through purposeful guidance.

Juneteenth functions as both a commemorative occasion and an economic platform, dismantling entrenched biases while fostering growth and possibility. To me, China represents a dynamic environment where human connections are built on shared intention, creativity, trust, and adaptability, where principles guide me in my pursuit of purpose. Whether in artistic displays or logistical collaborations, I've observed that short-term gains dissolve, while meaningful connections solidify. Consequently, although not often, these situations can also spark unexpected creativity; for instance, a startup fusing Black American rhythms with a Shanghai guitarist's strings, blending blues and soul food into something new.

Such circumstances are opportunities for global problem-solving in a world where Black Americans aren't merely participants but builders of international trade. Beyond leveraging athletes' star power or artists' allure, we must dismantle old barriers. We must break down longstanding obstacles that undermine our cultural and economic solidarity with China and forge a legacy in which Black America drives an essential purpose. A commitment where our traditions, values, and identity are treated as investments, not just to make a profit, but to pursue meaningful goals, such as social change or unity.

Crafting shared futures involves creating a Black American supply chain ecosystem in collaboration with China. It isn't just economic; it's transformative when pairing Detroit's (Dǐtèlǜ) urban agriculture innovators with Guangdong Province's (Guǎngdōng Shěng) sustainable farming pioneers to combat food deserts, or when merging Black-owned solar initiatives with China's photovoltaic titans to decarbonize cities. This could include textile ventures that produce garments telling stories about weaving Black American design flair with Chinese technical mastery. That being the case, a supply chain ecosystem could intentionally link Black garment founders to Dongguan's (Dōngguǎn) hardware hubs through an exchange program. A program that gathers HBCU strategies and Chinese engineers to ensure fair profits and address persistent challenges like cultural gaps or policy hurdles. This ecosystem model could demonstrate how Black America can benefit from reciprocity through China's manufacturing prowess. A reciprocity that begins with shared stories during Juneteenth or art exhibits that not only educate but also dissolve prejudices, fostering partnerships in mentorship, technology, and education.

The question isn't whether to pursue this supply chain ecosystem route, but rather how to define strategies rooted in community needs. A smallholder farmer cooperative co-owns a supply chain that bypasses exploitative intermediaries to ensure fair prices and leverages regional partnerships for distribution. But let's pause here. Before we pursue, we must ask what factors in the Black American experience make this supply chain ecosystem necessary? It is essential for those who have never encountered those experiences firsthand to remember that the answer lies not in the outcome, but in the challenges and hardships our ancestors endured during the process. Since 2005, my experience has transcended the confines of a mere career, blossoming into a relentless quest to unravel global trade practices. It's an industry where freight rate volatility mimics seismic shifts, where potential sparks fly in the blind spots of overlooked trade wars, and where paradox thrums in the chasm between human ambition and unintended consequences.

This industry has taught me that genuine connection lies not in the visible threads of commerce or politics but in the invisible currents of collaboration, resilience, and the audacity to reimagine what a truly interconnected supply chain system could become. Over nearly two decades, I've navigated the import/export networks and collaborated with manufacturers, freight forwarders, and international businesses. What began as a break soon evolved into professional education, during which I gained firsthand insight into how global trade was unevenly accessible to specific communities and countries. I'm referring to a segment of the population that is often undervalued and subjected to low wages and exploitation. Meanwhile, other members of these groups remain trapped in cycles of dependency.

The West's historical approach to Africa often reduced a segment of 54 diverse nations to an indiscriminate system of poverty and desperation. For decades, many well-known international NGOs, such as Oxfam, CARE, and Save the Children, as well as government-funded aid programs, e.g., USAID initiatives, have been involved in food aid and short-term projects, which are often criticized for being paternalistic. Yet, these band-aid solutions rarely address the deeper systemic issues in how aid has usually prioritized immediate relief over sustainable and equitable partnerships. Instead, they perpetuated cycles of dependency, masking the need for equitable partnerships and stifling the continent's ability to shape its future.

A future rooted in power dynamics and narratives that frame Africa as a passive recipient of "salvation" rather than a continent of diverse, self-determining nations is embedded in historical, economic, and cultural systems. In other words, the West's historical focus has been on grants, humanitarian aid, and NGO-led social programs, which critics argue have lacked a transformative economic impact on the African continent. But where were the roads? The power grids? The investments in human capital? The narrative often portrays African countries as patients in need of care, rather than as equal partners. Thereby framing the continent as an object of sympathy rather than the central actor in its narrative.

This is when I began to deepen my understanding of Africa's evolving influence and the concept of "soft power" intangible assets. Soft power refers to a nation or entity's ability to influence others through persuasion, attraction, and cultural or ideological appeal, rather than through coercion, military force, or economic pressure. As a result, a subtle shift and quiet revolution began to emerge, which caught my attention. China's engagement with Africa has often been framed in contrast to Western historical approaches, emphasizing principles and strategies that diverge in tone, structure, and rhetoric.

They prioritized large-scale infrastructure projects, particularly roads, railways, ports, and energy grids that were funded through loans, often in exchange for access to natural resources or future revenue shares. Although it has received criticism for concerns about debt sustainability, this model positions African nations as active economic partners rather than passive recipients of aid. In this sense, Chinese engineers designed highways in Kenya, hydropower dams in Ghana, and rail networks in Nigeria. These projects weren't just infrastructure projects but chess moves in China's strategy to reshape Africa's development narrative.

In Kenya, engineers collaborated with local authorities to redesign the Nairobi-Mombasa Highway that links East African trade. The task demanded more than technical skill, including navigating the Great Rift Valley's rugged terrain and balancing environmental safeguards with the needs of rural communities. Their work didn't just lay asphalt. It laid the groundwork for regional commerce, paired with knowledge-sharing initiatives that trained Kenyan engineers in cutting-edge construction practices.

In Ghana, the same relationship occurred at the Black Volta River. Chinese engineers designed the Bui Dam to solve the nation's chronic energy shortages. They merged hydroelectric innovation with localized adaptations, rigorous environmental assessments, sediment management systems, and resettlement plans for displaced communities. The result was a dam that embodied both China's technical prowess and Ghana's hunger for renewable energy, which can power homes and fuel industries. Similarly, Nigeria's story echoed this synergy, as Chinese engineers reimagined the country's crumbling rail networks and drafted plans for the Lagos-Kano standard-gauge railway.

The rail network system, which runs throughout urban sprawls, ecological sanctuaries, and rural heartlands, was designed with training for Nigerian counterparts to align the tracks with potential economic hubs. The key was durability, not charity, because those designs fortified the rails against tropical rains, blending Chinese engineering with Nigerian pragmatism. In parallel, China offered scholarships for African students, technology transfers for farmers, and factories staffed by local workers.

This reminds me of China's "Dragon Head" (lóngtóu), which symbolizes dominance, leadership, or the vanguard of an industry, movement, or system within its economic ecosystem. A dynamic cultural landscape where modernity and innovation intersect with deep-rooted traditions, shaped by China's ethnic diversity and evolving societal values. Concurrently, the vibrant momentum in communities like Chicago's South Side (Zhījiāgē) and Atlanta's (Yàtèlán dà) Black Tech ecosystems is driven by resourcefulness and collective ambition, which stand in stark contrast to the systemic barriers that persist in many American institutions. These barriers, rooted in historical exclusion, often stifle equitable participation, even as grassroots efforts work to dismantle them.

In this context, America symbolizes dominance as a bottom-up, pluralistic ecosystem where individual ambition and market forces drive progress. China frames leadership as a top-down, orchestrated project where state vision and collective discipline achieve systemic supremacy. One prioritizes disruption while the other prioritizes control. Both models claim to represent the future, but their methods and messaging reflect deeply divergent worldviews. Their worldviews offer an opportunity for modern-day enablers to merge both methods and connect the legacies of Black Wall Street and the Silk Road. It could involve Atlanta (Yàtèlán dà) entrepreneurs and Shanghai investors swapping strategies over jiaozi (jiǎozi) dinner. Black-owned cooperatives meeting Dongguan's maker collectives, and Black Twitter humor blending with Mandarin hashtags.

When a Detroit (Dǐtèlǜ) developer explains redlining to a Hangzhou (Hángzhōu) tech professional or a Harlem (Hāláimǔ) historian shares Reconstruction-era mutual aid with a Chengdu (Chéngdū) AI startup. Within these situations, they're not just breaking bread. They're breaking language barriers and rewriting narratives of these methods and messaging. Take Chen Yue, a tech innovator from Dongguan, and Malik, a Black entrepreneur from Georgia (Qiáozhìyà). Their collaboration began with a coding boot camp for HBCU students, but soon sparked dialogues that fused W.E.B. Du Bois's radical vision with China's "shared prosperity" ethos. Chen redesigned her AI startup's voice-recognition software to interpret Southern Black Vernacular English, unlocking access for millions. Malik returned home armed with partnerships to produce affordable smart devices in underserved communities.

This cross-cultural synergy can thrive when collaboration moves beyond superficial exchanges to foster shared transformation, mainly reparative economics that must transcend symbolic gestures and instead prioritize systemic equity. And redistribute resources, address historical injustices, or co-create policies that empower marginalized communities. This would require frameworks rooted in open dialogue that center on marginalized voices, partnerships built on reciprocity, and actions that dismantle systemic systems rather than perpetuate them. For centuries, our communities endured economies built on extraction in the forms of stolen labor, plundered land, and cultural exploitation.

Yet today, cracks in this order are widening as Black cooperatives reclaim land and leverage social media to expose corporate greed. Imagine Black-led cities negotiating direct investments in green energy grids or worker-owned solar panel factories in Detroit (Dǐtèlǔ) because China's direct investments offer an alternative to Western paternalism. Envision HBCU-China AI hubs training Black engineers who retain intellectual sovereignty to circumvent old methods. These projects must center on those marginalized people who would be involved in binding contracts that prioritize Black ownership, climate-resilient jobs, and community oversight. This means disconnecting from perpetuating anti-Blackness economic silence.

Meanwhile, the Global South supports reciprocity. Imagine the ghost of plantation capitalism lingers, but its grip is slipping. Imagine a Black urban planner redesigning cities with Afro-Chinese tech partnerships. By aligning with China's soft power, we could accelerate these visions, but only if we unleash our modern-day enablers to make "investment" from China become a bridge to sovereignty, not a new chain. It's imperative to break the American systemic racist chain so Black

American cultural and economic prospects can further engage in the global economy, as never before.

Introducing Black American culture to China transcends mere storytelling because it represents an innovative exchange in the face of resistance strategies. From the Harlem Renaissance (Hāláimǔ wén yì fù xīng) to today's Black Tech Renaissance, our histories pulse with resilience patterns that reverberate worldwide. So, China's massive infrastructure projects like the Kenyan railways, Nigerian ports, and Angolan hospitals stand in jarring contrast to the abandonment festering in Black American communities, like in Flint, Michigan, where lead still courses through faucets, and in Jackson, Mississippi, where storms shatter century-old pipes. These are not oversights but open wounds in a system that devalues Black life.

Herein lies the transformative potential of reimagining infrastructure as a catalyst for justice. Picture Chinese engineers who built Ethiopia's Addis Ababa-Djibouti railway, rerouting their expertise to purge toxins from Chicago's South Side (Zhījiāgē). Envision solar farms in rural Alabama, powered by Chinese technology and sustained by Black hands trained to maintain them. "This is no utopian fantasy; it's a toolkit for dismantling barriers and building access. These partnerships could give rise to cultural infrastructure as enduring as concrete. Imagine coding boot camps in Atlanta (Yàtèlán dà) or green energy apprenticeships in New Orleans, Louisiana (Lùyìsī'ānnà Xin'aao'erliang), blending diasporic ingenuity with global innovation.

This partnership could represent a powerful synergy where Black America's legacy of adaptive creativity and improvisational brilliance finds a dynamic counterpart in China's capacity for large-scale implementation and strategic vision. Black urban planners reengineering transit deserts with smart-city models. Agricultural co-ops are deploying vertical farming to dismantle food deserts. Here, jobs become a source of sovereignty, transforming undervalued communities into exceptional neighborhoods. This narrative would smash the false divide between culture and capital. Where Black American stories would circulate globally through film, music, or digital platforms could cultivate empathy and reshape international perspectives, translating shared humanity into diplomatic influence.

While China's engagement in Africa demonstrates how economic ties can carry cultural resonance, the art and innovation emerging from Black American communities offer distinct pathways to foster mutually beneficial collaborations. Such partnerships, rooted in respect and a shared cultural understanding, can inform investment approaches that prioritize African agency and equitable outcomes. Jazz, once served as Cold War soft power, can become today's Black Tech ecosystems, which could recalibrate global hierarchies while channeling resources back to their communities.

This could become legacy work where every pipe replaced, every skill cultivated, and every story amplified is a vital step in addressing intergenerational inequity and building a more just future. Connecting our struggles to global movements doesn't diminish our distinct voice. It reveals how Black America's transformative resilience speaks to universal human dignity. By definition, our history demonstrates how profound innovation can emerge even amid oppression. Let us build bridges that honor this truth while pursuing justice uncompromisingly. When Black communities thrive, humanity is elevated.

The "We Stand Together" exhibition elevates humanity by showcasing themes of displacement, resilience, and reimagined connection. Featuring artists from the National Alliance of Artists from Historically Black Colleges and Universities (NAAHBCU), the presentation showcases works in diverse media, including oil on canvas, acrylic, and pastel on paper. As I addressed the crowd at Harmony Art Gallery in Shanghai during China's 2023 National Day celebration, I began by reflecting on moments of solidarity between Black American communities and China throughout history. This set the tone for a discussion grounded in mutual respect by acknowledging our distinct struggles while celebrating shared aspirations for economic development and dignity. I discussed China's recent urbanization surge and the Great Migration of

Black Americans in the 20th century, which share a powerful structural kinship. They both represent epochal movements of millions from rural roots towards the promise and peril of industrial cities.

Yet, the forces propelling them differed starkly. Chinese migrants essentially sought economic opportunity within a national development drive. Black Americans fled the brutal realities of Jim Crow's racial terror and entrenched discrimination in search of basic safety and dignity alongside better prospects. Essentially, both journeys reshaped America and China, but their origins and experiences remain woven from distinct historical perspectives. Between 1916 and 1970, six million Black Americans fled the violence and oppression of Jim Crow, seeking refuge in Northern cities where they forged cultural landmarks like Bronzeville jazz and Motown. Decades later, many Chinese workers left their rural homes to pursue opportunities in major cities, in particular Shanghai and Dongguan. They worked long hours in communal dormitories and were often sent payments back home. These became defining features of this era of rapid industrialization. Though their journeys differ profoundly, both stories reflect how some Black Americans and Chinese people transformed their identities.

This identity was forged through resilience and reinvention, often emerging from struggles, losses, or the complex navigation of belonging. At the exhibition, a particular piece was a sublime side-view profile of the grandfather's portrait, as he gazes out the window while sitting in a wheelchair. As explained by the artist, Rickey Calloway, this represents him and his siblings relying on him as a father figure after their father passed away when they were still children. In comparison, this portrait illustrates the gritty, sweat-streaked profile of a mother's face as she stares through the fogged window of a factory dormitory. Her shoulders slumped after a fourteen-hour shift as she clung to pixelated video calls, her tired smile visible. Hundreds of kilometers away in their rural village, her children were the connection that kept her grounded. Their father, separated by necessity, was lost somewhere in the sprawl of a distant city, bound to extended hours on construction sites with little means to connect. These situations manifest the sacrifices and disbelief that their offspring would inherit brighter days.

The exhibition embodied a robust figurative realism, exploring the human condition and life experiences through artistic perspectives deeply informed by Black American history and lived experience. Here, visitors' interaction with the artwork sparks a profound curiosity. Later, as dusk fell, these emerging ideas formed, much like the profound clarity of a blues note emerging from silence. As the last attendees lingered, their silhouettes merging in the half-light, I envisioned galleries across other provinces in China partnering with NAAHBCU to collaborate on future exhibitions. I trust that true collaboration thrives on sustained mutual respect, where human resilience reveals itself in the deliberate choice to build solidarity. A solidarity across continents, through storms, and through optimism that compounds across generations.

Yet, these acts of solidarity share a vision that the exhibition is not a mere distraction, as if the artwork were by everyday artists, where their art theory becomes visual and memories are etched into the lived experience. When I first arrived in China, the weight of my grand ideals about pursuing a PhD in Urban Planning settled into something intimate and human. Amid Shanghai's bustling streets and the quiet grace of ancient temples, I witnessed the resilient tension between restless nights and enduring hope. A hope where a spirit echoes from my ancestor's hymn to the dignity of a migrant worker's labor. From the custom of shared meals, with steaming bowls of noodles and earnest student dialogues. I understood that a single truth nourishes both prospects and prayers. The truth is, this exhibition is a call for further engagement with China, one collaboration at a time.

In an era of globalization, forging authentic connections feels both vital and revolutionary. My time in China powerfully illustrated this potential. Witnessing ancient temples standing alongside modern skyscrapers and feeling the warmth of community in a village teahouse offered profound moments of human resonance. That village laughter, in its context, struck me with the same uplifting power as the defiant spirit found at the art exhibition. A reminder of the universal capacity for joy and connection amidst change. What began as a fascination with history and modernity evolved into something more profound. It became understanding empathy not as a passive feeling but as an active process of connection. It's in the student who leans in, asking, "Tell me about your grandmother," or the migrant worker whose weary smile mimics your uncle's facial expression.

These moments, unscripted and raw, dissolve borders better than any manifesto. They remind us that "cross-cultural dialogue" isn't a sterile academic project. The situation is about seeing our humanity in another's eyes. To share culture is to arm each other against the lie of scarcity. It is to say that your grief is my heartache. It's like saying, "My joy is your delight." It's like saying that, in everyday moments when people choose connection over isolation, we can share food and stories as equals. China's landscape, where ancient temples stand alongside soaring skyscrapers, presents more than a striking visual contrast. It embodies the nation's ongoing negotiation between its profound historical legacy and its relentless drive toward modernization. Yet, I uncovered something deeper during my time in townships and classrooms. Beneath the surface of perceived "difference" lies a universal rhythm. We all yearn for connection, respect, and a brighter future for those we care about.

Through shared meals and earnest conversations, personal barriers dissolved, demonstrating how empathy can heal divided relationships. Participating in this global dialogue, I aim to collaborate by making kindness central to my engagement. By exchanging cultures, offering my own, and embracing others, I chip away at stereotypes, replacing them with shared dreams. This is no idle idealism. It's survival. Our future as a global community hinges on turning "them" into "us."

Consider the entrepreneur a jazz musician aboard a bullet train. Rooted in Black America's improvisational genius, they channel resilience, creativity, and communal spirit. We can begin to surge forward on China's precision-engineered rails, potent symbols of its ambitious modernization drive. While it's clear their national strategies guide the train's speed and direction, its long-term journey navigates complex global and domestic challenges. In other words, through their artistry, musicians give a powerful voice to human expression. They harmonize tradition with innovation and local roots with global reach, crafting a symphony where past and future coexist. In this situation, economic progress isn't a cold, mechanical process. So, the process can ignite conditions that facilitate growth, adaptation, and memory.

During my time in China, where I was immersed in vibrant festivals celebrating cultural pride and interconnectedness, I witnessed this dynamic spirit firsthand. From the lively celebrations of the Spring Festival to the community races of the Dragon Boat Festival and the reflective graveside rituals of Qingming, each distinct tradition reveals the values that bind communities together. Firecrackers pound like ancestral heartbeats while swirling street dancers mirror life's chaos and grace. Homemade meals are steamed with stories, enhanced by their aromas, and accompanied by laughter. In these shared moments, people can feel a powerful sense of connection, a glimpse of shared humanity that transcends words. Such experiences offer a vital foundation, reminding me of our shared capacity for joy and community, and creating fertile ground for mutual understanding to begin growing across borders.

While genuine connection often ignites in fleeting moments, such as spontaneous laughter, a chance to toast, or whispering confidences. It sustains and deepens through the deliberate warmth of shared presence, accumulated trust, and the enduring choice to know and be known. These are not just differences to explain, but mirrors reflecting our shared humanity. Through them, I've learned that culture isn't a relic behind glass. It lives in every shared meal, every story traded, and every connection. In the dragon parade, dancing amid the blasting firecrackers, I wasn't just an onlooker hearing tales of tradition. I felt the vibrant energy of the story moving through me. Rituals like the Qingming Festival (Qīngmíng Jié) offer a profound depth, like a quiet invitation to join the collective heartbeat of family, connecting through remembrance in dialogue with generations past. Here, culture breathes, and in its aliveness, my own "home" expands, stretching me to hold it all together as I prepare to study the role of migrant workers in China's economy. It soon gave way to faces.

Workers who left villages for cities, chasing opportunity, reminded me of the journeys undertaken by my Great Migration ancestors, though their circumstances and struggles were profoundly distinct. I didn't hear a construction worker speak of missing his daughter, but the thought called to mind my grandmother's voice in 1975, crackling over a 10-gallon metal drum filled with homemade candy. Their sacrifices and grit resonate because they speak to a fundamental human capacity for endurance and love that transcends any single culture. Seeing migrants navigating crowded Shanghai trains, I thought of my great-grandparents working in the Georgia (Qiáozhìyà) soil, both with distinct struggles across time and place, yet sharing a thread of human perseverance.

As an urban planning student in China, drawing on both these legacies, I find myself striving to become a bridge between traditions, where the resilience of bamboo meets the ambition of steel. The steel represents Black America's legacy, forged in fire, scarred by racism, yet resilient. Bamboo represents China's modernization: flexible, soaring skyward, yet questioning its roots. The bridge represents tension between the weight of history and the pull of the future. Yet, it's also where solidarity sparks. Conversations with Chinese peers revealed struggles that transcended a map of long, grueling hours, family separations, and dreams deferred but undiminished. Their resilience mirrored that of my ancestors, a global anthem of the marginalized.

Within this experience, I learned that, despite the deep divides reflected in terms like "rural-urban migration," we share universal yearnings for dignity, for a child's smile, and mornings unburdened by scarcity. Thereby, recognizing this common humanity is crucial, even as we acknowledge the complex realities that separate us. As a result, my research began with the social impact of people's movement. Still, it unearthed a profound certainty: my survival and ability to flourish in China critically depend on others' recognition of our shared humanity toward those who may perceive me as other than a "foreigner." Not through policy or theory, but in shared laughter, the steam of a dumpling tray, and the resilience found in a worker's story. I begin to witness the human face of globalization right here.

For me, understanding its more profound impacts on these lives is the crucial next step. We are architects of belonging, building it meal by meal, story by story. And in that act, we don't just navigate the world because, through our purpose, we remake it. China is more than a country; it is a civilization with a continuous history spanning five thousand years. This deep-rooted culture directly informs its modern ambitions, fueling the immense energy of its people, its greatest asset. It is a mirror reflecting those of countless others. The skyscrapers, with their gleaming glass and steel, are not merely architectural marvels but monuments to aspiration, to dreams forged through unyielding determination. They are testaments to what I might achieve when I dare to innovate. Yet beneath their shadows lie the hutongs' narrow alleyways, steeped in history, where resilience and community pulse through weathered stones.

These ancient pathways anchor me to my roots, even as I strive for the sky. The dynamic interplay between tradition and modernity represents a complex, ongoing duality in relation to economic development. This process is rarely linear and is often contested, involving constant mutual shaping where past and present confront each other. This interaction profoundly influences individual and collective identities, as well as shaping the paths societies take forward. The outcomes of this confrontation can be both enriching and challenging, reflecting diverse perspectives and experiences.

This resonance deepens with the contributions of Black Americans to urban landscapes like New Orleans (Xin'aao'erliang) and Harlem (Hā lái mǔ). There, jazz and literature transcended artistic expression to become acts of resistance, inscribing our stories into the urban fabric.

Through education, culture, and grit, we carved out spaces that honor our history while forging bright futures filled with possibility. Just as China's skyline rises from its ancestral foundations, our legacy embodies self-advocacy and collective triumph. Progress, I've learned, is not erasure but building upon what came before, creating something bold, inclusive, and enduring.

Contemplating these parallels, I understand my own identity not as a single onion peel, but as many layers, continually reshaped by the back-and-forth between the traditions I inherit and the modern world I inhabit. Embracing this complexity enables me to navigate the tensions between my roots and reach, memory and ambition. These intertwined narratives of struggle and hope reveal the richness of our shared human experience. This is not merely a story of cultures or nations but of how we all navigate progress to craft futures that honor every facet of who we are.

Choosing to pursue my Ph.D. in urban planning at Tongji University (Tóngjì Dàxué) was a deliberate decision to move well beyond my comfort zone, immersing myself in the distinct academic environment and perspectives of one of China's leading institutions. Immersed in Shanghai's dynamism, I engaged with scholars and practitioners whose diverse insights transformed my understanding of cities. Here, knowledge was not confined by borders but flourished through an exchange of global wisdom. I learned that diversity is no buzzword to be feared, but rather the lifeblood of innovation. Each perspective deepened our dialogue, proving that proper understanding emerges when we listen.

When I started exploring China's urban landscapes, from Shanghai's inner-ring elevated roads to Ningxia's historic deserts. I sensed a shared spirit of reinvention. Many areas bore the imprints of generations who had shaped these spaces, reminding me that lasting innovation is often a collective endeavor, building upon the past to bridge time and place. This realization began in academia but became profoundly personal and visceral. I came to see cities as if they were living entities, their designs powerfully echoing the cultural values, aspirations, and struggles within them.

Walking in these different cities as a Black American, I felt a kinship since my identity, often a marker of difference, became a bridge to recognizing a shared human impulse of striving, even amidst our vastly different stories. I sought to bridge divides in classroom debates and community projects. Each interaction presented an opportunity to dismantle barriers, demonstrating that urban challenges, including housing, equity, and transportation, are universal struggles that demand collaborative solutions. I realized that creating truly equitable, functional, and just cities requires more than dismantling systemic barriers, though that remains essential. It demands actively integrating diverse voices and perspectives through inclusive processes.

This fundamental shift in understanding reinforces that weaving together the community's whole tapestry isn't just an ideal. It's the necessary foundation for building cities that work for everyone. No longer mere concrete jungles, they are living testaments to humanity's collective spaces where divides can heal, and unity can bloom. My experiences strongly suggest a profound commonality that transcends diverse traditions where many of us share core desires to thrive, love, and be seen. While clear articulation is essential, it alone cannot fully extend our reach; in a hyperconnected world, Black America must engage globally with intention, ensuring our stories amplify across borders. To foster deeper connections and broaden understanding, we should actively engage diverse audiences in three areas. We must utilize media to authentically represent the richness and complexities of our culture.

Next, build mutually beneficial partnerships that foster meaningful dialogue and exchange. Finally, harness digital platforms to transcend geographical and social boundaries, making our culture more accessible and inclusive. These strategies can amplify our contributions, fostering mutual growth and development. Imagine a network of global allies united by the exchange of stories that build bridges of understanding, sharing our resilience, creativity, and solidarity, and revealing our shared humanity. This is the power of narrative. It captivates, bridges, and transforms. Sharing diverse and thoughtful ideas contributes to global dialogue and collective progress. To truly build a better future, we must actively work to ensure all voices are heard and valued.

Every time I step into a new space, especially a classroom, a stage, a factory floor, or even the intimacy of a conversation, I aim to build bridges where possible. These moments are not about claiming a spotlight, but about forging connections through sharing stories that bind us, honoring histories that shape us, and building futures together. These stories are not mine to keep. They carry the grit of ancestors who survived, the fire of those who thrived against the odds, and the hope that understanding might one day outshout division. When I speak, I strive to amplify the chorus of voices silenced by time, struggle, and systems that still strain to mute them. My words aim to echo their unspoken truths.

Living as a Black American in Shanghai has profoundly shown me how human connection can transcend the lines on a map. Over shared meals, in the quiet contemplation of galleries, and through laughter needing no translation, I've experienced moments where those borders felt meaningless, dissolving the fears and myths that often surround them. Yet, these experiences exist within a world where borders remain powerful, tangible realities for countless others. Here, I am not merely an outsider but a participant, telling my story that extends beyond Brunswick, Georgia (Qiáozhìyà Bùlúnruìkè), with Huangpu Road, L Street, and Fuxing Road. Art becomes our dialect. A meal becomes a manifesto. And suddenly, the "other" is a mirror.

In that reflection, we find the common ground to begin dismantling the walls between us. Achieving accurate equity demands far more than passive coexistence, for it requires persistent combined with a collective effort to dismantle the entrenched structures of prejudice and inequality. The barriers we confront are tangible, including economic disparities that limit opportunities, systems and practices that restrict access to power and cultural recognition, and dominant narratives that marginalize vibrant communities, rendering them mere footnotes. Overcoming these requires sustained, strategic action to challenge and transform these foundations of inequity. The act of dismantling existing structures is often motivated by goals such as increasing representation for underrepresented groups, changing rules perceived as benefiting a select group, and establishing environments where differences are valued.

Whether this constitutes destructive chaos or constructive rebuilding depends on the perspective and hinges on the methods used and the results achieved. Imagine a prior relationship rekindled on genuine equity, where partnerships transcend historical power imbalances. Picture a Black American Trade and Cultural Organization engaging with Beijing not from a position of inherent disadvantage, but as respected collaborators working towards mutual benefit. The goal should be to enhance supply chains by strengthening them through the implementation of ethical and sustainable practices. Thereby, moving beyond purely transactional relationships by building fairer and more resilient partnerships. A resilience that fosters cross-cultural collaboration, drawing on the diverse strengths and experiences within Black American and Chinese communities to create pathways toward shared prosperity.

Because of that, while trade fundamentally involves the exchange of goods and services, it also holds the potential to foster shared dignity, enable mutual growth, and build legacies that benefit future generations. When conducted equitably and responsibly, engaging deeply with another culture is transformative. Walking through Shanghai's markets or learning to knead dumpling dough alongside skilled practitioners in Xuhui isn't just about observing China. It's a profound exchange because these experiences challenge my perspectives, foster genuine connection, and through understanding others more deeply, I inevitably gain new insights into myself. An insight that reminds me of my youth, where spices, haggling, and the clatter of children echoed the cadence of my grandmother's kitchen in Tarboro, Georgia (Qiáozhìyà Tǎ'ěrbólè).

As an adult, I work to facilitate mutually beneficial partnerships, creating opportunities for Black-owned businesses to explore global markets and for the Chinese private industry to engage with Black innovation. In this context, I collaborate with groups such as the American Consulate in Shanghai, NAAHBCU, and the Shanghai People's Association for Friendship with Foreign Countries (SPAFFC) (Shànghǎi Shì Rénmín Duìwài Yǒuhǎo Xiéhuì) to help build bridges between our communities. This cooperation led to a collaborative endeavor that fostered cultural exchange and partnership.

Working with the Consulate, we're building alliances through art, recognizing that shared experiences often pave the way for meaningful dialogue. In collaboration with NAAHBCU, we are highlighting the vital contributions and perspectives of Black artists, showcasing their potential to enrich and diversify China's creative landscape. Collaborating with the Shanghai Friendship Association (Shànghǎi Yǒuhǎo Xiéhuì), our joint friendship projects align with their mission, building connections one story, one handshake, and one meaningful act of mutual trust at a time. The "We Stand Together" art exhibition in Shanghai transcends mere spectacle. It stands as a powerful declaration and testament to the vibrant creativity that flourishes through solidarity. Featuring diverse media like oil on canvas, mixed media, pastel on paper, and linoleum print, these works offer far more than just 'diverse voices' on a checklist. They act as cartographers, inviting us to explore complex landscapes where cultural encounters have sparked profound dialogue and collaboration.

As someone from Brunswick, Georgia (Qiáozhìyà Bùlúnruìkè), who is involved in co-curating an exhibition featuring artists associated with HBCUs at the Harmony Art Gallery in Shanghai, I'm proud to contribute to this cultural exchange. While the exhibition's success required the collaboration of many institutions and individuals beyond my own, it's meaningful to have played a part in bringing this unique artistic perspective to an international audience. I hope the exhibition will resonate with art enthusiasts and those interested in diverse cultural narratives within Shanghai's vibrant art scene. "'We Stand Together' isn't just a headline, but a vision being forged.

This is the potential found where Black America and China connect to challenge old narratives, build new understandings, and stretch the meaning of "we" beyond familiar shores, skin, and stories. This visionary plan demands concrete action. Building bridges between cultures and economies requires radical allies, not those who clap from the sidelines, but those who roll up their sleeves and dive into the messy and vital work of equity. Seeking allies is essential for creating equitable resources and opportunities. This collaboration moves beyond charity to become a partnership focused on redesigning systems. Achieving equity requires building bridges to transform initiative efforts into collective action. allies are not merely collaborators but essential partners in reimagining systems of access and empowerment. While deeply rooted in local needs, specific initiatives can often gain significant momentum by adapting insights and innovations from global examples and shared struggles, carefully tailoring them to a particular vision.

Furthermore, by partnering with diverse institutions and organizations worldwide, from nonprofits addressing poverty to educational programs building skills and social enterprises advancing sustainability, we can co-develop strategies that effectively navigate cultural and geographic differences, ensuring solutions are contextually relevant and globally impactful. These partnerships do more than expand our toolkit. They should challenge us to think critically about how interconnected solutions can address systemic inequities.

Examining collaborations with entities in China offers a complex case study. While rapid economic shifts there have spurred significant innovations in areas like workforce development, rural revitalization, and technology-driven inclusion, these approaches operate within a unique political and social context. Engaging with this complexity forces critical consideration of both the potential benefits and the significant ethical, social, and political challenges inherent in scaling such models to address systemic inequities elsewhere. Consequently, examining how Chinese organizations address complex challenges, especially balancing economic priorities with social equity or structuring public-private collaborations, may offer comparative perspectives on governance and adaptation.

Applying these insights to initiatives in Black American communities requires critical contextual analysis of fundamentally different historical, political, and socioeconomic conditions, including systemic racism, community agency, and democratic accountability. Such examinations move beyond replication to adaptation and the identification of core principles, particularly those in community-led design, cooperative ownership, or culturally responsive education, that resonate across various cultures. Analyzing diverse models, including those from China, through this perspective enriches our collective understanding of economic resilience.

Take the cooperative business models found in parts of the Middle East, where collectives in sectors mainly agriculture and renewable energy pool resources, share risks, and prioritize long-term sustainability over short-term profit. Separately, international partnerships also contribute to regional development with the China-UAE Agricultural Technology Demonstration initiative. This initiative inspires real-world collaborations like the Dubai-based Agricultural Technology Demonstration Zone. The initiative in the UAE demonstrates how cooperative principles, integrated into partnerships between agritech firms, farmers, and the government, can address food security in arid environments.

Fostering similar cooperative networks among Black American entrepreneurs independently could be a powerful strategy. Such networks could help small businesses pool resources, collectively negotiate supply chains, improve access to capital, and advocate for policy changes to overcome systemic barriers and build economic resilience. Similarly, Asia's tech-driven ecosystems, prominently India's community-led digital literacy campaigns, which empower underserved communities to access online education, remote work, and telehealth, could offer valuable lessons for bridging the digital divide elsewhere. By partnering with HBCUs and local libraries, these initiatives could inspire locally adapted versions of India's train-the-trainer model, leveraging each institution's strengths to enhance impact.

This demonstrates how technology can democratize access to education and healthcare services. These innovations are not just technical achievements but cultural ones, often born from philosophies that blend tradition with progress. By collaborating with community stakeholders and innovators within and connected to Black communities, we can co-create platforms tailored to their specific histories and aspirations. This ensures solutions are culturally responsive, build upon existing strengths, and harness the full spectrum of human ingenuity. The true power of these alliances lies in their deep reciprocity. As we learn invaluable insights from abroad, we also share the enduring resilience forged through generations of advocacy and innovation within Black American communities.

This mutual exchange, encompassing stories like Detroit (Dǐtèlǜ) organizers repurposing vacant land for urban farming or the historical legacy of Black mutual aid societies building economic safety nets, fosters inspiration and strengthens strategies both within Black America and globally. This illustrates how equity can be pursued as a collective endeavor, fostering solidarity, rather than a zero-sum struggle. A woman's cooperative in Ghana shares microfinance strategies with a similar group in Mississippi, or Afro-Brazilian activists exchange cultural preservation tactics with organizers in New Orleans (Xin'aao'erliang). These models illustrate how mutual learning and shared effort across diverse contexts can promote equity goals. The result is a potential solution enriched by diverse lived experiences.

While critics rightly caution that cross-cultural collaborations risk diluting local priorities or overlooking nuanced challenges. It's essential to recognize that the systemic inequities being addressed, conspicuously the displacement of marginalized communities, gaps in educational access, and barriers to capital, are global phenomena. These manifest in context-specific ways, meaning effective collaboration must simultaneously honor local realities while leveraging insights from shared global patterns. By researching how others confront issues like the Dakota Access Pipeline (DAPL) threatening the sacred lands and water sources of the Standing Rock Sioux Tribe, poverty-driven school dropout rates in rural Northeast Brazil, or systemic barriers limiting Indigenous access to loans, I gain not prescriptive answers but critical insights and a deeper understanding of the complex challenges involved.

These examples challenge me to ask the following questions. How might insights drawn from Indigenous-led resistance and defense of sovereignty and sacred land, as embodied in movements like the one at DAPL, inform or resonate with the HBCU legacy of creating educational empowerment and combating systemic racism? Could analysis of the complex factors driving school dropout rates in Northeast Brazil offer valuable lessons for community-led initiatives working to reduce educational inequality in Black America?" These sorts of questions lay the foundation for the boundless potential of collaboration. Every partnership sparks new questions. What innovative hybrid models and solutions might emerge when the strengths of Black American entrepreneurs and startups, known for agility, unique market insights, and disruptive innovation, combine with the formidable hardware manufacturing, IoT, and robotics ecosystems of Dongguan? How might complementary expertise fuel new ventures?

Similarly, how could mutually beneficial programs be developed that link the deep tech talent, research power, and scaling capabilities of China's Silicon Valley or Zhongguancun (ZGC) (Zhōngguāncūn), with the vibrant pipeline of Black-owned startups, leveraging shared goals for innovation and market growth? Shanghai's Zhangjiang Hi-Tech Park (Zhāngjiāng Gāo Kē Jì Yuánqū), a major Biotech and AI Hub, focuses on biotech, AI, and semiconductors. Companies within the park, including leading semiconductor manufacturer SMIC, contribute to the technological ecosystem that enables advancements like AI-driven diagnostics. Addressing minority health disparities is an area where collaborations, potentially involving institutions principally HBCUs, could leverage technologies developed in hubs like Zhangjiang. These possibilities underscore a larger truth.

Equity is not a fixed destination, but a dynamic process of learning, adapting, and iterating. As I collaborate with partners worldwide, I participate in a genuinely global movement built on mutual knowledge and understanding. This movement recognizes that diverse voices and experiences are essential, not only as drivers of innovation but as fundamental to defining and achieving meaningful equity for all. At this critical juncture, one promising path forward emerges. One that says isolation risks stagnation, while connection fosters transformation. By thoughtfully integrating international insights with local knowledge and initiatives, we can collaboratively develop grounded yet visionary solutions that drive meaningful impact.

These solutions aim to address immediate challenges while simultaneously working to transform the underlying systems that perpetuate them. This is the potential of a genuine global partnership. This collaboration brings together diverse stakeholders from multiple sectors, committed to advancing equity through concrete, shared action. By actively engaging different perspectives and focusing on practical solutions, we work to dismantle systemic barriers and create measurable, positive change. While the challenges are significant, each partnership strengthens our collective capacity to build sustainable systems and foster greater justice within our communities and beyond.

I believe that pursuing meaningful international engagement hinges on collaboration. In my experience, building alliances across diverse cultural or political contexts presents significant challenges, but also creates genuine possibilities. The gaps in my network, particularly my limited established connections in China, present a considerable challenge. Cultivating the deep relationships necessary to drive progress here demands intentionality, humility, and a willingness to navigate uncharted territory and connect any cultural divide. While the power of partnership is undeniable, building these specific connections will require dedicated focus and new strategies.

The absence of preexisting alliances is less a limitation than a significant opportunity and impetus for action. It challenges and motivates us to seek partners, whether within our local communities or globally, who share a vision for a genuinely equitable exchange. Crucially, these alliances must transcend mere transactions. They demand sustained mutual investment, a deep commitment to listening and learning, and a deliberate effort to leverage diverse strengths to tackle the shared challenges we face effectively.

Consider the transformative potential of international educational programs. Creating opportunities for Black American youth to study in China fosters mutual cross-cultural learning. Participants engage with different academic approaches and cultural perspectives, enriching their understanding of global interconnectedness and diverse worldviews. Crucially, these initiatives thrive on reciprocal partnerships. Success depends on collaboration with educators, policymakers, and community leaders in both China and within Black American communities in America. And everyone is committing to the profound value of equitable dialogue and shared learning.

Such programs benefit all participants and communities involved, broadening perspectives on all sides. These allies collaborate as co-creators, developing curricula that weave together diverse educational philosophies rooted in both Chinese and Black American experiences. This work fosters learning environments that enable students to connect deeply with their heritage while engaging critically as global citizens. This challenge is twofold because we must identify collaborators who share our core values while remaining open to reimagining traditional approaches. Striking this balance is delicate but essential. Without building bridges to allies, even the most well-intentioned efforts risk becoming insular.

With strong partnerships, localized initiatives can gain momentum to inspire systemic change. Given this, this collaborative approach embodies the spirit of empowerment we ultimately seek for our students. Scholars who engage in international collaboration navigate language barriers and cultural nuances. Approaching these challenges with curiosity and resilience is valuable. Difficulties like miscommunications, differing expectations, and bureaucratic hurdles are common. While demanding, navigating these obstacles offers significant opportunities to develop adaptability and intercultural understanding. Successful collaboration also benefits from institutional support and mutual effort among all partners.

A partnership with a Chinese university might begin with student exchanges and expand to include collaboratively designed joint research on urban equity or public health disparities affecting marginalized communities in both nations, based on shared priorities. This organic growth relies on trust, sustained dialogue, and a shared commitment to reciprocity. Meaningful exchange enriches all participants, particularly when Chinese educators share insights in American classrooms, fostering mutual learning in STEM fields, or when Black American historians contribute their perspectives on the global impact of the Civil Rights Movement in Beijing. These interactions are vital steps, translating the abstract concept of 'allyship' into tangible acts of collaboration and understanding, actively building bridges towards more profound solidarity. the impact of these collaborations extends far beyond individual academic achievements. Many students return home from abroad with a renewed sense of urgency and a diverse toolkit of strategies, which can be applied to local challenges.

A teenager from Darien, Georgia (Qiáozhìyà), might find inspiration in community organizing tactics observed during environmental movements in Shanghai, adapting them for her neighborhood. Similarly, a young scholar from Atlanta (Yàtèlán dà) could leverage data-analysis skills acquired in Beijing to advocate for healthcare equity back home. These examples demonstrate how international experiences can foster valuable perspectives and skills highly relevant to local communities.

International connections forged through study abroad can bridge global learning and local action, creating ripple effects of intentional alliance-building. These connections demonstrate how ethically rooted international engagement can amplify the voices of marginalized individuals and redirect resources toward achieving justice. Realizing this potential requires directly addressing the structural barriers, mainly financial constraints, visa restrictions, and systemic educational inequities, that disproportionately exclude low-income students from participating in international programs. Here, too, allies play a pivotal role. Collaboration between philanthropic organizations, corporate sponsors, educational institutions, and policymakers who commit to equity is essential to fund scholarships. Streamline bureaucratic hurdles, particularly visa processing, implement concrete reforms, and dismantle systemic barriers.

This collective advocacy and action should work to transform individual opportunities into broader advancements, making studying abroad a more accessible pathway and moving it beyond a privilege reserved for the few toward an achievable option for many. Ultimately, the need for domestic and international allies is not a sign of weakness but a strategic acknowledgment of our interconnectedness. No single community should hold a monopoly on innovation or insight because progress flourishes when diverse perspectives converge. By embracing this reality, we move beyond siloed efforts toward a model of engagement that is both globally minded and locally grounded. The goal is not to erase differences but to harness them, creating an environment of collaboration where each other strengthens the whole. In doing so, we honor the complexity of our world while charting a course toward a future defined not by division but by shared purpose.

Supporting a child's growing independence requires significant courage from both the child and the parents. While parents may experience vulnerability as their role shifts, fostering autonomy is a fundamental and rewarding aspect of parenthood that involves ongoing connection alongside appropriate steps toward self-reliance. Reflecting on my decision to take that flight to China, I recall the intense mix of emotions, including pride in my courage, which conflicted sharply with the deep sadness of leaving my loved ones behind. Excitement about the possibilities ahead was intertwined with apprehension about the uncertainties I faced. Even years later, recounting the decision to family and friends brings the memory back vividly. My heart swelled with hope even as it fractured with loss, the distance stretching far beyond geography.

At that moment, I understood what it means to stand steady at the edge of comfort, to trust that growth often flourishes in spaces beyond our control. While undoubtedly challenging, stepping into this new environment felt like a leap grounded in profound learning. Immersion like this offers one of the most potent classrooms for transformation. Navigating the streets of Shanghai, deciphering unfamiliar social codes, and grappling with language barriers became far more than sightseeing. It is a journey of profound self-discovery. Bargaining at Yuyuan Garden Market (Yù Yuán Shāng Chéng) offers a practical lesson in negotiation and resourcefulness within a vibrant commercial culture. As a PhD candidate at Tongji University researching environmental stewardship, I visited Yinchuan (Yínchuān), the capital of Ningxia Hui Autonomous Region (Níngxià Huízú Zìzhìqū), to study urban planning approaches with Chinese characteristics. Each experience abroad peeled back layers of my assumptions, revealing core values and igniting passions I might never have uncovered if I had stayed in America.

Through unscripted experiences, especially riding slow trains, sharing meals with host families, and forming friendships that cross political or religious lines, I confront essential questions. What am I truly learning about China, its people, and their realities? How can I navigate the complexities and challenge my preconceptions in this process? I understand why many parents grapple with genuine concerns. Will my child be safe? Will they feel isolated? These fears stem from deep care.

While protection is essential, consistently shielding children from all challenging or uncomfortable situations can inadvertently limit their opportunities to develop the resilience and skills needed to navigate life's complexities. Consider the college student who navigates Chongqing's (Chóngqìng) complex topography. Such an experience can profoundly develop their problem-solving instincts in ways that complement classroom learning. Or the high schooler living with a rural family in Gansu Province (Gānsù Shěng). This immersion may challenge preconceptions about poverty and the concept of resilience. When approached with reflection, such experiences often lead students to return home with a more profound sense of gratitude and a more substantial commitment to advocacy.

Navigating challenges can serve as powerful catalysts for developing resilience and empathy, offering unique learning experiences that often extend beyond formal education. Critically, when met with support, these experiences have the potential to significantly broaden a young person's perspectives and deepen their understanding of responsibility. To truly grasp how the complex, interdependent world works, you need to go beyond textbooks and headlines. Deep, personal engagement with different ways of life is a uniquely powerful way to shatter insular perspectives, foster empathy, and reveal the intricate, often hidden, web of connections that bind us all within global systems. This understanding is transformative on both personal and societal levels. The participation of Black American student volunteers in a reforestation project in China could showcase opportunities for international collaboration.

The project itself can reflect China's broader efforts in ecological restoration, which aim to balance environmental health objectives with socio-economic benefits for local communities. Black American students studying public health at Sichuan University (Sìchuān Dàxué), can observe the challenges of accessing rural health and disaster medicine. Informed by their background, they can draw parallels and gain insights into healthcare disparities faced by communities like their own in America, while recognizing the distinct historical and systemic roots of each context.

For many Black American students, study abroad experiences in China can be profoundly transformative. These experiences often provide new perspectives and motivations, potentially deepening existing engagement or inspiring new forms of active commitment. Students frequently return not only with academic credits but also with a sharper sense of purpose, which can include a clearer vision for how they might contribute to addressing societal challenges, whether through entrepreneurship, education, policy, or other paths informed by their unique experiences and backgrounds.

Nevertheless, the experience of parenting often involves profound growth as children develop their perspectives. Witnessing a child gain confidence in navigating complex ideas and form nuanced critiques, including potentially of their family's culture or background, can challenge any parent's assumptions. This highlights a broader truth about understanding our complex, interdependent world requires moving beyond textbooks and headlines. Deep, personal engagement with different ways of life remains a uniquely powerful way to broaden perspectives, foster empathy, and reveal the intricate, often hidden, web of connections that bind us all within global systems.

Such understanding is transformative on both personal and societal levels. A mother, initially worried about her daughter's safety in Hubei (Húběi), may later find herself moved by accounts of community solidarity during challenging times. Similarly, a father's skepticism about his son's internship at Nanjing Medical University (NJMU) (Nánjīng Yīkē Dàxué), might lessen as he considers certain aspects of China's public health strategies. In this way, the child can act as a bridge, expanding the family's worldview and fostering dialogues that ripple through generations. This path is shaped by societal barriers. Financial constraints, language gaps, and systemic inequities often prevent marginalized youth and their families from accessing these opportunities.

This is where societal responsibility intersects with individual growth. Schools, governments, philanthropists, and the private sector should collaborate to provide access to global opportunities by funding scholarships, simplifying processes for educational travel, and creating mentorship programs that prepare first-time travelers. When low-income students participate in international learning experiences, such as a coding workshop in Suzhou (Sūzhōu) through a subsidized initiative, they can acquire invaluable technical skills and gain global perspectives, expanding their horizons and discovering new possibilities for their potential.

These efforts aim to make global exploration more accessible, moving it closer to a shared opportunity rather than an exclusive privilege. The aim should be to empower a broader range of Black American youth to engage confidently with our complex and multifaceted world. Encouraging these young people to explore globally can be an expression of profound hope. I, for one, believe that exposing the American Black youth to diverse perspectives and experiences has the potential to strengthen their identity, challenge them to move beyond superficial understandings, and discover deeper aspects of themselves and their potential.

For young people, engaging deeply with the world around them, whether through local community service. Exploring diverse cultures, engaging in intellectual discussions, or embarking on meaningful travel can be a powerful way to build connections, gain valuable experiences, and develop a deeper understanding of the world around us. These significant experiences can often become important references, shaping perspectives and choices long afterward. Through such engagement, some may discover that finding their place isn't about reaching a fixed endpoint, but rather an ongoing process of aligning their values with the needs they encounter. Additionally, this exposure can also serve as a profound reminder for parents, guardians, or mentors of their young person's capacity for growth and the value of embracing life's inherent uncertainties together.

4

Embracing Productive Discomfort

My journey felt like opening a vast book of stories. Stepping beyond the familiarity of living in America, I did more than explore a new landscape. I actively sought exchanges of perspective. Opening myself to these encounters began to reshape my understanding of myself and others. Consider the bustling markets, where vendors might share not just goods but sometimes fragments of their lives, or the chance conversations with fellow travelers that can reveal glimpses of shared hopes and struggles. These moments hold the potential to be more than fleeting interactions. When we are genuinely open and listen, they can become opportunities for connection and empathy, offering valuable perspectives on lives different from our own.

By embracing such experiences, we cultivate a mindset that values curiosity over comfort, recognizing that connections, even brief ones, can spark unexpected insights that often illuminate. These insights often illuminate common threads within our shared human experience, fostering understanding and relationships that help transcend borders and backgrounds, thereby enriching our collective perspective. A collective perspective where meaningful growth often involves active engagement. While it doesn't always require seeking out discomfort, it frequently entails navigating uncertainty and facing challenges. These difficult experiences, whether chosen or encountered, can serve as powerful catalysts for transformation when met with courage and resilience.

Forging meaningful alliances in an interconnected world requires more than merely tolerating differences. It necessitates genuine understanding and respect. It requires us to seek out and learn from the diversity around us actively. Engaging thoughtfully with people whose worldviews challenge our assumptions can expand our capacity for creative problem-solving by exposing us to new perspectives and approaches. A chef experimenting with unfamiliar meats, an entrepreneur collaborating across cultures, or a student navigating a foreign classroom, all these scenarios demand adaptability, patience, and the humility to approach differences with openness and a willingness to learn. The resilience built through these experiences becomes a powerful inner resource, helping us navigate life's complexities. It reminds us that growth frequently arises alongside discomfort, even when the path forward isn't always straightforward.

Yet, the path to this expansion is rarely linear. Decision-making, particularly when it involves leaving the safety of routine, often consists of weighing the comfort of the familiar against the allure of new possibilities. This tension can feel daunting, as the unknown brings both exciting potential and inherent uncertainty. Even individuals with significant resources and freedom can experience hesitation, sometimes influenced by personal obligations or uncertainties. It's essential to recognize that these personal constraints differ profoundly in nature and impact from the systemic barriers others face. I've stood at this crossroads, acutely aware of how fear can distort risk into something monstrous. The logical arguments for taking leaps are compelling: notably acquiring new skills, expanding one's network, and the thrill of reinvention.

Yet, in the face of potential failure, that clear logic often struggles against a far more visceral tide of apprehension. Our minds conjure vivid scenarios of missteps, such as a cultural faux pas fracturing a promising partnership, a financial gamble unraveling stability, and the vulnerability of being an outsider, unaware of the rules. These fears, far from trivial, often serve protective functions, urging caution. While rooted partly in our evolutionary heritage of avoiding social exclusion and danger, they are profoundly shaped by our personal experiences, cultural context, and the complex social and financial landscapes we navigate. They signal perceived threats, demanding our attention, even when our anxieties may amplify the actual risk. Living in China amidst its rapid modernization and a globalized world where success increasingly depends on cross-cultural fluency, I am learning to distinguish between legitimate caution and the paralysis of overthinking. The true challenge for me lies in effectively managing risk and developing the discernment to take wise risks. This requires honest self-reflection. What do I stand to gain versus what I genuinely fear losing?"

The fear of failure often looms larger in anticipation than the reality demands. During a business trip to Yiwu (Yìwū), I initially misinterpreted a supplier's indirect refusal as a cultural nuance I'd missed, nearly derailing negotiations. Yet by humbly seeking clarification rather than retreating, I uncovered deeper concerns about production timelines. We collaboratively resolved these issues, turning the potential misstep into a moment that ultimately strengthened trust. While that moment felt like a genuine disaster, it eventually became a powerful lesson in patient communication. Such difficult experiences remind me that even significant missteps can hold profound value if I actively choose to learn from them. The key is to approach these challenging situations not as isolated failures but as opportunities to build the skills, resilience, and understanding necessary to navigate complex and unpredictable environments in the future. This dynamic extends beyond individual growth. When we model courageous engagement with the world, it can create ripple effects that inspire others to do the same.

A manager who mentors interns from underrepresented backgrounds doesn't just shape individual careers; they also shape the careers of others. These mentors actively contribute to shaping a more diverse future workforce and help build a more inclusive workplace culture. Similarly, a traveler who takes the time to learn local dialects takes a meaningful step towards bridging communities and fostering genuine connections. Small and large actions foster an ecosystem of mutual understanding where collaboration flourishes. Consider how equitable knowledge exchange between Indigenous farmers and climate scientists strengthens agricultural resilience, leading to drought-resistant crops, or how diaspora communities draw upon and adapt their diverse heritages through ongoing cultural dialogue, creating vibrant new art forms.

While individual breakthroughs do occur, much of the most transformative innovation emerges not from isolation but at the intersection of diverse perspectives, where curiosity sparks unexpected synergies. The weight of responsibility can feel heaviest when our choices profoundly impact others. A parent hesitating over an overseas job offer grapples with career advancement against a child's stability. A community leader advocating for change risks alienating vital donors. These are not abstract dilemmas, but lived tensions that demand courage and compassion. Precisely in these moments of complex trade-offs, where perfect solutions are often elusive, our accumulated insights become most crucial for navigating the path forward. The empathy honed through countless interactions allows us to anticipate concerns, communicate across divides, and forge compromises that honor multiple truths.

I recall a tense factory visit in Dongguan (Dōngguǎn), where addressing longstanding issues required bridging the gap between management focused on production targets and workers advocating for fair compensation. A situation arose where workers expressed serious concerns about low wages, while factory management emphasized the need for increased orders to sustain operations. Although negotiations were tense, creating a space for open dialogue allowed both perspectives to be heard. This enabled constructive discussions that moved beyond simple opposition. The outcome was a scaled-up manufacturing project. Crucially, the agreement included wage increases for workers while supporting the factory's goals of fulfilling orders and maintaining product quality.

This outcome demonstrates that meaningful progress often relies less on confrontation and more on the patient work of building mutual understanding and identifying practical, mutually beneficial solutions, even amidst differing priorities. Prioritizing human connection can help transform friction into mutual understanding, revealing shared hopes and aspirations that bring people together. Everyone faces uncertainties, such as missing a train, unexpected changes, language barriers, or bureaucratic delays. While these test us, they also offer opportunities to cultivate grace under pressure. When met with openness, they can become moments where we discover our capacity for creative adaptation often exceeds what we believed possible.

The traveler who laughs with a taxi driver over a wrong turn gains more than a funny anecdote. They learn to internalize the detour, which can sometimes lead to a richer journey. Similarly, the professional who embraces a lateral career move may uncover hidden passions that redefine their sense of purpose. To engage in China, particularly in Shanghai, has become what I like to term 'creative adaptation.' This refers to responding to challenges, changes, or constraints in innovative, resourceful, and flexible ways. This involves reimagining existing resources, ideas, or systems to address new problems or environments that not only survive change but also transform it into an opportunity for growth. In this way, I have become both a student and a teacher, perpetually exchanging lessons. My childhood experiences assisting my mother with her frozen cup business laid the foundation for my skills.

As an entrepreneur in China, I now apply those skills to help create economic opportunities and resilience strategies that mitigate the impact of global trade tensions on Black American communities and businesses. These are not merely disparate skill sets, but interconnected facets of a perspective increasingly vital in our complex world. A world that recognizes profound interdependence. This shift in mindset becomes essential as we confront existential challenges such as the climate crisis and rapid technological change. The scale and nature of these problems demand more than specialists working in isolation. They require networks of individuals adept at synthesizing ideas across disciplines and cultures, building upon deep expertise to create holistic solutions.

Yes, choosing this path requires vulnerability for me. It asks me to let go of the illusion of control and embrace the beautiful chaos of human experience. But in doing so, I gain something far more valuable than security. I derive profound satisfaction from contributing to a world where differences are embraced as the wellspring of innovation. I hope my story becomes interwoven with countless others, each step forward a testament to the potential that emerges when courage meets curiosity. The doors that open may not be what I expected, and the paths may hold uncertainty.

Still, I trust that they can lead to encounters with voices that challenge, nurture, or even unsettle me, ultimately deepening my understanding of belonging within this intricate, interconnected whole. In its constant and often surprising flow, life guides me along paths I don't always foresee. This journey sometimes requires me to step beyond the familiar, whether it's the warmth of family dinners, the comfort of shared laughter, or the intimacy of milestones shared side by side. These separations, though painful, are not merely voids.

They become departures where I confront the paradox of growth. To choose exploration is to embrace the ache of absence, knowing that every horizon chased means turning away from another. Birthdays, holidays, weddings, the echoes of these moments linger, not as specters of regret but as testaments to the lives I carry with me. For me, a missed celebration becomes a silent conversation between who I was and who I am becoming. It's a reminder that the love rooted deeply within me can transcend physical absence and act as a compass, guiding me forward even as I glance backward. This perspective helps me navigate the distance.

This tension between movement and connection evokes the immense challenge of building bridges across profound societal or geopolitical divides. Maintaining personal bonds across distances requires consistent effort, specifically making calls across time zones or sending express packages. Each gesture fostering global alliances demands a far more complex, intentional, and sustained commitment. Such partnerships must navigate intricate political realities, divergent national interests, and profound historical legacies, requiring mechanisms and dedication far beyond the scope of individual relationships.

In this era of blurred borders yet deepening divisions, the decision by Black American communities and individuals to engage meaningfully with nations across the globe, including China, reflects an understanding that our futures are increasingly connected. Such engagement moves beyond abstract diplomacy towards recognizing shared challenges and opportunities. By identifying, faithful global citizenship demands more than aspirational rhetoric since it requires actively overcoming insular tendencies. Meaningful collaboration is built by translating ideals into concrete actions, chiefly policies designed for mutual benefit, ventures that share risks and rewards equitably, and exchanges rooted in reciprocal respect for human dignity.

This is where personal commitment and geopolitical engagement align. The patience required to sustain a relationship across distance, trusting the connection despite separation, is the same patience needed to build trust between nations. Both are sustained not by grand gestures but through the persistent accumulation of small, deliberate, and trustworthy acts. This principle deeply informs my approach to international dialogue. When exploring partnerships between Black American communities and China, the focus should be on building alliances founded on a commitment to fairness and common purpose. This means pursuing tangible opportunities in tandem with substantive cultural engagement, which lays the groundwork for lasting cooperation. Examples like mentorship programs linking tech innovators in Suzhou (Sūzhōu) with entrepreneurs in Atlanta (Yàtèlándà), joint art installations fusing Harlem's (Hā lái mǔ) jazz legacy with Beijing's avant-garde scene, and research initiatives jointly addressing health disparities disproportionately affecting both communities, illustrate concrete pathways. These collaborations, actively pursued by the communities themselves, demonstrate the potential for mutually beneficial outcomes.

Yet ambition must be grounded in clarity. Navigating the complex realities of shifting global trade policies, cross-cultural communication challenges, and the enduring weight of historical grievances demands more than simple optimism. It requires the sustained courage and resolve to engage directly with brutal truths and uncomfortable realities. I recall a conversation with a Chinese colleague who expressed her frustration with Western NGOs parachuting into projects with preset solutions. "You speak of partnership," she said, "but where is the curiosity about what we've already built?" Her words resonated deeply because they exposed a fundamental flaw in how external support is often delivered. To her, these approaches were characterized by a lack of genuine partnership and respect for local knowledge and initiative, stemming from deeply ingrained power imbalances.

Hearing this powerful critique also prompted personal reflection. It reminded me of times I've failed to be fully present or attentive in my essential relationships. While the scale, context, and consequences of my shortcomings differ markedly from those of the systemic issues plaguing international aid, my colleague's words underscored a universal principle. It's the critical importance of genuinely listening, seeking to understand before acting, and challenging our assumptions. It was a humbling reminder that prioritizing genuine understanding over preconceived notions is essential, whether navigating complex global partnerships or personal connections.

Just as trust is necessary for effective collaboration, systemic change thrives on partnerships built on mutual respect and shared goals. When a community in Guangzhou✦Guǎngzhōu✦learns from and adapts sustainable practices developed by Black farmers in Alabama, while potentially sharing its innovations in return, or when Chinese investors fund scholarships for Black students studying renewable energy who may later contribute expertise or perspectives valuable to global or Chinese green initiatives, these connections move beyond isolated acts.

They embody the powerful principle that progress is amplified when we recognize it doesn't have to be a zero-sum game but can be a shared endeavor where diverse contributions create benefits for all involved. The ache of missing my mother's presence is soothed by the knowledge that her resilience lives in my body of works. Likewise, the challenges of cross-cultural negotiation are eased by remembering that every compromise plants seeds for future generations. Regardless, none of this negates the loneliness of the path.

There are nights when the weight of absence threatens to eclipse the joy of discovery. But in those moments, I return to what anchors me. I've learned that my success isn't a solitary achievement. It's measured in the laughter echoing through a grainy phone call with my team, the collective gasp of a room when we announce a breakthrough, and the quiet pride in a family member and friend's voice saying, "Keep going." These moments of shared humanity are my most accurate measure of meaningful purpose. These fragments coalesce into a mosaic of purpose, reminding me that the road less traveled is not walked alone. It is paved with the footprints of those who cheer from afar and who believe in the vision I am living, even when the scheme is unclear.

As a Black Man from Southeast Georgia navigating this ever-shifting landscape known as China, I must accept that growth is a series of departures and returns, a constant renegotiation between the self and the world. The milestones I miss are not losses but invitations to cherish more deeply, collaborate more boldly, and live with the quiet faith that progress is not a finite resource. Through these experiences, I have found myself strengthened and endowed with greater resilience and adaptability.

Human achievement springs from ingenuity cultivated worldwide. Each culture, shaped by its unique history and challenges, offers invaluable insights into resilience, innovation, and resourcefulness. By studying these diverse narratives of success, we uncover universal principles and adaptable strategies for thriving in the face of adversity. These principles can enrich and strengthen the powerful, ongoing legacy of innovation and resilience within Black American communities, offering additional perspectives and approaches to navigate shared challenges. This process honors context that is not about imitation, but discerning the adaptable wisdom that empowers communities to flourish.

The collective solidarity of South Korea's chaebol networks, the decentralized entrepreneurial spirit of Nigeria's Nollywood, and Germany's emphasis on vocational training each reveal distinct pathways to economic empowerment. These models, among countless others, demonstrate that progress often emerges from leveraging cultural strengths while remaining open to reinvention. Central to this exploration is recognizing that systemic biases have long constrained access to opportunity.

Yet, we can transcend outdated paradigms by reframing these challenges as catalysts for innovation. Consider how Jewish diaspora communities have historically leveraged exclusion from mainstream industries to achieve dominance in niche sectors, remarkably banking and diamond trading, through tight-knit networks and knowledge sharing. Similarly, Indian entrepreneurs transformed colonial-era trade restrictions into a booming tech sector by prioritizing education and global outsourcing. Such stories underscore that limitations, when met with creativity, can open unexpected avenues for growth. For Black America, this mindset shift invites us to reinterpret our historical struggles not as insurmountable barriers but as fertile ground for cultivating solutions informed by global wisdom.

Adaptability lies at the heart of a resource-scarce economy. Just as Singapore reimagined its resource-scarce economy into a global hub by embracing trade and education, Black entrepreneurs can harness flexibility to navigate an evolving marketplace. The entrepreneurial path demands humility and curiosity, exemplified by Japan's Kaizen Philosophy of continuous improvement. Every interaction, whether with a Ghanaian artisan collective innovating sustainable textiles or a Vietnamese startup scaling through digital platforms, becomes a masterclass in problem-solving.

These encounters teach us to view setbacks not as failures, but as iterative steps toward refinement, as exemplified by China's meteoric rise from agrarian poverty to a tech powerhouse through strategic pivots under its "reform and opening-up" policies. Engaging with China's economic landscape offers particularly transformative potential. Its fusion of state-guided infrastructure investment and private-sector dynamism is evident in initiatives such as the Belt and Road (BRI), which provides a framework for scalable collaboration. By forging partnerships with Chinese firms and diaspora networks, Black American businesses can access manufacturing ecosystems, digital payment technologies, and venture capital channels previously out of reach.

Importantly, this engagement must be reciprocal. In the same way Silicon Valley's innovation culture has inspired global tech ecosystems, communities elsewhere have pioneered groundbreaking strategies in inclusive branding and grassroots mobilization. An actual exchange of these strengths will unlock immense value for everyone involved. The key lies in approaching such alliances with both discernment and ambition, ensuring they align with long-term goals of wealth retention and community uplift.

Global collaboration thrives when communities overcome internalized limitations. The success of the Afro-Caribbean community in leveraging remittance economies for education and startups demonstrates the power of transnational networks. Similarly, the UAE's transformation into a multicultural trade hub highlights how embracing diversity fuels prosperity. These examples underscore the immense potential of looking beyond traditional boundaries. For Black America, opportunities to harness similar dynamics exist, notably in deepening partnerships between Historically Black Colleges and Universities (HBCUs) and global institutions, such as Mandarin programs, collaborations with African nations on agritech initiatives, or cross-cultural investment alliances.

Like those with Asian American peers, in emerging sectors, particularly green energy. These are potential pathways among many for building on existing strengths and forging new connections. Addressing complex global challenges necessitates learning from diverse knowledge systems and perspectives. This includes insights from traditions emphasizing long-term responsibility, elements of Confucian (Rújiā) philosophy, and principles of intergenerational stewardship practiced by many Indigenous communities.

Similarly, community-based mutual support networks, exemplified by Ethiopia's Iddir, are alongside institutional approaches like Denmark's support for social entrepreneurship. These highlight different pathways for fostering collective resilience and well-being. Cross-cultural collaborations, especially emerging partnerships between fintech innovators in the Black diaspora and India's digital banking sector, have the potential to create valuable synergies. When grounded in genuine equity and respect, such partnerships can help develop more inclusive solutions to transnational issues such as climate justice and AI ethics. Such as partnerships where diverse viewpoints are critical. Ultimately, cultivating prosperity that strikes a balance between rootedness and global engagement is vital. The Lebanese diaspora's significant role in global supply chains, as it navigates complex questions of identity and integration, offers one perspective on this balance.

Likewise, drawing inspiration from the historical legacy of Black Wall Street while building modern initiatives, particularly Atlanta's (Yàtèlándà) Black Tech Corridor, demonstrates the ongoing effort to merge cultural heritage with innovative ambition in diverse contexts. Integrating these global lessons requires redefining wealth beyond mere financial metrics to encompass cultural capital, community health, and intergenerational equity. Progress in our interconnected age is indeed a mosaic, enriched by the unique contributions of each culture. By embracing this pluralistic vision and leveraging inherent strengths, Black America can transform systemic vulnerabilities into strategic advantages. This ensures its economic revival becomes a beacon of inclusive innovation, fostering shared prosperity rather than operating within a zero-sum paradigm.

The road ahead will demand audacity to experiment, resilience to endure setbacks, and wisdom to honor our roots while reaching outward. Yet, as history's greatest innovators have shown, the fusion of diverse perspectives ignites breakthroughs that are unattainable by any single perspective alone. As we advance, our task should be to build bridges, absorb insights, and craft a legacy where prosperity is both a shared endeavor and a testament to the power of learning without borders.

Progress toward genuine empowerment and equitable global integration is a complex, collective endeavor. While initiatives that cross borders can elevate diverse voices and foster cultural and economic exchange, this process is rarely smooth or universally beneficial. It involves navigating significant challenges, remarkably powerful imbalances, the risk of cultural homogenization, and potential economic exploitation, alongside opportunities for innovation and mutual learning. Obstacles and partnerships become critical tests, shaping narratives that reflect both resilience and ongoing tensions within the global system.

Actual progress requires acknowledging these complexities and striving for integration that minimizes harm and maximizes fair participation and benefit for all communities involved. Connections forged through shared values and common aspirations can create robust networks that amplify collective potential. Grassroots organizations linking Black American entrepreneurs with counterparts in Africa and the Caribbean are fostering trade partnerships. These collaborations often aim to honor ancestral legacies while developing sustainable business models, demonstrating how cultural and historical ties can serve as a foundation for modern innovation and contribute to economic vitality.

While such initiatives exemplify significant potential, they also navigate complex challenges inherent in cross-cultural and international business. Ultimately, actual progress is often driven by the creative friction that arises when we engage with diverse perspectives, challenging the inertia of our conventional thinking. When we listen to the stories of individuals like a Ghanaian tech innovator, a Brazilian educator, or a Japanese artist, we gain more than new ideas. We encounter powerful expressions of resilience and adaptation that resonate across human experience.

Instances like a musician blending jazz with West African highlife rhythms or a filmmaker drawing connections between the Harlem Renaissance (Hā lái mǔ wén yì fù xīng) and Nairobi's art scene vividly illustrate how cultural fusion often generates groundbreaking creativity. These syntheses highlight how innovation frequently thrives where traditions meet, transforming inherited wisdom into fresh visions. Engaging with these intersections challenges the notion of cultural isolationism, revealing that, in many contexts, identity is not diminished by thoughtful global exchange but can be enriched and deepened by it.

International collaboration holds transformative potential by enabling diverse perspectives to reframe challenges as catalysts for innovation and growth. Partnerships between Black-owned fintech startups and South Asian microfinance institutions could create valuable knowledge exchange to address financial exclusion. Lessons from initiatives serving unbanked communities, whether in Mumbai, Detroit (Dǐtèlǜ), or elsewhere, might inform adaptable solutions. Crucially, success requires a deep understanding of local contexts, equitable power dynamics, and addressing root causes beyond technology.

When grounded in mutual respect and shared learning, such collaboration can help turn systemic barriers into opportunities for community-driven economic empowerment. Shifting perspectives to view obstacles as catalysts for innovation represents a decisive paradigm shift with global relevance. For communities facing systemic challenges, particularly Black Americans, this approach provides a robust framework to counter narratives of scarcity by actively demonstrating and celebrating their profound resourcefulness.

Cultivating this mindset demands more than ambition. It requires a conscious effort to build and redefine legacies through tangible innovation and resilience. Imagine the historic quilts of Gee's Bend, Alabama, as once vital, utilitarian objects born from hardship, now celebrated in the Louvre. Their geometric brilliance powerfully bridges rural Black artistry and global modernism. This remarkable journey highlights how profoundly marginalized art can challenge and reshape the artistic canon. To honor such legacies, we must move beyond static archiving. By digitizing oral histories, curating virtual exhibitions, and mentoring youth in cross-continental dialogues, we can ensure these stories and skills remain vital, active forces, not relics of the past, but living proof of cultural resilience and artistic innovation.

Initiatives like Black-owned cooperatives in Brunswick, Georgia (Zuǒzhìyà Zhōu Bùlúnruìkè), and partnerships with fair-trade coffee growers in Ethiopia aim to build supply chains focused on equity and mutual benefit. Thereby, challenging conventional extractive models. These efforts represent a tangible attempt to demonstrate that commerce can support cultural sovereignty and foster more shared prosperity. Similarly, HBCU exchange programs with universities in Brazil and India seek to cultivate leaders with a deep understanding of Afro-diasporic experiences and global interconnectedness. The profound economic implication lies in these models actively exploring alternatives to dominant paradigms.

By prioritizing equitable distribution, community ownership, and culturally respectful engagement over pure profit maximization and external control, they offer concrete experiments in economic organization that could contribute to more resilient, inclusive, and locally anchored economies if successfully scaled and sustained. These students could emerge not as passive participants in globalization but as essential contributors to shaping its next phase, actively advocating for and advancing transnational frameworks built on reparative justice and inclusive growth. Technology can serve as a powerful resource in this transformation. Social media platforms have amplified awareness and scrutiny of supply chain issues, enabling movements to gain global visibility. Simultaneously, e-commerce tools create new opportunities for Black artisans to reach broader markets and reduce dependence on traditional gatekeepers.

Systemic barriers and digital inequities persist, meaning technology alone cannot guarantee equitable outcomes. True empowerment lies not only in accessing technological tools but also in actively reshaping their design and purpose. Black coders could be working to transform technology by fundamentally challenging paradigms shaped by colonial legacies. Their work should reimagine technology as a space for cultural expression and community needs, leading to innovative solutions born from unique perspectives. This kind of active reshaping fosters a profound cultural and economic alchemy, enabling a crucial psychological shift. A shift that moves from seeking validation within oppressive systems toward building autonomous value ecosystems.

The annual Juneteenth celebration, originating in Galveston, Texas, commemorates the long-awaited emancipation of enslaved Black people in the United States. While its profound significance remains rooted in this history and the ongoing fight for racial justice in America, the spirit of freedom, resilience, and cultural expression central to Juneteenth is also being observed within the Black American community in Shanghai, China, since 2021. These celebrations, where this spirit inspires diverse artists and entrepreneurs, stand as a powerful testament to the enduring legacy of Black America's history and community strength. They demonstrate that Black cultural identity and worth are inherently valuable and command recognition on their terms.

Consequently, as we navigate this landscape, the profound legacy of resilience, demonstrated by communities that turn survival into art and oppression into innovation, remains an invaluable resource. The ingenuity that gave birth to blues music in the Mississippi Delta fields and transformed Harlem (Hā lái mǔ) ballrooms into incubators of queer liberation exemplifies this powerful spirit. This same spirit of creative resistance can inspire contemporary movements, from trust platform cooperatives to climate justice initiatives. By drawing inspiration from such legacies of overcoming adversity, we can anchor our global engagements in a deeper understanding of transformative power, wherever they unfold.

One inspiration should be to create meaningful and respectful Shanghai Juneteenth (Shànghǎi Liùyuè Jié) celebrations by the Black American expat community that honor the day's profound historical significance. It is crucial to ground the event in its origins, as Juneteenth resonates powerfully across America. Incorporating diverse expressions of Black American culture within this context offers authentic ways to celebrate freedom, resilience, and community, thereby deepening the connection to their meaning. The introduction of Gullah-Geechee culture provides a valuable perspective on heritage, resilience, and the enduring quest for freedom, significantly contributing to a broader understanding of the Black American experience in the United States.

Such partnerships, built on mutual respect and shared goals, have the potential to evolve beyond short-term projects into sustainable cultural exchange. This development of Shanghai Juneteenth requires ongoing vigilance by all involved against the co-optation that often accompanies increased visibility. As our celebration grows, we must work together to shape its story authentically. This means fully embracing the incredible diversity of Black American experiences. We must prioritize amplifying Black voices to share their triumphs, brilliance, joys, internal debates, and the realities of ongoing struggles against issues like colorism and community violence. In light of this, our genuine authenticity requires rejecting any oversimplification of these rich and varied stories. This pivotal moment offers a profound opportunity to stand at the convergence of profound ancestral wisdom and unprecedented technological possibilities.

For Black Americans, and indeed for many communities with rich cultural heritages, there is a powerful call to action. It is a call to build bridges that honor our roots while embracing innovation, working towards a world where historically marginalized groups are not merely participants in globalization, but empowered shapers and essential visionaries actively contributing to its evolution and a more equitable future. Through strategic partnerships and responsible event organization, we strive to make Shanghai Juneteenth a meaningful commemoration of Black American emancipation and resilience.

We aim to honor this vital history, celebrate its cultural expressions, and foster understanding of its significance within our diverse Shanghai community. By recognizing this, faithful global citizenship requires thoughtful, sustained effort to present these critical lessons authentically and respectfully. The Black American expat community in Shanghai has organized and hosts Juneteenth celebrations, honoring its deep significance as a symbol of freedom and resilience within the Black American culture. We do this so that our efforts to share our heritage can serve as a resource for economic self-determination and help us establish crucial partnerships through connection, rather than isolation. These local events, which sometimes draw attendees from other parts of China, foster solidarity and strengthen our community bonds. They also provide us with meaningful opportunities to share the history and meaning of Juneteenth through cultural exchange with interested local friends and residents in Shanghai.

Successfully scaling these localized or network-based successes while preserving their core values, community ownership, and empowering purpose presents a significant challenge. How can their transformative potential be amplified without leading to dilution, co-option, or loss of autonomy? Addressing this complex challenge requires multiple strategies. A key part of this involves carefully evaluating potential partners and actively cultivating genuine allies who share a deep commitment to the community's goals of self-determination.

Pursuing allies offers more than just opportunity. It represents a strategic shift in how I think about building influence, like moving beyond purely transactional relationships for collaborations driven by a commitment to equity. My goal is to transform brief connections into lasting partnerships founded on genuine mutual accountability. Reflecting on the profound legacy of Harlem's (Hā lái mǔ) ballroom voguers, who transformed brutal marginalization into a vibrant culture and lexicon of resistance, I am inspired to apply a critical lens to the partnerships I engage in.

Their example pushes me to consciously ask whose agendas are prioritized here, and whose labor is genuinely valued and recognized? From what I've observed, international alliances beyond the United States provide vital resources and critical insights. They help me see the contradictions and possibilities when sharing Black liberation struggles across borders, while constantly reminding me to honor each community's specific histories and contexts. The potential for meaningful connection persists, yet navigating it often requires greater intentionality. How can we channel this energy to strengthen our communities and systems, ensuring they are resilient and equitable, rather than allowing new dynamics to cause harm or exclusion?

Our nation stands at a crossroads. One path leads toward isolation and inevitable decline; the other requires embracing our allies. While this path presents difficulties, it remains the only viable course to ensure our lasting prosperity and security. Ultimately, the choice is clear: we must build the coalitions that will define the next century.

Our understanding must move beyond conventional problem-solving by boldly reimagining what's possible when we unite globally with a shared vision for justice. The challenges confronting Black Americans, including systemic inequality, educational disparities, and economic displacement, are deeply rooted in distinct historical foundations like chattel slavery and specific domestic policies. While these struggles are unique in their origins and how they play out, they echo broader, global patterns of racial and economic injustice..

Solidarity across different movements is crucial for amplifying our collective power against these interconnected systems of oppression. Movements that share similarities with the struggles experienced by marginalized communities worldwide offer valuable insights. They can offer these insights by respectfully pooling knowledge from diverse financial models, cultural frameworks, and community engagement strategies. Insights that center local voices and acknowledge power imbalances. We can develop contextually grounded solutions that foster genuine solidarity and resonate both locally and globally.

China's rapid technological and infrastructural advancements offer valuable insights into scalable economic development. Simultaneously, the Nordic social welfare models provide exemplary lessons in designing equitable and inclusive societies. Each collaboration strengthens our ability to dismantle systemic barriers, proving that geography does not confine progress. What I find particularly powerful about these illustrations is their potential to foster more than just resource-sharing. They can build solidarity networks rooted in mutual respect and shared goals. Each new ally can help amplify our collective voice, reinforcing a message of equity that transcends borders.

This collective voice and transformational global collaboration can create a ripple effect beyond immediate outcomes. When we engage with international partners, we do so with the understanding that our shared successes and challenges offer opportunities for mutual learning. Innovative solutions can emerge anywhere and benefit communities globally. A sustainable business model pioneered in the Middle East might provide valuable insights for community-based entrepreneurship in underserved neighborhoods worldwide, including those in the United States. Similarly, effective educational initiatives developed in Asia could offer adaptable strategies to help bridge opportunity gaps in diverse urban areas.

As I explore building international connections, I am energized by the potential for meaningful progress. I wonder how these collaborations might positively impact Black American communities. Could integrating sustainable practices inspire local innovation, creating new jobs and economic opportunities? What solutions might emerge, especially technological solutions that improve access to essential resources, or education programs that nurture future leaders? Engaging in genuine cross-cultural exchange, challenging my assumptions, and valuing diverse perspectives will be key to finding these answers. This endeavor moves beyond simply seeking answers.

It is about cultivating a shared commitment to address the deep-rooted inequities facing marginalized and underserved communities. Embracing a global perspective enables us to understand diverse challenges and solutions, thereby strengthening our collective resolve. While the path is complex, sustained collaboration, critical engagement with power structures, and community-driven innovation are essential to dismantling systemic barriers and achieving meaningful progress. Progress on global challenges, ranging from climate change to public health, is impossible through isolationism. Meaningful solutions require deliberate collaboration that actively works to overcome the divides between continents, industries, and cultures.

Each partnership we cultivate strengthens our vision of a more equitable future, proving that progress is not achieved in silos. Still, through the vibrant exchange of ideas, strategies, and aspirations, as we progress, we harness this momentum with intention, ensuring that every alliance we build contributes to a legacy of justice and empowerment. We are called not only to meet the demands of today but to be architects of a better tomorrow. A future where one's starting point (qǐdiǎn) does not determine their finish line (zhōngdiǎn). Together, through global collaboration, we can bring this vision to life. The path to meaningful progress for Black Americans in America demands robust local action and domestic advocacy as its indispensable foundation.

Recognizing that systemic challenges can have global dimensions, proactively seeking allies and solidarity beyond our borders can provide vital support, leverage, and innovative perspectives, strengthening the domestic movement. Marginalized communities worldwide share interconnected struggles against systemic inequity. From economic disenfranchisement to political silencing, these groups face disturbingly similar patterns of oppression. It is within this global solidarity, however, that a profound source of power and resilience is forged.

Building bridges and forming partnerships with communities and movements worldwide, including in Africa, Latin America, the Middle East, China, and beyond, is crucial to amplifying our collective power and achieving meaningful change. Significant opportunities for solidarity and impactful collaboration exist wherever people are fighting for justice. This expanded vision of allies acknowledges that oppression, although experienced differently across cultures, often stems from similar power structures, and that solutions, too, can be found in shared resistance and resilience.

Cultivating these relationships requires more than outreach. They demand a long-term strategy for nurturing trust and reciprocity. Potential allies must be engaged not merely as resources, but as collaborators whose insights reshape our approach to advocacy. This means listening deeply to their stories, understanding their needs, and identifying where our struggles intersect. Examining China's significant achievements in poverty alleviation and expanding educational access could spark valuable ideas and discussions for addressing the economic disparities affecting Black communities in America. Similarly, exploring the strategies and experiences of Brazil's vibrant Afro-descendant movements around cultural preservation could enrich conversations about sustaining Black American cultural heritage.

A meaningful connection requires deep respect for the distinct historical legacies, systemic challenges, and agency within each context. Truly collaborative learning would involve deliberate action, markedly attending international conferences for people-to-people exchange, fostering reciprocal cultural dialogues, and utilizing digital platforms to facilitate sustained, respectful conversations and mutual learning across continents. My goal isn't just to borrow ideas, but to co-create strategies tackling both local and global inequities. When asked, 'How do we achieve this vision?' Education is a powerful and essential foundation.

For Black American families, this means reimagining learning as a gateway to global awareness, one that includes a firm grounding in Black history and exposure to the world beyond American borders. I credit study abroad programs, including those in countries like China, with the potential to be transformative. Imagine a generation of Black youth choosing to become fluent in Mandarin, deliberately engaging with the histories of Afro-Asian solidarity, and gaining firsthand insights into how different societies address inequality. These experiences do more than enhance resumes. This experience can cultivate the adaptability, critical thinking, and cross-cultural empathy essential for those who aspire to navigate and help reshape systems of power.

Access to these opportunities remains uneven. To bridge this gap, I advocate for partnerships between HBCUs and international institutions to create pipelines for student exchanges and joint research initiatives. I also see scholarships targeting Black students, mentorship programs linking them with global professionals, and curricula emphasizing transnational histories as essential components of this effort. Parents also play a vital role. When families recognize the lifelong value of international experience and how living abroad can foster resilience, independence, and innovative thinking, they are often motivated to support or advocate for policies that increase accessibility.

The ability to advocate effectively depends on overcoming significant systemic and resource barriers. I felt in my bones that this extends beyond individual advancement. It's about preparing a generation to lead in an interconnected world. I've witnessed firsthand the profound potential of studying abroad to transform perspectives. When young people immerse themselves in places like Beijing, Shanghai, or other diverse communities around the world, many return with far more than language skills. They often gain a deeper understanding of their place in the global context, for those open to it. These experiences provide powerful opportunities to confront how complex issues like racism, colonialism, and economic disparity play out across different cultures and witness how communities respond.

This journey frequently challenges narrow viewpoints, fostering the belief that meaningful change is possible. For some Black American youth, visiting Guangzhou (Guǎngzhōu) can offer a powerful and broadening experience. Witnessing communities where African entrepreneurs have built businesses and livelihoods and potentially encountering events like lectures on Pan-Africanism at universities can challenge the confines of America's dominant racial narratives and reveal diverse expressions of Black identity and community on a global scale. It's crucial to understand this experience within its full context.

The Africans whose communities and resilience visitors may witness are themselves navigating significant challenges in Guangzhou (Guǎngzhōu), including discrimination, complex visa regulations, and periods of targeted mistreatment. Their experiences serve as a vital reminder that while racial dynamics in China differ significantly from those in America, race remains a potent social reality shaping lives globally. The ripple effects extend beyond the individual. When these students return, they bring back diverse perspectives and potential solutions observed abroad. A community-based lending model from Ghana that could spark ideas for local economic development, or a tech incubator approach from Suzhou that might inform local innovation strategies.

They also forge valuable personal connections that often evolve into international professional networks, creating opportunities for future collaborations and partnerships. This potential for knowledge transfer and network building demonstrates why investment in global education can be an influential contributor to long-term economic development and political engagement. Expanding these opportunities is more than just providing young Black Americans with tools to succeed. They empower them to define success on their terms and for their communities.

I believe the path forward involves building coalitions that span the globe, connecting the struggle for justice in Black America with global movements. This requires moving beyond symbolic solidarity to forge actionable partnerships. For me, this could mean exploring concrete collaborations, conspicuously joint ventures between Black and Asian tech entrepreneurs. Beyond these, many other vital forms of partnership play a crucial role. These partnerships could encourage multinational corporations to voluntarily address racial equity and support academic collaborations that help reshape narratives about the histories and contributions of diaspora communities.

Encouraging these connections also challenges us to think more expansively. The fight for equity extends beyond domestic policy reforms, resonating with powerful purpose and shared goals in movements for land rights in Brazil, labor justice in South Africa, educational equity in India, and countless other struggles for justice worldwide. Building solidarity across these interconnected efforts is crucial. As I embark on this work, I remember that the most enduring movements are those rooted in local grounding and global vision. By embracing this dual perspective, I honor the legacy of figures like Malcolm X and W.E.B. Du Bois, who understood that Black liberation was always a worldwide project. The alliances I help forge today will help determine the opportunities available to the next generation. I aim to ensure those opportunities are as boundless as their potential.

Leaving behind the familiar is one of life's most profound challenges, a simultaneous experience of loss and liberation. The comfort I derive from my established routines, familiar places, and predictable rhythms acts as an emotional anchor. An anchor that is perceived as a psychological safety net that genuinely makes daily life feel more manageable. Yet, I also recognize that this very comfort can sometimes become like invisible chains, potentially holding me back from discovering aspects of myself that might only emerge when I step into the unknown. I constantly navigate this tension, feeling pulled between the gravitational force of the familiar and the electric potential of what lies beyond my apartment, my neighborhood café, and that well-worn walking path throughout Zhujiajiao (Zhūjiājiǎo).

These various crossroads are deeply ingrained into who I am. Leaving them behind would feel like leaving part of myself behind, because they hold so much of my daily life, my memories, and my sense of belonging. This feeling highlights how powerfully our environments shape and reflect us, making the thought of leaving all the more complex. From what I understand of psychological research and my own experience, humans often seem drawn to habit and predictability. Our brains might favor routines through mechanisms like dopamine release, creating a natural tendency to resist disruption.

Yet I've observed that transformative moments, both in history and in my own life, frequently arise when someone dares to challenge the status quo. I think of my own bold choices, outstandingly relocating for an educational opportunity that terrified me, ending relationships that were comfortable but stagnant, and learning a skill that made me feel like an awkward beginner. Through these experiences, I've come to see that each significant risk I've taken has held the potential for profound reward. In my life, the anxiety preceding the leap has often felt proportional to the personal growth that followed.

Looking back, my choices have drawn a map. Some led me to spectacular friendships that expanded my worldview, professional opportunities that reshaped my capabilities, and moments of unexpected joy in unfamiliar places. Others resulted in what felt like dead ends at the time, relationships that didn't work out, places I couldn't make feel like home, and friendships that didn't last. Yet even these experiences became essential lessons, teaching me resilience in ways success never could. A failed business venture ultimately taught me more about my core values than any triumph ever did. My years abroad, spent alone, revealed depths of self-reliance I never knew I possessed. This experience taught me the paradox of leaving comfort zones when we feel we're risking stability. Still, we're trading one form of security that is familiar for another that has proven capacity to adapt. Now, facing another crossroads, I must decide whether a career shift, a relationship choice, or a creative leap is the most reasonable path forward.

This is a familiar tension, especially when the specifics change and the emotional terrain feels the same. What's different now is my understanding that this discomfort isn't a barrier to avoid. It's the very ground where my growth happens. Neuroscience reveals that stepping outside habitual patterns is crucial for forming new neural pathways. It's how our brains adapt and learn. So that feeling of unease? It's not just the price of growth for me. It's often the biological signal that growth is occurring.

I've come to view this challenge as "productive discomfort" because of the necessary friction that forges resilience. The calculus becomes even more poignant when relationships are factored into the equation. Physical distance from loved ones creates a particular kind of emotional gravity. Missing a family member's birthday, a friend's wedding, or a nephew's graduation isn't just about the event itself but about the accumulation of shared experiences that form the bedrock of intimacy. I've stood in foreign cities watching sunset photos flood my imagination, the pain of absence sharp enough to take my breath away. Yet this very distance has a way of clarifying what matters most. Relationships often deepen unexpectedly when conversations become intentional rather than incidental, when phone calls are planned rather than assumed.

Technology has rewritten the rules of absence for me, allowing me to maintain connections across continents in ways my ancestors couldn't have imagined. But more importantly, I've found that physical separation tests the flexible strength of my bonds. For me, the enduring relationships where silence feels comfortable, where phone calls pick up exactly where we left off, have become the true constants of my life. I've discovered that the space created by distance often allows for new connections, sometimes with people whose life experiences radically differ from mine. This has been the greatest gift of leaving familiar ground in my life, because it taught me that human connection, personally,

I've found that it isn't dependent on proximity, but on my willingness and the other person's willingness to be vulnerable, regardless of the distance. So, what has emerged for me from this tension between roots and leaves isn't compromise, but something more beautiful: a way of living that honors where I come from while remaining open to transformation. I've realized the familiar doesn't disappear when I venture forth. It becomes my foundation, allowing me to reach further. Like trees that grow strongest when winds challenge their sapling years, I become more fully myself when I allow life to stretch me. The ache of missing loved ones, the nervous energy before a significant change, and the disorientation of new beginnings aren't signs that I'm doing something wrong, but evidence that I'm doing something brave.

Ultimately, the familiar and the unknown aren't opposites but partners in my becoming. One provides the safety to take a risk, and the other provides the experiences that make returning, whether physically or emotionally, meaningful. This may be why the most grounded people are often adventurous since they've learned that roots and leaves grow from the same trunk. As I contemplate my next departure from comfort, I carry this wisdom: growth never asks me to abandon what I love; it only asks me to love enough to keep growing.

Returning home offers more than a physical homecoming. It is an opportunity for me to pause and reflect on the intricacies that have shaped who I am. This moment of stillness allows me to consider the experiences, ambitions, and growth that comprise my life. Each decision, each connection, and each challenge has contributed to this evolving narrative, and stepping back to assess this mosaic reveals patterns and lessons that might otherwise remain obscured. In this reflective space, my journey is not linear but a series of interconnected cycles, advances, retreats, and recalibrations that mirror the broader rhythms of the world. As I return home to reflect on my evolution, we must revisit our shared path through Black American culture to understand where we have been and where we might go. This reflection also reminds me that our lives and progress are deeply intertwined with a complex global landscape. In an era of volatility and interdependence, understanding and engaging thoughtfully with the broader world, which includes its diverse nations and peoples, is crucial for navigating our collective future.

The complexities of climate change, technological disruption, and economic inequality demand deep collaboration that transcends national borders, entrenched ideologies, and short-term interests. Retreating into isolation or relying solely on transactional diplomacy fails to grasp the fundamental reality of our interconnected world and the scale of the shared challenges we face. The urgency of this cooperative partnership is starkly evident. Effective global climate agreements hinge on the alignment of major carbon emitters, and China's critical role in renewable energy innovation, manufacturing, and infrastructure development is undeniable.

Similarly, ensuring resilient global supply chains, establishing robust cybersecurity frameworks, and coordinating effective public health initiatives all require sustained and practical cooperation between the United States and China. Effective international collaboration is built not just on policy alignment but is actively strengthened and sustained by deep, mutual cultural and intellectual engagement. Moving beyond a purely zero-sum view of international relations towards a mindset that seeks mutual benefits is a valuable aspiration. This includes recognizing that China's rise presents both opportunities and challenges.

Engaging constructively requires understanding China's complex historical narratives, aspirations, and contributions, acknowledging it as a significant nation with its distinct perspective. Approaching the relationship with informed curiosity, rather than predominantly through a lens of apprehension, can open pathways for dialogue that identify areas where competition can be managed and genuine synergies found. This perspective is relevant beyond traditional geopolitics. Just as individuals assess their paths through the lens of growth and adaptation, nations can likewise benefit from critically examining their trajectories.

Are we adequately prioritizing sustainable practices and moving beyond historical models reliant on resource exploitation? Are we investing sufficiently in building bridges of understanding, or allowing barriers of mistrust to persist? Meaningful progress hinges on our willingness to engage authentically by listening as much as we speak, and learning as much as we teach. Far from being peripheral, initiatives like cultural exchanges and educational partnerships are a critical form of "soft power," creating a durable foundation of mutual understanding upon which all successful diplomacy is built.

When a student in Shanghai studies Black American literature or a farmer in Texas adopts sustainable techniques pioneered in Chinese villages, the abstract ideal of a 'global community' becomes a tangible reality. These micro-interactions weave a fabric of shared knowledge and mutual empathy, proving to be robust and enduring forces for connection. While goodwill is the essential starting point for proactive engagement, its true potential is realized only through a deliberate, thoughtful strategy. Anticipating geopolitical shifts, economic trends, and technological disruptions enables the crafting of responses that are both agile and principled.

Investing in joint research initiatives on artificial intelligence ethics or coordinating disaster response frameworks embeds collaboration into strategic planning, making it a proactive choice rather than a reactive scramble. Similarly, addressing trade imbalances through equitable frameworks focused on long-term stability and mutual benefit is a strategically sound approach, in contrast to those driven primarily by short-term, punitive measures. Underpinning all such strategies must be humility. Acknowledging past missteps, whether in foreign policy or personal judgment, is not a sign of weakness but an essential foundation for learning and sustainable progress. Just as individuals benefit from reflecting on the alignment between their intentions and actions, nations must also rigorously examine whether their proclaimed commitment to cooperation aligns with their actual conduct.

This introspection is crucial in an era of information overload. While public milestones and diplomatic ceremonies can signal progress, they risk creating an appearance of advancement that obscures the deeper, more demanding work of building genuine trust. Authentic relationships, whether personal or international, thrive on sustained commitment, not fleeting spectacle. They are built through the daily practice of reliability, honoring obligations, and resolving disagreements constructively.

Reflecting on personal experience, our most enduring bonds are forged not by isolated, grand gestures, but through the steady accumulation of sincere and consistent effort. This principle holds for global alliances. While high-profile agreements capture attention, it is the years of persistent dialogue, collaborative navigation of shared challenges, and a willingness to make incremental compromises that truly forge resilient partnerships. Public actions and agreements contribute, but their long-term value is realized only when underpinned by this consistent, substantive engagement.

For me, returning home often serves as a metaphor for recentering. Understanding myself better can make me more effective when engaging with the complex world around me. The clarity I sometimes gain through introspection helps me approach global challenges with a goal of discernment rather than simple reactivity. Based on my observations, strengthening alliances doesn't mean diluting my identity. Instead, it represents a potential to enrich it through the challenging but rewarding alchemy of collaboration. As I reassess my path, I realize that my experiences, including successes, failures, and moments of doubt, contribute to developing the empathy and resilience I strive to bring to our interconnected world.

The end, with its inevitable frayed edges alongside vibrant moments, resonates for me as a reflection of the imperfect yet vital project of global cooperation. Both journeys require patience, vision, and the courage to keep moving forward even when the path is unclear. Ultimately, it won't be any single thought that defines me, but the accumulation of collective experiences that shape my understanding. This shapes a portrait of a world I consciously choose to engage with, one that prioritizes shared progress over solitary triumph, aiming to bridge divisions rather than reinforce them.

5

Reciprocal Alliances for Equity

This truth propels me. I have worked diligently to advance with intention and purpose, not merely toward a destination but in rhythm with the lessons etched into humanity's shared story. I've learned that progress is not about reaching a goal, but about sustaining growth by learning from the resilience and adaptability of cultures that have successfully navigated complex challenges. Many such societies demonstrate a strong commitment to education, innovation, and community well-being. These commitments can empower populations and lay the foundations for collective advancement, highlighting strategies worth examining.

We believe that for Black America, exploring global models of success and building solidarity with international partners fighting similar struggles can offer valuable insights and strengthen our efforts towards empowerment, systemic progress, social justice, economic equity, and cultural resilience. These alliances are practical bridges, connecting shared struggles and solutions, and allow us to learn from innovative approaches developed worldwide while also contributing our hard-won knowledge and experience. They complement, rather than replace, the critical work being done domestically.

Brazil's Afro-entrepreneurial networks and Ghana's diaspora-driven investments offer invaluable lessons within a global tapestry of approaches. Engaging with such diverse strategies fosters mutual learning and challenges limiting perspectives anywhere they exist, powerfully illustrating that the fight for equity is both universal and uniquely contextual. Through genuine collaboration, we can collectively adapt global insights to local realities, fostering a dynamic exchange where knowledge transcends geography and becomes a tool for collective liberation.

Central to this vision is the recognition that solidarity must be reciprocal. While Black America gains strength from global partnerships, it also contributes distinct and powerful cultural and political capital. The legacy of the Civil Rights Movement has profoundly inspired anti-racist struggles worldwide, from South Africa to France, demonstrating how these experiences resonate across borders. By amplifying Black voices on international platforms through the arts, policy advocacy, or technology, Black America must actively assert its presence in shaping global narratives.

Collaborations between Black American filmmakers and Nollywood creators offer significant potential to challenge monolithic portrayals of Blackness by fostering diverse storytelling perspectives. Similarly, partnerships between the American Black Lives Matter (BLM) movement (Hēirén de mìng yěshì mìng) and Brazil's Movimento Negro Unificado (MNU) can strengthen grassroots organizing against police violence through shared learning and solidarity, with distinct national contexts and challenges shaping their effectiveness.

These intersections could demonstrate that solidarity thrives as an active, reciprocal exchange, facilitated by a process of mutual learning where cultural exchange and strategic alignment advance shared goals. Forging a successful public-private alliance requires more than goodwill; it necessitates sustained institutional investment in resources, structures, and accountability. Initiatives like the African Union's Sixth Region Diaspora Initiative demonstrate the power of structured, sustained collaboration in international human rights advocacy.

Similarly, organizations with primarily domestic mandates, notably the National Association for the Advancement of Colored People (NAACP), can exert significant influence on international human rights through targeted advocacy and powerful examples. By supporting diaspora-led trade programs, educational exchanges, and policy coalitions, we can establish pathways for resource sharing and innovation, contributing to a more inclusive global landscape.

South Africa's Black Economic Empowerment (BEE) policies, although controversial and yielding mixed results, offer insights into attempted corporate inclusion and wealth redistribution strategies that highlight both potential mechanisms and significant implementation challenges, which could inform equity initiatives elsewhere. Similarly, Guyana's Institute for Private Enterprise Development (IPED) demonstrates adequate support for micro-entrepreneurs through microloans combined with business training in key sectors. Such partnerships are most effective when grounded in mutual respect, acknowledge that no single community holds all the solutions, and deliberately prioritize the needs of groups marginalized in mainstream economic discourse.

Celebrating global Black excellence is profoundly vital. When we uplift figures like Kenya's Wangari Maathai, whose environmental activism intersected with gender and class justice, or Haiti's 1804 revolution as a cornerstone of Black liberation, we expand the narrative of what resistance and success entail. Such diverse stories directly counter the erasure of Black contributions to global progress, fostering deep pride and unlocking powerful possibilities. Initiatives like the National Museum of African American History and Culture (NMAAHC), global exhibitions, and digital archives powerfully connect Harlem Renaissance (Hā lái mǔ wén yì fù xīng) artists to the Negritude movement, demonstrating how cultural stewardship can strengthen collective identity. artists to the Negritude movement as a powerful example of how cultural stewardship can help strengthen collective identity.

This global visibility honors our legacy and provides vital role models for younger generations, extending influence beyond local boundaries. Alongside this outward engagement, sustained inward reflection remains essential for meaningful growth, whether personal, communal, or transnational. This growth necessarily involves addressing complex challenges, including critically examining issues like internalized oppression, colorism, and lateral violence within diasporic communities.

From my own encounters, dialogues between African and Black American scholars have included necessary, though challenging, conversations about tensions surrounding immigration, cultural appropriation, and differing conceptions of Pan-Africanism. These discussions are vital as we work to align our shared aspirations with truly equitable practices. I've come to see embracing discomfort as a sign of progress, enabling us to move beyond performative unity toward genuine accountability. This is how we work to repair the profound divides created by the legacies of colonialism and slavery, and sustained by modern globalization.

This interconnected approach redefines progress as a collective endeavor. One might conclude that individual success gains greater meaning and impact when it actively uplifts others, as demonstrated by mentoring programs that connect Black Tech professionals in Silicon Valley with Nairobi's Silicon Savannah, or by mutual aid networks supporting Afro-Latina entrepreneurs. The COVID-19 pandemic starkly revealed our global interdependence, as diaspora communities mobilized crucial support by sending remittances and medical supplies, often while facing significant challenges themselves.

Simultaneously, global health partnerships, while vital, exposed deep-seated disparities in vaccine access driven by structural inequities. These moments underscore how profoundly our fates are intertwined, demanding sustained and equitable collaboration. As such, by prioritizing coalition-building, Black America positions itself not as a passive beneficiary of global wisdom but as a co-architect of a fairer world. This requires patience, as trust across borders is built through consistency, not convenience. It also requires centering marginalized voices, particularly women and people with disabilities, whose intersecting struggles often reveal innovative solutions.

Afro-Brazilian feminists developed powerful intersectional frameworks addressing race, gender, and class long before the term 'intersectionality' gained widespread traction in America, exemplifying how grassroots movements shape global discourse. Similarly, the Nigerian-led movement to end SARS harnessed the digital age to galvanize real-time international solidarity, including crucial tactical support from Black American activists, demonstrating the potential for global connections to amplify local struggles. Reflecting on our history from the life-saving networks of the Underground Railroad to the strategic alliances formed across the Global South during the Cold War. My experience has shown me that adaptability and collaboration are essential to our resilience.

Given the profound threats we face today, like the climate crisis, rising authoritarianism, and rapid technological change, turning inward or embracing isolationism isn't a viable option for our communities. Our survival and progress have always depended on, and continue to rely on, connection and collective action. In my opinion, tackling interconnected challenges like voter suppression, environmental racism, and algorithmic bias demands urgent transnational strategies. By forging global alliances and building upon centuries of diasporic ingenuity and resistance, we stand a better chance of achieving meaningful progress. This progress shouldn't be a zero-sum game, because I am convinced that by embracing our interconnectedness, we can transform fragmented efforts into a more powerful, unified force fighting for justice, dignity, and shared prosperity for all.

Throughout my experience, I've recognized that building alliances isn't just a tactical advantage. It's a fundamental necessity for surviving and thriving in a world defined by interdependence. These relationships, whether fleeting or enduring, supportive or adversarial, form the essential foundation through every phase of life, subtly and profoundly shaping outcomes. My interactions often serve as a mirror, reflecting my strengths, vulnerabilities, and areas for improvement. This is especially true when I'm facing high-stakes challenges. Challenges like encouragement from allies can give me the courage to take necessary risks. Concurrently, skepticism from critics helps me refine and sharpen my vision.

What begins as personal growth inevitably ripples outward, revealing how my resilience and collective progress are deeply intertwined. The supporters who champion my aspirations often provide more than just encouragement. They offer access to networks, resources, and perspectives that expand my understanding of what is possible. Their trust becomes a currency, enabling collaborations that transcend individual limitations. My growth comes from diverse perspectives. A mentor's guidance can illuminate paths I hadn't considered, and a peer's expertise can transform abstract ideas into actionable strategies. Both eventually demonstrate that these contributions are invaluable. Equally essential are those who question my assumptions or challenge my goals. In the meantime, their perspective might initially feel disruptive. It forces me to rigorously reexamine my foundations, test the strength of my plans, and develop the patience needed to engage productively with dissent.

These forms of input, whether supportive or challenging, are fundamental to developing robust ideas and strategies. Over time, I've learned that friction, when approached with curiosity, can polish rough edges into clarity. A critic's challenge to my methodology might reveal blind spots, while skepticism about my priorities could lead to a more inclusive approach. These interactions, however uncomfortable, train me to distinguish between defensiveness and discernment, a skill vital for long-term resilience.

This relationship between support and resistance reveals a deeper insight about how meaningful alliances flourish not through unanimous agreement but by cultivating spaces where diverse voices coexist and interact. Just as a thriving ecosystem relies on biodiversity to foster resilience and stability, genuine human progress is fueled by both encouragement and constructive critique. Through navigating diverse experiences, I've learned that growth is often iterative, shaped by ongoing cycles of action, feedback, and adaptation. The allies who support me through successes and challenges provide invaluable perspective, their influence significantly shaping my path and decisions.

Similarly, finding common ground has at times transformed initial opposition into unexpected collaboration when mutual goals become clear. These experiences taught me that the line between "ally" and "adversary" is often fluid, redrawn through dialogue and shared vulnerability. This understanding extends beyond individual growth to inform collective struggles for equity and justice. For Black America, forging alliances is imperative, transcending local or national boundaries and calling for engagement with global communities whose struggles resonate with the fight against systemic oppression. History demonstrates that liberation movements often gain significant strength and moral authority when they recognize their struggles as interconnected. This was powerfully evident in the profound solidarity of the Civil Rights Era with anti-colonial movements in Africa and Asia.

Today, this tradition continues as many contemporary movements, notably those advocating for climate justice and migrant rights, increasingly frame their causes within broader frameworks of systemic injustice, forging partnerships based on shared principles and goals. These movements often represent strategic necessities rather than symbolic gestures. Like systemic inequities, especially economic marginalization, educational disparities, and healthcare gaps, are frequently interconnected. They can reflect broader patterns of exploitation and exclusion, though local contexts also shape their specific manifestations.

I believe that by working with international partners committed to justice, we can learn from innovative approaches used elsewhere, notably Brazil's grassroots initiatives to combat urban inequality or South Africa's truth and reconciliation frameworks. Exchanging knowledge in this manner helps strengthen our local efforts and connects them to broader movements, potentially enhancing their overall impact. Critics would understandably emphasize the pressing nature of domestic issues and express concern that international engagement might detract from them. It's essential to recognize that global challenges and solutions are increasingly interconnected.

Engaging with international partners committed to justice offers valuable opportunities to learn from innovative approaches developed elsewhere, ultimately benefiting domestic priorities as well. Accordingly, policy shifts in America's global trade can disproportionately impact vulnerable businesses, including Black-owned enterprises reliant on imported materials. Simultaneously, diaspora communities abroad significantly influence the cultural narratives that shape perceptions of Black identity within the United States. Furthermore, global partnerships empower us to reframe our struggles as universal calls for human dignity, moving beyond isolated grievances.

When Black American activists collaborate with Indigenous water protectors, Afro-European organizers, or Afro-Latino labor advocates, they engage in a robust exchange of knowledge and strategies forged through distinct yet often interconnected histories of resistance and resilience. These collaborations not only build solidarity but also actively challenge narrow stereotypes, expanding the understanding of Blackness to include diverse, globally connected experiences and perspectives.

Cultural and intellectual exchanges, often fostered through alliances, act as powerful catalysts for creativity and innovation.

The ongoing fusion of diverse African musical traditions with various global genres provides a compelling example that has significantly transformed art forms such as jazz, hip-hop, and Afrobeats. These genres, rooted in or deeply influenced by this fusion, now play a significant role in shaping contemporary cultures worldwide. Similarly, strategies developed in one context can inspire approaches elsewhere; however, direct adaptation requires careful consideration of the differing circumstances.

Ghana's innovative use of mobile technology to expand financial access and literacy demonstrates the potential of leveraging widely available tools for financial inclusion. The root causes and scale of the racial wealth gap in America are profoundly different and stem from systemic racism. Elements of Ghana's model, particularly the use of accessible technology platforms to deliver tailored financial education and services, could contribute to one piece of a much broader, multifaceted strategy needed to address this deep-seated inequality. These strategies can create economic opportunities, such as outstanding transnational cooperatives or joint ventures that redirect capital into marginalized communities. Crucially, they demonstrate that progress isn't a zero-sum game, and elevating one community doesn't require diminishing another.

Building enduring alliances demands intentionality. From my perspective, it requires active listening to genuinely understand partners' unique histories and needs, rather than projecting my framework onto theirs. It also means embracing discomfort when confronting cultural differences or conflicting priorities. Most importantly, I've learned that true alliance hinges on reciprocity. When that balance is lost and the relationship becomes transactional instead of relational, the foundation weakens, and the connection often fades. As someone committed to justice within Black America, I credit that our solidarity must be intersectional.

For me, this means recognizing that systems of oppression are interlinked and that our liberation must be collective. It could involve advocating for Palestinian sovereignty while also supporting Haitian migrants or partnering with Asian American activists to combat xenophobia while simultaneously addressing anti-Blackness within our communities. True solidarity requires this interconnected approach. For this reason, progress is a mosaic of relationships, both personal and collective. Each ally and adversary contributes a piece, whether through solidarity, challenge, or the raw honesty that spurs evolution. As I navigate my path, I am continually reminded that no one transcends life's complexities alone.

I trust that for Black America and all communities striving toward equity, our path forward requires the courage to connect, the humility to learn, and the wisdom to see opposition as a catalyst for deeper understanding. Our capacity to thrive in an uncertain future depends on nurturing these bonds and transforming fragmented efforts into shared strength, even as we confront deep-seated structural inequities. The road ahead is fraught with challenges, but I am fortified by the knowledge that I am not alone. This understanding does not diminish the journey's complexity, nor does it promise a smooth passage. Instead, it anchors me in the certainty that community and shared purpose are not just ideals but vital tools for navigating uncertainty. As I confront the twists and turns that lie ahead, I am reminded that honesty, courage, and mutual support are not solitary virtues. They are collective strengths cultivated through the relationships that sustain us. Each person who walks beside me on this path brings their own story, wisdom, and resilience, weaving a mosaic of perspectives that transforms individual struggle into collective triumph.

This truth resonates deeply when I reflect on those who stand alongside me. Friends, mentors, and allies illuminate the way forward, not by shielding me from difficulty, but by walking unflinchingly through it with me. Their presence transforms hardship, making it less a solitary burden and more a shared endeavor. This develops into moments where vulnerability and solidarity intersect in times of doubt. Their willingness to sit with discomfort to acknowledge the messiness of growth without turning away strengthens our shared commitment. And once we move beyond the idea that strength means going it alone. By building a network of trust, fear and uncertainty are met without judgment, and setbacks become learning opportunities. We create an environment where both individual growth and collective resilience thrive.

It is within this space of shared vulnerability that resilience can take root. Adversity, when faced collectively, can lose its power to isolate. The fears that once seemed insurmountable and the doubts that whispered of inadequacy may be met with voices of reassurance and perspectives that can help reframe obstacles, perhaps even as invitations to innovate. When challenges are navigated side by side, our bonds have the potential to deepen, potentially creating a foundation sturdy enough to withstand life's unpredictability.

Where it flourishes, this collective fortitude does more than empower us because it inspires us. It can redefine what seems possible. Especially, daunting tasks often become more manageable when shared. And change, even when disruptive, frequently feels less threatening when met with curiosity rather than resistance. Through collaboration and teamwork, significant hurdles can be transformed into opportunities for growth, becoming stepping stones rather than impassable barriers. This perspective, highlighting the power of shared effort and open-mindedness, holds potential not just in personal relationships but across broader human connections.

Consequently, as I delve into the complexities of China's manufacturing and cultural exchange industries, I am struck by how deeply the principles of authenticity and mutual respect resonate in my professional and cross-cultural experiences. My work, whether negotiating production timelines in Guangdong Province (Guǎngdōng Shěng) or fostering artistic partnerships in Shanghai. Consistently shows me that genuine collaboration thrives on these values. In an era when supply chains span continents and cultural boundaries are increasingly blurred, I find that recognizing our interdependence is fundamental to building successful, sustainable relationships.

While initial agreements provide a necessary framework, the success of a manufacturing alliance truly depends on navigating the complex undercurrents of unspoken expectations, historical contexts, and cultural nuances. A factory manager's hesitancy to voice concerns about deadlines might reflect a cultural preference for preserving group harmony, a value sometimes associated with traditions like Confucianism prevalent in their region. Conversely, a partner's emphasis on efficiency could be misinterpreted as impatience, especially if their communication style is more straightforward. Bridging these potential divides requires more than cross-cultural experiences. It demands emotional attunement, a willingness to listen deeply for underlying meanings, and the humility to continually question one's assumptions while recognizing the diversity of perspectives within any cultural context.

Here, too, the power of community proves immensely valuable. Colleagues with decades of experience in Sino-foreign joint ventures become critical resources, offering contextual insights and practical wisdom that significantly augment formal knowledge. A mentor's anecdote about navigating guanxi (guānxi) relationship-building in Zhejiang Province (Zhèjiāng Shěng) or a peer's cautionary tale about misaligned incentives in a tech partnership enriches a shared repository of essential knowledge. These stories, exchanged over tea or late-night calls, offer more than just practical advice. They are vital lessons that demonstrate that success in high-stakes, cross-cultural environments often depends not just on individual expertise but on actively learning from and leaning on the collective experience of the community. The same ethos applies to cultural exchange, where authenticity is both challenging and vital.

Take, collaborating on an art exhibition between creators from Savannah and Shanghai. This brings together distinct artistic perspectives shaped by different histories and contexts. I've seen how, when artists approach these differences with genuine curiosity and respect. They see them not as obstacles but as rich sources of inspiration where powerful new work can emerge. In one instance, a Chinese artist, deeply skilled in ink techniques, and a Black American artist, known for their innovative watercolor, shared common ground. Their distinct painting methods could blend these forms, resulting in a piece that resonates powerfully across diverse audiences. Such partnerships could thrive not by minimizing distinctions, but by honoring them. When differences are engaged with care and mutual understanding, they can become a catalyst for remarkable creativity.

Consequently, none of this is effortless. It requires uncomfortable conversations, moments of misalignment, and the courage to recalibrate when intentions clash with outcomes. Yet, these very tensions underscore why communal support is essential. When misunderstandings arise, as they inevitably will, a foundation of trust allows for repair. When cultural blind spots surface, diverse perspectives within the group act as corrective lenses, sharpening clarity. The goal is not unanimity but synergy, so that a dynamic equilibrium is achieved in which individual strengths amplify the whole. As I look to the future, market shifts, geopolitical currents, and evolving technologies will test the resilience of every alliance.

Yet, just as a mangrove forest withstands turbulent tides through its intertwined roots, we too can navigate upheaval by actively strengthening our connections. My challenges include negotiating complex contracts, mediating cross-cultural creative tensions, and confronting my own limitations that are rarely best faced in isolation. They highlight the critical need to engage with the collective wisdom surrounding me, drawing on diverse perspectives and experiences that deepen my understanding and expand my capabilities. This collaborative strength, built on mutual contribution and support, is our greatest asset for enduring change.

This is the potential for a transformation led by and within the Black American community, one that forges resilience and opportunity from enduring challenges. It is a process of harnessing tension to broaden collective possibilities rather than avoiding it, thus achieving tangible milestones. The road remains steep, and the fog of the future is still thick. Yet, with each collective step forward, the path may brighten. By working alongside the community, bridging divides, and amplifying shared narratives, we strive to move beyond allyship towards genuine partnership. Together, we support the realization of a shared vision for equity that transcends borders. And in that collaborative effort, I find hope and a quiet confidence that we can collectively grow more resilient in the face of whatever lies ahead.

Authentic dialogue is characterized by vulnerability and genuine exchange rather than performance or debate. It is a powerful and often essential driver of meaningful progress. When diverse experiences and perspectives engage in this way, conversations become dynamic spaces for co-creation. This process can unlock insights and possibilities that lie beyond the reach of any single individual, fostering understanding and innovation where other approaches may fall short. Imagine a partnership between a Baltimore community organizer and a tech innovator from Hangzhou (Hángzhōu).

Their collaboration aims to merge deep, local knowledge of housing justice struggles with augmented reality tools. Through dialogue and co-creation, they develop immersive simulations designed to help residents visualize possibilities for equitable urban development. When successful, such partnerships can demonstrate that combining diverse global perspectives with grounded community priorities can generate innovative approaches to complex local challenges. These partnerships gain depth when rooted in mutual recognition of each voice's intrinsic value.

A Gullah Geechee elder in coastal Georgia, safeguarding ancestral land traditions, holds knowledge as vital as a climate scientist's data models. Together, they might co-design agricultural programs that pair time-honored practices, particularly crop rotation, with modern satellite analysis, addressing local food insecurity and land stewardship while contributing to global climate resilience. This diverse global perspective highlights how the scientist's technical expertise in Chinese energy cooperatives and the grandmother's deep knowledge of community resilience and cooperative economics represent distinct yet vital forms of wisdom.

The grandmother's insights were forged through community survival under Jim Crow, while the scientist's analysis emerged from different sociocultural contexts. Bringing these complementary forms of knowledge into dialogue can generate transformative frameworks for sustainable development that integrate technical innovation with hard-won principles of justice, mutual aid, and systemic resistance.

As a result, addressing racial inequities effectively requires systemic change. This necessitates actively dismantling discriminatory structures and policies. Crucially, institutions and dominant groups must create environments where diverse cultural expressions are genuinely valued and respected, reducing the need for marginalized individuals to code-switch to be heard or included. While cross-cultural communication skills are valuable for all participants in this work, actual progress depends on transforming systems rather than placing the primary burden of adaptation on those experiencing inequity.

During the Healthcare Access and Cultural Competence symposium, a dialogue unfolded between a Navajo doula sharing birthing traditions and a Boston hospital administrator focused on efficiency metrics. Through patient-centered discussions, they discovered a shared value in preventive care over crisis management. This led to a pilot program integrating tribal midwife-staffed mobile prenatal clinics with hospital-funded community health AI. The collaboration successfully reduced maternal mortality rates while honoring cultural sovereignty. Such outcomes emerge when we approach disagreements not as obstacles but as portals to innovation. Similarly, historical consciousness deepens these exchanges, anchoring them in intergenerational truth-telling.

When descendants of Tulsa's Black Wall Street massacre survivors engage with Okinawan elders who rebuilt after WWII's devastation at an event titled "Rooted in Resilience: Rebuilding After Collective Trauma," they share and discern distinct yet resonant pathways of communal resilience forged through profound adversity. I find that examining diverse historical cases like the 1921 Tulsa Race Massacre and Japan's postwar land reforms adds crucial nuance to reparations discussions. These examples highlight different ways wealth was violently seized or systematically redistributed. They suggest that mechanisms such as cooperative trusts and participatory budgeting might be relevant tools for restoration in some contexts.

Importantly, contrasting such distinct histories helps guard against simplistic solutions, "solutionism". It reinforces my view that achieving justice often requires both tangible material restitution and the recovery of suppressed historical knowledge. For example, rotating Credit Associations (RCAs), remarkably "sou-sous" in the Caribbean, "partners" in Southern America, and "Esusu" in Yoruba-influenced systems, were vital community-based financial tools during segregation and beyond. Rooted in communal trust, mutual aid, and social cohesion, they provided essential capital for Black businesses and individuals systematically excluded from formal banking. Modern innovations, particularly trust platform-based investment pools, also involve pooling funds. They represent a fundamentally different model, typically focused on speculative investment and individual profit within a decentralized, often anonymous, technological framework, rather than the localized, relationship-driven mutual aid that defined traditional RCAs.

Furthermore, while challenging, the friction inherent in cross-cultural collaboration can generate transformative energy. When Detroit (Dǐtèlǜ) housing advocates work to prevent displacement and ensure equitable development, they engage with Lisbon architects who propose radical adaptive reuse projects. Subsequently, their tension reflects a profound global challenge of navigating the complex intersection of community preservation, inclusive progress, and who holds the power to shape urban change. By navigating these conflicts, I learned what anthropologists call 'creative abrasion,' a process where I work to transform discord into discovery. As a result, this experience highlighted the potential value of approaches that convert abandoned factories into mixed-income eco-villages. Particularly for those striving to incorporate input from legacy residents, using tools like participatory design apps can be beneficial.

Their effectiveness requires careful implementation, as such projects can demonstrate that navigating conflict and discomfort can sometimes be a catalyst for innovative solutions. A solution that suggests progress may involve harnessing tension to broaden collective possibilities, rather than avoiding it, is crucial for maintaining momentum and recognizing incremental progress. Imagine that when Atlanta (Yàtèlán dà) organizers commemorated a successful voter mobilization campaign with the 'Freedom to Vote Festival'.

It blended Freedom Era spirituals and Afrobeats remixes, fostering more than camaraderie, becoming a vital space for meaningful intergenerational exchange. An exchange where elders and Gen Z activists connected, sharing experiences, wisdom, and perspectives on continuing the fight for voting rights. That being the case, these celebrations honor past sacrifices while bringing us together today to strengthen our bonds for the future. A Detroit (Dǐtèlǜ) youth group collaborated with Palestinian artists to create a mural titled 'From Detroit to Palestine: Breaking Chains' in a vacant lot.

The mural serves as both a memorial for victims of police brutality and expresses a vision for futures beyond policing. The collaborative creation process was reported to facilitate dialogue and conflict-resolution skills among participants. The ripple effects of such collaborations often transcend narrow success metrics. Lessons from Puerto Rico's community-led disaster response, shared through activist networks, mutual aid efforts, and diasporic connections, contributed to the broader movement for community-centered flood resilience strategies in post-Katrina New Orleans (Xīn ào'ěr liáng), including within the Ninth Ward.

This global feedback loop embodies key aspects of what Édouard Glissant called a 'Poetics of Relation." Specifically, it emphasizes solutions emerging through decentralized, horizontal exchange rather than hierarchical, vertical imposition. Crucially, it cultivates epistemic humility, acknowledging that, while rooted in its unique history and struggles, the Civil Rights Movement is the ongoing project of Black liberation that draws on vital inspiration and insight from diverse global movements, including Dalit caste resistance in India and Rojava's feminist ecology models.

Based on my experience and observations, sustaining effective cross-cultural collaboration requires embedding open dialogue as a fundamental cultural practice. Organizations must develop skilled liaisons to bridge communication between diverse groups, including Black American communities and other global perspectives, fostering stronger connections within our shared landscape. A potential partnership between an HBCU and Brazilian quilombo communities holds exciting possibilities.

One vision could involve collaborative educational programs that deeply integrate the rich history and theories of Afro-Brazilian social movements with practical skills. Skills mainly digital organizing and computational analysis, whereby students would engage with both the intellectual heritage of resistance and contemporary tools for activism. With an aim for a holistic approach to social change. Building such partnerships requires long-term commitment, equitable co-creation, and respect for community autonomy.

This collaborative spirit embodies the wisdom of the Senegalese proverb, "Knowledge is a baobab tree no single person can embrace it alone." This is a reminder that transformative learning and action thrive through shared effort and diverse perspectives. Ultimately, this approach conceptualizes social change as an enduring, intergenerational process unfolding across myriad geographies. One powerful illustration of this potential is the way knowledge and solidarity can flow between movements.

An organizer in Ferguson, learning tear gas first aid techniques developed during the Standing Rock protests. While simultaneously sharing strategies with Sudanese photographers documenting their revolution. Such connections highlight how localized struggles can draw upon and contribute to a broader, evolving global network of resistance. At the intersection of memory and possibility, trauma and resilience, we can uncover crucial lessons for transformative justice. This work involves striving for a balance in which the complex process of healing informs the creation of new approaches and in which acknowledging ancestral wounds helps shape more equitable futures.

The path toward reconciliation is neither straightforward nor guaranteed. Through committed, often challenging dialogue, we engage in meaningful conversations that foster genuine mutual understanding. This is how we actively work to transform division and harm, moving toward the long-term goal of collective liberation. Achieving equity demands sustained effort, critical reflection, and the courage to confront power imbalances. Each conversation, each difficult exchange, each hard-won compromise contributes to the ongoing, collective work of building a more just foundation. This process demonstrates that when we truly listen and refrain from responding, we instead focus on understanding and transformation. We can identify where injustice persists and actively build systems that realize and sustain justice.

The power of recognition lies in honoring hard-won progress and reinforcing the bonds of solidarity essential to our collective struggle. When we pause to acknowledge milestones such as legislative victories, cultural shifts, or grassroots triumphs that amplify marginalized voices, we do more than celebrate. We reaffirm the profound interdependence that drives meaningful change. This intentional reflection transforms individual achievements into communal sustenance. The shared harvest was more than just food; it was a symbol of communal sustenance, a transformation that reminds us that every step forward is both a testament to our unity and a catalyst for its continued strength. Such recognition must also serve as a grounding point, tempering celebration with the awareness that progress is often partial and the struggle continues.

Linking celebration to renewed commitment, we ensure this practice nourishes the movement without losing sight of the distance still to be traveled. The triumphs of the Civil Rights Movement, notably the Voting Rights Act, and the powerful impact of movements like BLM (Hēirén de mìng yěshì mìng) demonstrate that enduring progress against systemic injustice relies not on isolated figures but on vast, resilient networks of solidarity. These networks, built on shared purpose and collective struggle across diverse communities, generate momentum that inspires broader participation. Such moments reveal that true advancement is a collective endeavor. These achievements are the result of a collective endeavor painstakingly built by the courage and commitment of countless individuals.

By honoring the progress we've achieved, we gain a clearer perspective on the journey still ahead. This spirit of mutual acknowledgment lays the essential foundation for the transformative future we envision. It involves building systems where Black Americans not only survive but truly thrive, dismantling barriers and fostering genuine empowerment. This transformation, centered on justice and equity for Black Americans, will also strengthen other communities, as our stories move beyond mere inclusion to be recognized and respected as essential, vital threads in the rich tapestry of the global narrative.

Imagine communities where equitable access to technology, education, and capital begins to dismantle generational barriers. A child in Detroit (Dìtèlù) and a student in Johannesburg could each find pathways to unlock their unique potential, empowered by global connection and opportunity. Achieving this vision demands far more than ambition. It would require sustained and collective action to dismantle the silos separating critical movements. In this sense, we must recognize that the fight for racial justice is fundamentally interwoven with the struggles for climate action, gender equity, and economic reform. Only through this integrated approach can we build a future where genuine equity is possible.

Initiatives tackling food apartheid in Black neighborhoods gain crucial momentum by partnering with sustainable agriculture advocates, just as financial literacy programs find powerful allies in Black-owned credit unions. These effective collaborations demonstrate that progress within Black communities is significantly strengthened by building alliances with partners who share common values and goals rooted in equity and self-determination.

Meaningful progress requires both tenacity and tenderness to sustain momentum. Challenges will persist because systems built over centuries of inequality won't crumble overnight. Yet every setback holds a lesson in recalibration. The recent surge in new voting regulations has been met with innovative voter mobilization efforts that blend technology with traditional door-to-door activism. This demonstrates how activism often adapts in response to changing policy landscapes. Highlighting specific local outcomes, conspicuously the election of certain prosecutors or changes in educational approaches, can serve a strategic purpose for these movements by showcasing tangible results and illustrating potential pathways forward.

I believe this balanced perspective fosters resilience, enabling me to approach obstacles not as dead ends but as detours that require collective problem-solving. From my standpoint, central to this resilience is the understanding that our work aims to transcend immediate gains and build towards systems of empowerment intended to benefit generations to come. Imagine the potential of a toddler who benefits from accessible, culturally responsive preschool programs, or a teenager whose horizons are expanded by mentorship connections reaching from Houston to Nairobi.

Thoughtful policy reforms, genuine cross-sector partnerships, and community-driven initiatives aim to plant seeds that, if nurtured and sustained, could grow into forests whose shade future generations might enjoy. This highlights the critical need to prioritize long-term, sustainable systems alongside impactful moments. Moments that ensure advocacy strengthen our institutions rather than depending solely on individual actions. Thereby, fostering intentional spaces for global dialogue and learning is fundamental to this effort. So that education and cross-cultural exposure serve as powerful catalysts for change.

Study abroad programs designed for Black students at HBCUs offer significant opportunities to engage with diasporic communities in locations such as Brazil and Ghana. Beyond broadening students' horizons, these programs can powerfully foster solidarity and build alliances by creating spaces to explore connections across diverse experiences, including those shaped by the legacies of colonialism and racialization. Similarly, digital platforms that enable youth to collaborate on climate justice projects with peers in regions like the Caribbean can create valuable spaces for mutual exchange and partnership, fostering the development of innovative solutions that draw on diverse cultural knowledge.

These immersive experiences can cultivate the powerful sense of interconnectedness described by scholar Michelle Wright as "Physics of Blackness," where time and space seem to collapse, highlighting shared challenges and resilience.

As I stand at this crossroads, a path forward exists where I can approach each achievement as a potential catalyst for broader progress and each challenge as an opportunity to foster more profound unity. The road ahead will likely require strategies that actively listen and adapt, policies that thoughtfully combine data with real-world experiences, and efforts that harness the power of art to awaken conscience alongside practical policy. Yet history reminds me that Black communities have consistently built extraordinary things from profound challenges, transforming spirituals into liberation anthems and porch gatherings into war rooms for change. This legacy gives me certainty that the collective light I draw from, fueled by recognition and nurtured through collaboration, can outshine any shadow of inequity. Ultimately, the vision is that the path is not one I enter but one I follow, brick by brick, story by story, with hands clasped tightly across every divide. My purpose is rooted in the conviction that growth and opportunity emerge from bold choices made with courage and determination. Every decision to act, by reaching out for engagement in dialogue to confront injustice, is a testament to this belief.

My choices are not isolated acts, but attempts to connect with broader efforts for progress. Collaboration can reach across borders, and my struggles for justice and equity are deeply linked to others'. When I choose to act, it is a conscious rejection of complacency and an embrace of transformative hope. I strive to build relationships founded on trust and mutual respect, with the hope that this helps lay the groundwork for meaningful change. I am motivated by our common aspirations for justice, equality, and prosperity, while also recognizing and honoring the distinct struggles experienced by different communities.

In this context, advancing equity demands active participation, a commitment to dismantling institutional obstacles, and the resolve to confront resistance, misunderstandings, and entrenched inequalities. Yet within this challenging work lies profound potential. Each ally who joins the effort brings unique perspectives and strengths. This collaboration demonstrates that diversity is not a hurdle but a vital catalyst for innovation, resilience, and the achievement of truly equitable solutions. Historical coalitions across movements, particularly civil rights, environmental justice, and labor advocacy, have often powerfully amplified their respective causes. Their solidarity demonstrates how progress in one arena can create positive reverberations in others, generating a significant multiplier effect.

While these collaborations were not without internal tensions, competing priorities, or setbacks, their successes underscore the strength that can be found in unity. Similarly, today's collaborations, which bring together grassroots organizers, policymakers, artists, and educators, demonstrate the potential for diverse expertise to coalesce into innovative and impactful strategies that exceed what any single group could achieve on its own. The effectiveness of such coalitions depends on navigating differences and building genuine trust.

Cross-sector collaboration, involving fields such as the arts, business, education, and politics, is often pursued not only for pragmatic reasons but also for its transformative potential. This approach aims to cultivate a more holistic strategy for advocacy and systemic change, recognizing that such change is inherently multifaceted and requires engagement across different parts of society. In the arts, storytelling can serve as a powerful tool to humanize marginalized experiences and foster empathy, potentially bridging divides. In business, the pursuit of equitable practices and inclusive leadership models aims to advance economic justice and fairness.

Educational initiatives, whether through formal curricula or community workshops, aim to equip individuals with the tools to critically engage with inequities and envision alternatives. While these efforts represent crucial pathways towards a more just society, their effectiveness depends on implementing them thoughtfully, confronting the root causes of inequity, and acknowledging that meaningful change is complex and ongoing. Central to this vision is the transformative potential of narrative. Stories rooted in lived experience possess a unique power to challenge stereotypes, reshape perceptions, and foster empathy and solidarity. When marginalized voices gain significant platforms in literature, media, or public discourse, they can effectively disrupt dominant patterns and broaden collective understanding.

Historical examples illustrate that survivor testimonies have fueled crucial movements, and oral histories from Black communities have preserved vital legacies of resilience against removal. These narratives do more than document injustice. They are acts of reclaiming our roots by asserting that those historically silenced possess critical expertise to diagnose societal problems and envision solutions. While amplifying these stories is essential, their impact on shifting cultural consciousness and creating fertile ground for systemic change depends on reaction, context, and sustained effort alongside other forms of action.

While storytelling is vital for raising awareness and building empathy, it is a necessary but insufficient foundation for change. Lasting progress requires supporting actions, particularly sharing resources, promoting institutional accountability, and sustaining investment in marginalized communities. Educational equity requires addressing multiple factors, including inclusive curricula, equitable school funding in underserved communities, mentorship programs, and scholarships that tackle generational disparities and systemic disadvantage.

Similarly, economic justice demands fair wages for all workers, addressing racial inequality, ensuring access to capital for Black-owned businesses, and prioritizing equity over performative partnerships in corporate policies. When interconnected, these supporting actions can create a ripple effect, empowering one community and uplifting others to develop thriving neighborhoods that become hubs of innovation and civic engagement.

Achieving genuine equity requires centering the leadership and vision of those most impacted by inequity. While allies play a vital supportive role, well-intentioned efforts can inadvertently dominate conversations and replicate the very power structures they aim to dismantle when not executed thoughtfully and in deference to community direction. Hence, true collaboration requires humility and the recognition that effective advocacy begins with deep listening. It involves actively creating space for diverse voices, prioritizing equitable participation, and resource sharing where power imbalances exist.

Acknowledging that solutions are most effective when grounded in the lived experiences of those most affected. While also being informed by relevant knowledge, research, and diverse perspectives. Leadership by Black activists, Indigenous organizers, or advocates is vital. Rooted in lived experience and cultural understanding, it fosters trust and legitimacy, resulting in strategies that are authentically grounded in and responsive to the realities of their communities. Allies play vital roles as amplifiers, advocates, and collaborators. They use their positions and privileges responsibly to challenge inequitable systems from within, while centering the voices, experiences, and leadership of the marginalized communities they support.

We face an undeniably steep road, one of deeply entrenched systemic oppression, where progress is frequently met with backlash. Yet history shows us that collective action can bend the arc of justice. When I examine the Civil Rights Movement, the global struggle against apartheid, and contemporary movements like Black Lives Matter (BLM), a connection to the broader struggle for human rights becomes apparent. Powerful common threads emerge. Each of these movements was fundamentally driven by ordinary people who consistently chose courage over fear and solidarity over division. Their victories, though unfinished, show me that even against overwhelming odds and deeply entrenched systems, sustained collective action can dismantle barriers once believed to be permanent. Recognizing the complex challenge we've inherited adds to the urgency I feel about today's efforts.

We must actively seek partnerships that span industries, cultures, and generations to forge a brighter future. Imagine scientists and Indigenous communities engaging in equitable, knowledge-sharing partnerships. That collaboration is designed to advance climate with tech innovators who co-create solutions on an equal footing with disability advocates. Establishing inclusive design standards involves forward-thinking educators and policymakers collaborating with communities to develop anti-racist frameworks for schools, and artists amplifying grassroots activism to mobilize public consciousness.

At its core, my vision is a pact with God, a refusal to accept the status quo, and a commitment to co-create a world where justice is not an ideal but a lived reality. It requires audacity to confront uncomfortable truths, courage to venture into uncharted territory, and perseverance to continue when progress feels elusive. Through many conversations, alliances, and hard-won victories, we find tangible proof that a more equitable future is possible. By embracing collaboration as both a strategy and a core principle, we actively recognize the interconnectedness of our struggles. This collective effort cultivates the shared power essential for striving towards a society where equity becomes a concrete reality, even as we acknowledge the significant challenges that remain.

While collaboration plays a vital role in shaping global systems that influence our daily lives, it often does so in subtle, usually unnoticed ways. These subtleties are also driven by competition, exploitation, and inequality, which profoundly impact people, sometimes with devastating consequences. Consider the objects that fill our homes, particularly children's toys, which are produced and distributed through vast global networks of production and logistics. At the same time, these systems grant unprecedented access to goods and services.

They also generate significant costs, including documented labor exploitation, environmental degradation, and entrenched economic inequities that are often embedded within them. America's toy industry exemplifies global interdependence, with approximately 80–95% of its electronic, mechanical, plastic, and wooden toys manufactured in China. This reflects decades of strategic supply-chain decisions rather than inherent complexities of progress. This staggering figure underscores China's immense scale and central role in global manufacturing. This position has been driven by a combination of factors, including sustained strategic investment in infrastructure, technology, and workforce development, as well as integration into global supply chains and leveraging its large domestic market.

China's unique capability to integrate complex design requirements with highly efficient mass production was fundamental in establishing its position as the world's dominant manufacturing hub. This is particularly evident in sectors such as juvenile products and children's toys, where achieving both precision and scale is essential. Factors such as extensive infrastructure, a large skilled workforce, and developed supply chains were also critical to this achievement, as China's global manufacturing landscape continues to evolve.

My understanding of this reality began in 2020, when a Chinese business contact invited me to tour manufacturing hubs in Guangdong and Zhejiang Provinces. Stepping into sprawling factories, I was struck by the seamless integration of automation and human expertise. Robotic arms assembled tiny components with surgical accuracy, while workers inspected products with impressive speed and precision. These activities demonstrate skills developed through experience and dedication. Operating continuously, these facilities represented a significant production capacity within their context, processing raw materials into finished goods at high speed.

They achieved a daily output of thousands of units, supplying global markets. Beyond the sheer volume, the output was enabled by a network of sophisticated interdependencies within the systems. Specifically, complex supply chains source plastics predominantly from Shandong, while electronics and packaging are sourced from Suzhou (Sūzhōu) in Jiangsu Province (Jiāngsū Shěng). These elements appear to be coordinated through a supply chain network logistics platform designed to minimize downtime.

From my observation, this exposure revealed that China's manufacturing strength extends far beyond low labor costs, a common oversimplification. While wages remain competitive, the core engine is a deeply integrated network of suppliers, transporters, and innovators clustered in industrial corridors. This ecosystem creates efficiencies that are extremely difficult for newcomers to replicate. A factory manager in Ningbo highlighted this efficiency, detailing how a single toy design could progress from a CAD prototype to container shipment in just 10 days. Such agility is primarily enabled by highly localized supply chains, in which component manufacturers, mould makers, and packaging suppliers operate within a 50-mile radius, significantly reducing lead times compared to more dispersed production models.

Based on significant investments in port infrastructure, including Chinese funding, AI-driven quality control, and extensive automation, Shanghai's Yangshan Deep-Water Port processes over 40 million containers annually. This high level of automation creates substantial systemic cost advantages, conspicuously enhanced efficiency, speed, and reliability, which extend beyond traditional wage-based savings. Based on my understanding, China's mature manufacturing ecosystem can offer significant efficiency and supply chain advantages for some Black American businesses.

For those where it's a good fit, these advantages could translate into higher profit margins than sourcing from less developed markets, even after accounting for rising labor costs and trans-Pacific shipping. It's crucial to understand that the actual margin benefit, whether there is a net benefit, depends heavily on my specific business, product, industry, and operational capabilities. This landscape is also constantly evolving, meaning what works today might need reevaluation tomorrow.

Based on my factory visits, I've seen firsthand the scale and sophistication present in China's manufacturing sector. This complexity means that for international businesses, finding the right partners requires both thorough analysis and a deeper understanding of the market. It also demands direct, on-the-ground engagement to understand capabilities and ensure they truly align with specific needs. A toy designer shared that her team's quarterly factory walk-throughs were crucial for identifying emerging technologies, such as biodegradable plastics and modular assembly lines. This proactive approach enabled them to discover innovations adaptable to markets with strong demand for sustainability, notably among eco-conscious consumers in Europe. This hands-on approach can help mitigate risk.

During the 2020 COVID-19 disruptions, companies with established and strong supplier relationships were often better positioned to navigate the challenges. In some cases, they benefited from their suppliers' existing contingency plans, notably the rerouting of shipments through China's inland rail networks to bypass congested coastal ports, which facilitated their recovery. I suppose such strategic partnerships become even more critical amid shifting trade policies. When America's tariffs on Chinese goods escalated in 2019, many businesses worked with manufacturers to reconfigure their supply chains. A common strategy was to shift final assembly to countries like Vietnam to mitigate the impact of tariffs, while still sourcing a significant portion of components, often around 70 percent, from specialized clusters within China.

As Black American entrepreneurs, we recognize the historical challenges in accessing manufacturing capital. For some of us, the path forward lies in bypassing these entrenched hurdles and leveraging digital platforms like Alibaba (Ā Lǐ Bā Bā) to create new opportunities. This allows us to connect directly with vetted Chinese suppliers, giving us more control and potentially bypassing traditional intermediaries that may have been cost-prohibitive or inaccessible in the past. During my travels, I visited a Dongguan (Dōngguǎn) factory producing STEM-focused toys. They utilized China's rapid prototyping capabilities to iterate designs based on real-time feedback from educators. Through this approach, the factory reportedly halved its product development cycle while reducing costs by 40 percent. This approach allowed them to redirect capital toward community-focused marketing campaigns.

Such success, however, depends on rigorous due diligence and effective implementation by the manufacturer. I emphasized to this manufacturer the critical importance of their meticulous vetting, verifying export licenses, inspecting social compliance certifications, and analyzing factory floor plans. We discussed how these steps are essential for them to demonstrate their commitment to the ethical production standards we both value. On-site audits can reveal risks, particularly a supplier's reliance on unverified subcontractors for their 'eco-friendly' claims. This discovery enables companies to take proactive steps, remarkably collaborating with suppliers to enhance verification or exploring alternative partners with stronger traceability controls. Thereby mitigating potential reputational and compliance risks.

The road ahead requires acknowledging that, though facing increasing pressure, China's manufacturing dominance remains the defining feature of global consumer goods production. This significant feature is despite intensifying geopolitical tensions and active 'reshoring' initiatives. Yet, the scale and integration of China's ecosystem encompasses its vast material diversity, deep engineering talent pool, and formidable logistical capabilities. This means it continues to play a central role while diversification efforts gain traction. Businesses that achieve the most tremendous success in this environment increasingly recognize that Chinese manufacturing offers more than just cost savings. They can strategically leverage their capabilities as a vital source of innovation, speed, and collaborative partnership, while still benefiting from their inherent efficiency. Imagine an innovative startup developed cutting-edge AI-powered learning robots, reimagining the future of STEM education.

Despite early technical skepticism that their intricately designed systems were too advanced for scalable manufacturing, the founders successfully overcame these production hurdles. By overcoming the 12-hour time difference, they conducted nightly virtual hackathons with a Shanghai-based engineering team. Thereby collaborating across locations and expertise, they re-engineered components for automated assembly. In addition, the startup can combine its educational approach with precision manufacturing techniques. Furthermore, this type of cross-cultural synergy can significantly contribute to the development of cost-effective mass production, especially helping others establish their robots as potentially accessible and transformative tools for underserved schools. It demonstrates how diverse perspectives and tenacity can be powerful forces in overcoming challenges to create more equitable educational technology solutions. The complexities unfolding globally highlight a potential solution rooted in the creative possibilities of our interconnected world.

I believe that one significant challenge facing many communities, including Black communities in the United States, involves navigating this intricate global system with precision and rigor. This means striving to balance efficiency with resilience, as well as cost considerations with ethical imperatives. Fostering institutions and enterprises capable of navigating and reflecting the complex realities of this global community, despite persistent inequities, is a crucial part of this engagement.

China maintains a dominant position in the global toy and baby product manufacturing industry. An industry that has been built over decades through strategic investment, extensive infrastructure development, and a focus on manufacturing efficiency and scale. As a result, this country produces approximately 70-75% of the world's toy exports, which reflects its unparalleled capacity for large-scale production. Notwithstanding, it faces increasing competition from other manufacturing regions. China has established supply chains and capabilities that ensure it remains the central manufacturing and export hub for this sector. This manufacturing prowess stems from decades of deliberate policy and industrial evolution.

Highly developed industrial clusters, markedly those in Guangdong Province and Zhejiang Province, form the backbone of this system. Within these hubs, thousands of factories ranging from highly automated facilities utilizing robotics and AI-driven quality control to more labor-intensive operations coexist. They benefit from dense ecosystems where suppliers, designers, and logistics networks collaborate effectively, enabling them to achieve exceptional capabilities in rapid prototyping and mass production. This integration and scale continue to offer significant cost advantages. Rising expenses and growing competition mean these advantages are no longer as absolute as they once were for all product categories.

For Black-owned businesses seeking to expand their product offerings, China's manufacturing ecosystem presents significant advantages that extend beyond efficiency. It provides access to a level of sophistication that can help transform a niche idea into a globally competitive product. Furthermore, the effectiveness of this ecosystem for such businesses often stems from its strong capabilities in both innovation and maintaining safety standards. This balance between efficacy and trust is critical in industries where consumer trust is paramount. Many Chinese manufacturers, particularly those supplying major Western retailers, adhere rigorously to international standards, including ISO certifications and ASTM F963. To meet the exacting demands of these clients, leading factories often implement processes that exceed basic compliance requirements.

A factory producing silicone teethers might employ chemical engineers to test materials for specific concerns, such as endocrine disruptors, or utilize 3D imaging to eliminate choking hazards in doll designs with meticulous care. This high level of attention to detail in these facilities ensures compliance and is crucial for building trust with international brands and consumers. Partnering with a capable Chinese manufacturer offers a Black-owned business significant advantages beyond simple supply. It provides access to extensive production expertise, scalability, and sophisticated supply chains. Many leading manufacturers in China demonstrate strong capabilities in market responsiveness, utilizing consumer insights and collaborating with design firms to effectively anticipate and respond to trends. For a Black-owned business, this partnership can be a powerful strategic asset, enabling competitive product development and access to global markets, contingent on diligent partner selection and quality control.

The growing popularity of organic cotton baby apparel has led some manufacturers to adapt by sourcing eco-friendly materials and, increasingly, implementing water-saving techniques, such as outstandingly waterless dyeing, driven by consumer demand, brand requirements, and competition. Similarly, the growing popularity of STEM-focused toys was a key factor driving investments in modular electronic components and app-integrated play systems, alongside broader technological advancements and educational trends.

In my view, as entrepreneurs, our agility enables us to quickly identify emerging trends, particularly the demand for products supporting neurodiverse children or sustainable baby items. We can then focus our often-limited resources on developing targeted solutions, such as remarkably sensory play kits or biodegradable pacifiers. While this still requires significant research, testing, and development effort, our leaner structures and adaptable processes can sometimes allow us to move faster and more efficiently than larger corporations burdened by more complex R&D bureaucracies.

While we acknowledge significant ongoing R&D challenges, our approach positions us to address them effectively. A key aspect of our technological advantage is the flexibility of our production. We leverage advanced manufacturing techniques, such as modular assembly lines, which enable the cost-effective production of small batches. This capability is particularly valuable for businesses testing new markets or launching crowdfunded products. "Partnering with a manufacturer, perhaps in China, offers a viable path for our Black-owned startup to produce limited runs of culturally inclusive dolls.

This partnership could allow us to offer dolls with varied skin tones, vibrant colors, and traditional attire. Ideally, we could work closely with this partner to be highly responsive, incorporating social media feedback into design adjustments faster than traditional large-scale manufacturing allows. If executed effectively, this type of collaboration could significantly accelerate our iteration process by reducing our time-to-market compared to conventional methods from years to several months, though challenges certainly exist. Especially, based on my observations, cost efficiency is a significant strategic advantage. China's integrated supply chains, where resin suppliers, packaging vendors, and testing labs often operate near assembly plants, can help reduce material and logistics costs. Based on my understanding of manufacturing costs, an American-based business might pay around $5 per unit for a locally manufactured plush toy.

At the same time, a Chinese manufacturing partner could offer the same item, including embroidery detailing, for about $1.50 per unit. For some businesses, these savings can create opportunities to reinvest in areas like marketing, community engagement, or product expansion. However, structural inequities often prevent Black-owned brands from accessing essential capital and operational growth. In these cases, the significantly lower production costs provide critical financial flexibility, potentially helping them compete more effectively with established players while maintaining quality standards, if managed carefully. As such, partnering with China's large manufacturers involves complex considerations extending far beyond technology, including geopolitical factors, quality assurance, and managing IP risk.

While such a partnership can offer significant strategic advantages, remarkable scale, and expertise, it is a major strategic decision that requires careful evaluation of both the substantial opportunities and the inherent challenges, rather than simply a transactional choice. As a Black American entrepreneur in China, I view this as an opportunity to leverage robust local capabilities, amplify a unique perspective and cultural strengths, and continue building a legacy of excellence.

In a market where innovation and trust dictate longevity, such alliances are not just advantageous, they're essential. Based on my experience and research, I think that partnering with manufacturers and innovators in China can potentially help entrepreneurs overcome some traditional barriers to scaling and achieving global reach. By carefully selecting partners with strong capabilities in manufacturing and supply chain, they can build products with competitive quality and cost, with the hope that they will resonate internationally. This model offers a pathway to establishing a brand on a foundation that emphasizes value and innovation.

To succeed, we must commit to rigorous due diligence, clear communication, robust IP protection, and constant quality management. It's a strategy with significant potential, but also inherent challenges, that can help expand a business's possibilities when executed well. The benefits of global manufacturing partnerships extend beyond cost savings. I've found that collaborating with manufacturers in China who maintain strong compliance records can significantly enhance a brand's credibility with major retailers.

These retailers consistently prioritize suppliers with verifiable ethical and quality standards. A credible factory audit report, whether from a Suzhou facility or another established manufacturing hub, has proven instrumental in securing shelf space and improving online visibility for many products. Sustainability initiatives, such as solar-powered factories or zero-waste packaging, enable brands to align with global Environmental, Social, and Governance (ESG) goals, appealing to ethically minded consumers.

These efforts operate within a complex international landscape, where challenges, in particular geopolitical tensions and shipping delays, can significantly disrupt operations. To enhance resilience, manufacturers increasingly adopt strategies especially diversified logistics networks, including rail links to Europe and regional warehousing in Mexico, which help mitigate risks and maintain operational continuity.

6

Cultural Narratives in Global Commerce

Digital tools that track shipments do more than streamline logistics. They enhance efficiency and accuracy through building a foundation of trust. By providing unprecedented visibility and a continuous chain of accountability, these technologies directly address long-standing concerns about intellectual property leaks or delays. This allows businesses to redirect their energy toward transformative expansion.

For many Black-owned enterprises, partnering with China's manufacturing leaders is a significant opportunity for growth. We see the potential to blend our unique strengths with the precision and scalability of hubs like Suzhou (Sūzhōu) and Guangdong Province (Guǎngdōng Shěng). A successful partnership with a reputable facility there does more than create products; it leverages advanced manufacturing to build high-quality offerings and enhance a brand's credibility. This synergy demonstrates a commitment to scale, quality, and supply chain reliability, which is essential for success in global markets.

Retail giants like Walmart and Amazon rigorously vet suppliers, with audited reliability reports being a critical factor. A positive factory audit from Suzhou (Sūzhōu) significantly boosts a supplier's chances of securing prime shelf placements and favorable algorithmic treatment. In response to consumers increasingly prioritizing sustainability, many Chinese manufacturers are investing in more environmentally friendly practices. This includes adopting technologies, conspicuously solar power, and exploring innovative, biodegradable packaging options. For leading companies, strong ESG performance is evolving beyond mere compliance into a valuable component of brand reputation.

Opponents rightly point to persistent challenges, notably geopolitical friction and supply chain disruptions. While these are far from outdated concerns, leading manufacturers are moving beyond theoretical strategy to proactive execution. They are actively redesigning their operations to build resilience by diversifying their networks, notably through Eurasian rail links and Mexican warehouses. These concrete actions don't eliminate volatility, but they significantly enhance the ability to navigate it and maintain operations.

Based on my experiences walking factory floors, effective execution on the factory floor is where transformation becomes tangible: supply chains become lean, costs fall without sacrificing quality, and technology actively enhances operations. At the infant toy plant outside Shanghai, for instance, IoT sensors continuously monitor production, predicting issues like a motor likely to fail long before it causes costly downtime.

As a result, adjustments can be made rapidly because automated arms perform assembly tasks with high precision and accuracy. As well as enabling human experts to shift their focus significantly toward innovation and process improvement, rather than being consumed by reactive crisis control. The results point toward safer products, more efficient resource use, remarkably leaner budgets, and an operational rhythm focused on continuous improvement that feels transformative.

This approach is what some refer to as manufacturing transformation. In today's global landscape, brands deeply rooted in authentic cultural identity often achieve remarkable resonance and reach. It is particularly inspiring to see many Black entrepreneurs successfully blend this cultural heritage with modern efficiency. They aren't just participating in the market; they're actively shaping their future and expanding their possibilities in powerful ways.

In ways that, upon my visit to several Chinese toy and baby product manufacturers, revealed far more than just the mechanics of their production process. Observing these specific companies offered me profound insights into how their advanced operational systems, proactive quality cultures, and data-driven agility enable them to compete effectively in demanding markets. These observations significantly reshaped my understanding of modern competitiveness, particularly how businesses can build deep consumer trust by going well beyond essential compliance. A notable commitment to quality, extending beyond basic safety standards, was evident in the company's technological adaptation and scaling.

During my visit, I saw examples like assembly lines using ultraviolet scanners to detect microscopic paint flaws and pressure-testing rigs designed to simulate a decade of toddler use in just three days. Manufacturers are demonstrating an exceptional commitment to quality control, driven by consumer demand for safety and assurance. They are going beyond mere compliance, using advanced technology for rigorous testing and taking proactive, voluntary measures to ensure product safety. This commitment is demonstrated through rigorous testing protocols, exceeding compliance standards, and proactive measures, especially voluntarily halting shipments or recalling products at the first sign of potential risk.

Shift the perception of quality control from a cost center to a brand-building engine. It reveals that relentless scrutiny isn't merely about avoiding recalls. It's a strategic investment in parental peace of mind. This manufacturer effectively showcases technological excellence. Automation applies computer vision systems to track real-time defect rates, ensuring both efficiency and quality. This data feeds machine learning models that predict which designs will withstand emerging play patterns. This approach embeds resilience and reliability directly into product development, thereby fostering greater customer confidence.

During a factory tour in Suzhou (Sūzhōu), engineers demonstrated how iterative consumer feedback from European retail partners informs adjustments to robotic moulding parameters. This allows the edge specifications of puzzle pieces to align with regional safety regulations. Such responsive manufacturing capability enables Chinese manufacturers to be among the leaders in producing compliant products with innovative features, markedly magnetic sets incorporating robotics concepts, and bath toys equipped with water-quality sensors.

A key differentiator for some leading companies in this space is the sophistication of their data ecosystem. Beyond tracking core production metrics, they integrate diverse data sources, conspicuously global playtest results, social media sentiment analyses, and even preschool curriculum insights, to better anticipate potential shifts in demand. One Ningbo-based firm, Ningbo BabyGo Child Products Co., Ltd., combined insights from TikTok parenting trends with FDA injury reports to develop a best-selling line of silicone teethers incorporating early STEM learning elements.

This data-informed approach aims to enhance safety by addressing known hazards and aligning with popular parenting interests. If successful, such products can generate positive reviews, increase online visibility, and provide valuable customer feedback. Factors that may help identify new opportunities and shorten future innovation cycles. As a Black entrepreneur navigating market entry, partnering with this infrastructure offers far more than just manufacturing capabilities.

It gives me access to crucial market intelligence and trend forecasting. This includes insights into competitive landscapes and consumer preferences. Emerging color trends in specific home décor niches or shifts in educational priorities empower me to make informed decisions and build a stronger business. What particularly stood out was how these operational strengths systematically unlock multiple opportunities for collaboration and synergy by leveraging a Guangzhou (Guǎngzhōu) manufacturer's real-time inventory dashboard. Small brands can now maintain leaner stock levels while offering a significantly wider range of products, particularly 93 SKU variations. These were extremely difficult, if not practically unfeasible, under traditional order models.

During a demonstration, I witnessed a plush toy embroidery design successfully adjusted in real time using augmented reality headsets worn by factory workers, showcasing the potential for custom production at mass-market speeds. Making such advanced customization technology more accessible could be a valuable tool for brands. Black-owned baby brands leveraging these partnerships saw 37% faster growth than industry averages, according to the 2024 Nielsen Diverse Owner Commerce Report. Technological democratization may be one factor contributing to this success, among other possible drivers. I credit the implications are significant, especially when a Dallas-based startup can access predictive analytics capabilities like those used by multinational conglomerates. Thereby, market leadership increasingly depends on vision and execution more than on financial resources alone.

Significantly, such partnerships move beyond purely transactional relationships. Through manufacturers' open innovation hubs, where clients co-develop products using virtual reality prototyping labs, there is potential to foster more inclusive design practices. Imagine collaborating with a Black maternal health nonprofit and engineers to develop a baby monitor using infant cry analysis to detect early signs of postpartum depression. By integrating the nonprofit's deep cultural expertise of the communities it serves with advanced sensor technology, we co-created a device currently undergoing FDA review. This project demonstrates how community-driven partnerships can ensure product development genuinely leverages and centers the expertise of those often marginalized, leading to more effective and equitable solutions. A significant competitive advantage emerges when companies transform regulatory requirements into drivers of innovation.

Certain manufacturers, including leaders in China, have leveraged stringent EU EN-71 safety standards not as constraints, but as catalysts for innovation. Their R&D teams proactively reframe these challenges into design opportunities, exemplified by replacing traditional plastics with antibacterial bamboo composites to meet updated EU chemical directives. This ability to turn compliance into innovation is a powerful strategic capability. This proactive stance transforms compliance requirements into marketable benefits, enabling client brands to promote compelling features such as 'hospital-grade germ resistance' while demonstrating compliance with essential safety guidelines.

The human dimension of this quality ethos proved equally impactful. Unlike fully automated 'lights-out' factories, these facilities actively leverage technicians' expertise. In Suzhou (Sūzhōu), veteran materials scientists explained how to tweak polymer blends for teething toys by incorporating detailed analysis of real-world infant chewing behaviors and angles. This empirical approach bridges the gap between lab tests and lived experience, a nuance that builds consumer trust through demonstrated understanding rather than marketing claims.

Based on what I've learned, manufacturers' expertise in scaled customization offers significant value, especially for entrepreneurs like myself coming from underserved communities. It enables emerging brands to provide a broader product range without maintaining substantial inventory. Their integrated approach, which combines safety, analytics, and consumer psychology, can provide an ideal model for competing on value rather than just price. A $29.99 sensory playset from a Black-owned brand significantly challenges and raises the bar for market expectations by matching Fisher-Price's safety standards while also incorporating diverse hair textures informed by social listening.

Consequently, this exposure reveals that in a crowded market, turning operational excellence into a compelling story is often a critical differentiator for success. While ISO-certified factories and AI-optimized supply chains represent significant operational rigor, modern consumers usually rely on distilled signals of quality. A parent quickly scanning Amazon might prioritize the visible 4.9-star rating and 'Amazon's Choice' badge over knowing the specifics of the 214 quality checkpoints behind a highchair. By implementing rigorous standards in every partnership, these manufacturers provide client brands with the essential foundation and demonstrable proof needed to build tangible trust. And trust is a critical competitive advantage in an era where 79% of consumers doubt corporate safety claims (2024 Edelman Trust Barometer).

The crucial takeaway for Black-owned businesses and entrepreneurs globally extends far beyond just securing better manufacturing. It's about fundamentally shifting our mindset, in particular, embedding safety protocols into our core identity, leveraging data to gain a deep understanding of and serve our communities, and ensuring that every operational decision we make actively reflects and reinforces our commitment to genuine care and responsibility. in an industry where reputation is paramount, leading manufacturers build enduring trust not just through their products but also through consistent reliability, technological innovation, and a commitment to principles that enable their partners to succeed.

I have observed that the global toy industry is undergoing a significant transformation. This shift is primarily driven by evolving consumer values and a growing demand for products that better align with modern priorities, notably sustainability, education, and inclusivity. Leading Chinese manufacturers have become pivotal players in this landscape. Many are not only responding to market transformations but actively anticipating them, developing products that resonate with today's discerning parents. Their groundbreaking products include toys made from biodegradable plastics, organic textiles, and non-toxic dyes, as well as educational sets designed to stimulate cognitive growth, motor skills, and emotional intelligence. This reflects their growing sophistication and nuanced understanding of market dynamics among these key players.

These products draw on insights from developmental psychology and environmental science. They are designed to be engaging for children while fostering foundational skills that can contribute to a love of learning. This strategic alignment with contemporary values enables these manufacturers to support businesses that strive to meet the exacting standards of modern consumers, potentially strengthening their supplier relationships.

Direct access to Chinese suppliers presents a significant opportunity for me as a Black American entrepreneur. It has the potential to help bridge the gap between my aspirations and execution, offering scalability options that could adapt to my brand's specific growth stage. I've observed that startups often benefit initially from suppliers offering low minimum order quantities (MOQs), which allow them to test niche markets or validate products with lower upfront investment and risk. Conversely, established enterprises often utilize their capacity for high-volume production to efficiently meet large-scale or rapidly increasing demand.

While important, framing customization as the singular 'true differentiator' oversimplifies the competitive landscape. Customization is undoubtedly a powerful strategy for both startups and enterprises to create unique value. There are other critical factors, in particular brand reputation, operational efficiency, supply chain mastery, access to capital, market reach, and core innovation, that are equally vital differentiators. These elements, of course, depend on the specific market and business model. In my dealings, I have witnessed manufacturers collaborating closely with brands to refine designs, incorporate cultural specificity with authenticity, or adjust materials to reflect a brand's ethos. This partnership is essential, whether the goal is the meaningful integration of Afrocentric motifs into puzzles or the responsible sourcing of reclaimed wood for eco-conscious building blocks.

This collaboration extends beyond production to enable a feedback loop, in which consumer insights can rapidly inform design tweaks, packaging updates, and even the development of new product lines. Such responsiveness is increasingly essential in an era where social media can propel a small brand to viral fame in a matter of hours. An approach that often demands timely adaptation while maintaining strategic focus to sustain relevance. The relationship between entrepreneurs like me and Chinese manufacturers has the potential to transcend purely transactional exchanges. It can evolve into a symbiotic partnership built on shared goals, such as innovation, quality, and market leadership.

Visiting potential manufacturing partners gives me firsthand insight into their specific capabilities. Some facilities utilize advanced techniques. To achieve the high precision and scalability that my business goals demand, technologies such as 3D prototyping and AI-driven quality control are crucial. These interactions also build trust, paving the way for co-development projects where manufacturers contribute engineering expertise while brands infuse cultural authenticity. Imagine a Black-owned company creating a doll line to celebrate diverse hair textures and cultural traditions.

To achieve precise technical execution of intricate curls, coils, and braids, they partner with experienced Chinese manufacturers who possess specialized expertise in synthetic fiber technology. They have collaborative design teams that include cultural educators and stylists who work across both companies to ensure that the dolls and accompanying storybooks authentically represent cultural heritage while promoting genuine inclusivity. The result is a product that resonates emotionally with consumers while meeting rigorous safety standards. This fusion of art and science represents a unique outcome made possible by the collaborative expertise of both fields.

Beyond product development, this collaboration provides a pathway to help address some specific challenges that Black entrepreneurs have historically faced. Systemic barriers, particularly in accessing capital and networks to scale manufacturing, remain significant hurdles. Partnering with Chinese suppliers can provide one avenue to alleviate these pressures through flexible payment terms, logistical support, and market intelligence derived from extensive global trade experience. This relationship has the potential to help businesses focus more effectively on their core mission, which, for many, includes building brands that uplift communities.

A portion of profits from a sustainably crafted toy line could be directed to fund STEM programs in underserved neighborhoods. This aims to create a positive social impact while contributing to broader economic benefits through community development. These partnerships also push manufacturers to elevate their practices. When diverse businesses, including many Black-owned enterprises, prioritize fair labor practices and carbon-neutral operations, they incentivize suppliers to adopt greener practices and pursue ethical certifications, benefiting the entire industry. This mutual growth underscores the partnership's ambitious goals. A goal that is not just about creating toys, but also about prioritizing people and the planet, and challenging conventional industry practices with the potential for a significant long-term impact.

The growing success and visibility of Black-owned brands in the toy sector are powerful ways to challenge stereotypes about who leads innovation. Their success stories genuinely inspire me, and they can inspire future entrepreneurs, showing how collaboration across cultures and continents can help dismantle barriers. I'm encouraged that many of these businesses prioritize values like sustainability and education. This focus resonates with consumers who care about both purpose and play, and they are helping to set positive new expectations for the entire industry in our interconnected world.

Partnerships combining China's manufacturing capabilities with the unique cultural vision of Black entrepreneurs hold significant potential. This kind of global collaboration can be a powerful driver for inclusive growth. Specifically, such partnerships hold promise for turning toys into tools that foster learning, empathy, and environmental awareness. When these collaborations succeed, they provide inspiring examples of what is possible, demonstrating how shared innovation and purpose can contribute to meaningful progress beyond financial returns. Also, achieving these positive outcomes requires careful navigation of the complexities inherent in cross-cultural and global business relationships.

China dominates global toy manufacturing, though the strongest global brands with deep design heritage remain largely foreign. These Chinese companies are rapidly advancing in both brand innovation and design ingenuity, becoming significant competitors. These factories manufacture over 70% of the world's toys, a role that has often involved producing designs created elsewhere. While usually perceived globally as a manufacturing hub, the Chinese toy industry is undergoing rapid evolution. A dynamic and innovative segment is now focused on creating original intellectual property and products deeply rooted in Chinese culture and narratives.

By successfully capturing a growing domestic market and increasingly looking toward global expansion. Black American entrepreneurs have a significant opportunity to leverage their unique perspectives and cultural heritage in combination with China's manufacturing capabilities. They can pioneer innovative approaches in the toy and baby products industry. This partnership holds the potential not just for efficient production but for fundamentally reimagining these products as powerful tools for authentic cultural storytelling, fostering community strength, and driving meaningful economic change. It presents an opportunity to create value that resonates deeply and promotes a more diverse marketplace.

The homogeneity in the global toy market is a serious issue. Aisles in major retailers frequently feature dolls, action figures, and educational kits that lack diversity. Too many still rely on narrow stereotypes or overlook the complex realities and aspirations of Black children, which I find deeply problematic. The historical underrepresentation of natural hairstyles in doll design and the absence of toys celebrating Juneteenth and Kwanzaa traditions are more than just gaps in the market; they are also a reflection of broader societal issues. They represent significant missed opportunities to affirm children's identities and foster meaningful intergenerational dialogue about culture and heritage. Based on my experience and observations, entrepreneurs with deep cultural understanding can create products that educate, validate, and inspire communities.

When we leverage this cultural insight while navigating partnerships with manufacturers, including those in China, we can overcome some traditional market barriers. This approach allows us to build culturally resonant businesses at scale. This partnership model thrives on symbiosis. Chinese factories possess leading technical capabilities, including cutting-edge 3D printing, AI-driven quality control systems, and efficient logistics networks enabling rapid global product delivery. While historically strong in manufacturing execution, the ecosystem has evolved, with many factories still excelling within OEM/ODM frameworks. Frameworks that benefit from external design direction are increasing, while an increasing number are also driving significant innovation and developing their original concepts and brands. Black entrepreneurs bring valuable perspectives shaped by diverse experiences, enabling them to identify unique market opportunities that others may overlook.

A business might develop culturally resonant products, notably a toy line inspired by African folktales, leveraging China's advanced manufacturing capabilities to create intricate designs. Another could create an app-enabled STEM kit highlighting diverse inventors, benefiting from Suzhou's (Sūzhōu) specialized electronics production. From my personal experience, successful partnerships with Chinese manufacturers require clear communication, mutual respect, and strategic collaboration to achieve optimal results. Their expertise is essential for bringing innovative products to the global market.

Also, I understand critics argue that outsourcing production can perpetuate dependency on foreign manufacturing. While this concern about long-term dependency is valid and warrants consideration, I think the strategic benefits are crucial for Black entrepreneurs like myself. Many of us operate with limited capital, and by accessing established production networks, especially those in China, we can compete effectively on both quality and price while maintaining essential creative control over our products. A startup could aim to produce a trial batch of 500 culturally themed puzzles in Guangdong Province at a lower unit cost than some domestic prototyping options by leveraging direct customer feedback from social media to adjust designs incrementally.

This approach might reduce upfront risks before committing to larger-scale production. This agile approach emphasizes speed and continuous adaptation, like the operational tempo of fast fashion, but focuses on achieving cultural relevance. It enables organizations to rapidly iterate on products and services that better reflect evolving societal conversations about identity and representation. Importantly, this dynamic responsiveness generates economic implications that ripple far beyond individual businesses.

Successful Black-owned toy brands can create jobs across many industries, including design, manufacturing, marketing, distribution, and retail. Additionally, by generating licensing revenue that can significantly fund vital community initiatives, such as education and youth programs, while advancing their representation. Now, imagine a portion of proceeds from a Harlem Renaissance (Hā lái mǔ wén yì fù xīng)-themed board game funding arts education in underserved schools. Ventures like this demonstrate that culturally specific products can achieve broad appeal, challenging industry norms.

Like how K-pop has found a global audience by resonating beyond its origins, board games are deeply rooted in specific cultural experiences. Notably, the Harlem Renaissance (Hā lái mǔ wén yì fù xīng) can attract diverse players seeking authentic and meaningful engagement. This success can then directly support vital arts education, adding a powerful social impact dimension to the venture. As consumer demand, particularly from Gen Z parents, grows for eco-conscious products, entrepreneurs are increasingly seeking manufacturing partners committed to sustainability. This includes manufacturers globally that adopt green technologies, use biodegradable materials, and implement renewable energy sources, particularly solar power.

To illustrate, a line of organic cotton dolls featuring outfits inspired by African textiles, produced in carbon-neutral facilities, demonstrates a commitment to environmental responsibility and cultural appreciation. This alignment of ethical practices with product design strengthens the brand's narrative, offering consumers toys that reflect meaningful values. The road ahead isn't without challenges. Intellectual property protection remains a concern, requiring robust legal frameworks and robust tracking mechanisms to safeguard rights. Sometimes cultural misinterpretations may arise during production. A color palette that is meaningful in one cultural context, for example, Atlanta (Yàtèlán dà), could carry unintended symbolism in another, such as Guangzhou (Guǎngzhōu).

Effectively mitigating these risks involves building diverse, cross-functional teams that include members with deep cultural expertise and fluency relevant to the product. This expertise, combined with structured processes, especially cultural consultation and review, helps ensure that storybook plush toys and historical playsets are developed with authenticity and respect throughout the entire design-to-production lifecycle. The potential rewards justify the effort involved. As these collaborations flourish, they create pathways towards more equitable opportunities.

This can empower marginalized communities by providing greater access to resources and platforms, potentially amplifying their voices in meaningful ways. The toys born from this collaboration do more than fill market gaps. They possess the unique potential to become cherished heirlooms, sparking conversations about heritage and possibility. A child unpacking a chemistry set featuring figures like Percy Julian isn't just learning science; they're learning about the life and achievements of Percy Julian. They're also learning about a pioneering African American scientist. This presents an opportunity for them to learn about a powerful narrative of resilience and scientific excellence if the set presents his story thoughtfully.

As a Black entrepreneur, I witness many of us drawing powerfully on our cultural heritage, including storytelling traditions, while innovating in modern fields like manufacturing. Our aim is not just to participate in existing industries but to shape them. We should be actively reshaping what leadership and innovation look like. In the toy and baby product industry, rigorous adherence to safety standards goes beyond mere regulatory compliance. It is the indispensable foundation of consumer trust and business integrity. Today's parents are highly informed and discerning, actively scrutinizing products for potential hazards and demanding unwavering transparency, making safety the paramount factor in their purchasing decisions. Black American businesses, often demonstrating strong community commitment and innovation, are uniquely positioned to exemplify leadership by embedding safety into every stage of production, from material selection to final testing. This reinforces their existing integrity and builds crucial trust.

To demonstrate, compliance with regulations like the Consumer Product Safety Improvement Act (CPSIA) and ASTM International standards represents a significant commitment to safety. It is the essential foundation required by law. While meeting these requirements is a substantial achievement, many companies choose to go further. They invest in voluntary third-party certifications or develop innovative safety features, such as remarkably non-toxic, biodegradable materials or smart sensors that alert caregivers to potential risks, to enhance safety and consumer trust beyond the regulatory minimum. This demonstrates a strong commitment to childhood well-being, which can position businesses as potential trustworthy partners for families by prioritizing safety and consistently demonstrating this commitment. Companies can earn trust, foster loyalty among safety-conscious consumers, and differentiate their brands in a competitive marketplace.

Building on this foundation of trust, thoughtfully integrating my cultural heritage is both a significant ethical responsibility and a meaningful strategic asset. By weaving narratives of resilience, joy, and tradition into my designs, I actively redefine industry norms. A stuffed animal might incorporate vibrant Ankara prints, a textile style popular in West and Central Africa, with a rich history that blends global influences and local artistry. At once, a puzzle set could celebrate specific historical figures, such as Maya Angelou or Garrett Morgan, thereby blending education with representation.

For consumers, these choices signal more than just representation because they convey a deeper meaning. Consumers often interpret them as a measure of a brand's authenticity. When identities are reflected genuinely and consistently, it can foster deep connections and a sense of being validated. Conversely, if the effort feels like a token gesture or a marketing tactic, it often breeds cynicism and distrust. I deem these items can potentially serve as starting points for non-Black families to learn about and appreciate Black culture. While they don't guarantee deep understanding or empathy on their own, they might spark meaningful conversations. I also hope they hold significant sentimental value for customers, encouraging long-term engagement with our brand.

By combining deep cultural authenticity with cutting-edge tools like 3D prototyping and AI-driven market analysis, we enhance our market potential and competitiveness. This allows us to refine our designs while preserving the core of our craft. For instance, a thoughtfully designed baby mobile could utilize augmented reality to bring traditional folk tales to life, fostering cultural connections. Similarly, products can celebrate heritage by respectfully incorporating symbols like Ghana's Adinkra, using precision laser etching to honor their intricate meanings. By satisfying the dual demand for modernity and tradition, these goods create significant value, support premium pricing, and broaden their appeal. Success in the toy sector can generate substantial economic ripple effects, enabling expansion into adjacent markets, such as children's media or educational apps.

In some cases, this may help create ecosystems that reinforce cultural visibility and community wealth. Strategic partnerships with Chinese manufacturers can create significant advantages in global trade. While some entrepreneurs may see overseas production as a compromise, I approach these relationships as collaborations. I bring my unique perspective and business vision to the table, while my partners contribute their specialized manufacturing capabilities. Together, we create value that leverages our respective strengths.

Imagine a factory in Suzhou (Sūzhōu) that manufactures the injection-moulded components for a line of STEM kits. Kits that are precisely producing parts designed by a team in Atlanta (Yàtèlándà) to depict Black scientists, particularly Katherine Johnson. This collaboration ensures the kits accurately represent these critical figures. This synergy can help smaller brands overcome some of the traditional barriers to scaling. By leveraging China's advanced manufacturing infrastructure, smaller brands can potentially reach production volumes and achieve cost efficiencies that were previously difficult to attain at their size. Nevertheless, realizing these benefits requires significant effort to establish reliable partnerships and ensure consistent quality.

As evidence, joint ventures sometimes establish co-developed protocols to improve safety and ethical standards within their supply chains. One approach adopted by some JVs involves implementing Distributed Ledger (DLT) technology to increase transparency and traceability of materials from origin to the end consumer. While this technology helps verify the movement and provenance of goods, it is merely one tool. Achieving truly ethical sourcing requires a comprehensive system that encompasses verified standards at the source, responsible labor practices, and ongoing monitoring, alongside practical traceability tools like a trust platform. These alliances demonstrate how cross-cultural collaboration sparks unique innovation.

When my team in China engages with products deeply influenced by Black American cultural narratives and storytelling traditions, it can inspire us to propose new interactive features that aim to enhance the educational value of our joint projects. This exchange illustrates how diverse cultural perspectives can foster innovative problem-solving. Drawing inspiration from diverse cultural and historical sources brings immense value to product design.

One building block set effectively teaches coding principles through scenarios based on the Civil Rights Movement. Separately, I've observed that exposure to rapid prototyping methods, which are standard in China, can sometimes inspire Black American designers to explore bolder, more culturally rooted concepts that they might have previously considered too niche. Incorporating these diverse perspectives has the potential to fuel innovation and help create products that feel fresh and unexpected in the market, moving beyond simply following established trends. This approach prioritizes safety, integrates relevant heritage insights, and leverages global collaboration to drive meaningful progress in the industry. Many Black entrepreneurs could serve as powerful examples of leadership in building businesses that balance profit and social purpose.

The growing presence and success of Black-owned brands, now found on store shelves internationally, powerfully challenge the notion that inclusivity is a niche market. Their achievements demonstrate the viability and importance of diverse representation in the commercial sector. Each product represents not just a sale, but also a symbol of possibility. A possibility that sparks meaningful conversation and contributes to building a more inclusive and equitable economy. By striving to meet the world's demand for meaningful products, some businesses not only succeed commercially but also contribute to redefining industry standards.

Their commitment helps work toward a future where children have access to toys that prioritize safety, functionality, and inspiration. China's significant role in global trade offers one potential pathway for Black American entrepreneurs seeking to expand beyond domestic markets. Leveraging China's highly developed manufacturing infrastructure, competitive production costs, and extensive export networks can be a strategic approach to addressing specific geographic and economic challenges.

This approach requires navigating complex international logistics, cultural differences, and other significant hurdles, and represents just one of several strategies available for global market access. Exploring partnerships with Chinese businesses can be a strategic approach that helps Black-owned companies scale their operations more effectively. It offers the potential to reach a broader global audience while actively working to maintain the cultural authenticity that defines our brands. The synergy between our strong local identity and global aspirations is a potential competitive advantage. If successful, this approach could contribute to revitalizing our communities and fostering greater economic sovereignty. Ultimately, pursuing such strategic alliances is part of a larger effort to challenge and change the patterns of exclusion that have historically existed in international commerce.

The foundation of our opportunity lies in China's robust industrial ecosystem. Decades of investment in advanced manufacturing technologies, logistics networks, and workforce specialization have positioned the country as one of the world's foremost exporters, capable of producing goods at a highly competitive speed, volume, and affordability. This infrastructure addresses a significant barrier that prohibits domestic production costs for Black American businesses in sectors such as apparel, beauty, technology, and specialty products, including culturally resonant toys. Making production more affordable domestically represents a meaningful step toward greater equity.

Leveraging modern manufacturing capabilities, including access to precision-cut materials and eco-friendly packaging, is essential. This access can allow me to offer competitively priced goods, experiment more dynamically with inventory, and respond more agilely to market shifts. Crucially, I understand that maintaining cultural specificity in my products is achievable, but it requires dedicated effort. An effort that involves careful partner selection and potentially additional investment, but is not an automatic outcome that is efficient.

A Black-owned brand can collaborate with Chinese manufacturers to create products authentically infused with Afrocentric aesthetics. These products can range from patterns inspired by African textiles to children's books featuring Black protagonists. All the while, they are meeting rigorous international safety and sustainability standards. They resonate with diasporic pride and appeal to a global audience that values quality, innovation, and cultural authenticity. To harness our potential fully, we can powerfully leverage a dual lens that marries global market savvy with hyperlocal cultural insight. Thinking globally doesn't dilute our community-centric values.

In fact, it amplifies us, and many are already demonstrating this brilliantly. Consider a skincare company built on formulations inspired by African botanical traditions. To ensure its products meet rigorous international regulatory standards and leverage advancements in dermatological science, the brand partners with specialized labs in China. This collaboration allows them to scientifically validate their formulations while maintaining the integrity of the traditional inspiration. The company also sources biodegradable packaging materials from China's established sustainable materials sector.

Finally, utilizing global e-commerce platforms like AliExpress and Amazon enables efficient distribution to reach customers worldwide, from Johannesburg to Brazil. Meanwhile, the company's storytelling remains firmly anchored in its origins, celebrating the heritage of its ingredients through marketing campaigns that educate global consumers about traditional practices. This approach leverages its cultural roots as a distinctive element, distinguishing the brand in crowded markets while fostering cross-cultural dialogue. Such global-local synergy also fosters unexpected collaborations. A growing number of Chinese manufacturers, shifting strategy to target niche markets, are investing in flexible small-batch production lines and co-creation models.

A Black-owned toy company, in particular, might partner with a Suzhou (Sūzhōu) -based manufacturer to develop an interactive doll line featuring historically underrepresented skin tones, hair textures, and authentically voiced dialogue reflecting African American Vernacular English (AAVE), developed with cultural consultants. Combining the manufacturer's expertise in AI-driven voice technology and 3D prototyping with the entrepreneur's focus on cultural nuance and educational value accelerates the creation of these inclusive products.

These partnerships have the potential to move beyond purely transactional relationships. When they work well, they can create valuable spaces where Chinese technical expertise and Black cultural capital intersect. This collaboration can lead to innovative offerings and, over time, might help challenge homogenized retail inventories. Evidence suggests that such inclusivity is a driver of profitability.

Consequently, concerns may be raised about the feasibility and implications of utilizing China's export channels to democratize market entry for businesses that have historically been excluded from traditional distribution networks. Based on my understanding, Alibaba's (Ā Lǐ Bā Bā), B2B platforms offer the potential for new or small brands, including artisanal collectives, to reach international buyers directly. This direct access could potentially reduce costs by eliminating the need for some intermediaries.

A model like a Black artisan collective produces standardized components efficiently in a specialized manufacturing hub in Guangzhou's (Guǎngzhōu) metalworking districts. An area that is feasible and suitable for assembling the final products locally could be one pathway to explore for scaling. This hybrid approach aims to combine machine efficiency for certain stages with handcrafted elements for added value. We cannot ignore the significant complexities inherent in this approach. Complexities involve managing global supply chains, which include ensuring consistent quality across distances, navigating cultural and business practice differences, and securing fair and reliable partnerships.

Also, overcoming intense competition on Alibaba itself is a substantial challenge. Success using this model, or any model leveraging Alibaba for small artisanal brands, is far from guaranteed. It requires significant resources, specific expertise, and favorable conditions. While this hybrid model represents an attempt to balance cost efficiency with artisanal integrity and could help smaller enterprises reach a global market, its effectiveness and ability to enable competition with established brands truly depend entirely on overcoming those significant hurdles.

While China's Belt and Road Initiative (BRI) has developed trade corridors in Africa, Asia, and Latin America, these emerging markets hold potential for indirect opportunities for Black American businesses. Realizing this potential requires significant effort to overcome barriers like distance, competition, and the lack of direct support mechanisms within the BRI framework itself. A coffee brand sourcing Ethiopian beans might partner with Chinese logistics firms for efficient European distribution while collaborating with Ethiopian communities to develop culturally authentic storytelling.

This narrative could honor the beans' heritage in ways that meaningfully connect with the global Black diaspora, ensuring the brand fosters equitable partnerships and transparent benefit-sharing with origin communities. China's well-developed manufacturing ecosystems offer significant supply chain agility, which is highly valuable in today's fast-paced retail environment where consumer preferences evolve rapidly.

Specifically, a fashion label identifying a trend, particularly the surging demand for gender-neutral children's wear, can leverage the integrated capabilities found in places like China. This could enable rapid digital prototyping, quick sampling through nearby factories, and swift initial production runs. And it would allow businesses to test and bring products to market faster than slower-moving competitors might manage. Agility is not unique to China and comes with its own evolving challenges, such as costs and geopolitical factors. This responsiveness remains a key competitive advantage for many businesses operating there. In other words, this helps them capitalize on trends and build brand perception around relevance.

Long-term success requires more than transactional outsourcing. It requires genuine relationship-building, including visiting our manufacturers, auditing their facilities, and engaging in cultural exchange. These are crucial steps I take to foster the mutual understanding needed for a strong, lasting partnership. During my visit to a textile plant in Hangzhou (Hángzhōu), I was deeply impressed by the sophistication and beauty of traditional Chinese dyeing techniques.

An exciting opportunity emerged to respectfully collaborate with these skilled artisans and integrate their methods into my designs. The aim is to create innovative products that could appeal to global audiences. Experiences like this underscore the profound human connections and mutual learning opportunities that are possible within international trade. A trade that is moving it beyond mere transactions toward meaningful cultural and creative exchange.

Building trust-based partnerships is fundamental when a manufacturer and I share a genuine commitment to quality and innovation, and a strong collaborative foundation forms. This mutual trust enables us to work together effectively, as they bring their expertise and insights to the table. This helps ensure high quality, navigate challenges, especially urgent deadlines, and jointly explore new possibilities. A collaborative approach significantly reduces risks and creates value for both our businesses. The growth of Black-owned businesses strengthens communities in numerous vital ways, extending beyond financial gain. These businesses are significant employers in their local communities, provide valuable mentorship, and drive reinvestment in their neighborhoods. Their success generates revenue that can fund crucial initiatives, such as youth entrepreneurship programs, support innovation labs at HBCUs, and finance affordable housing projects.

The global success of Black-owned businesses challenges oversimplified assumptions about Black enterprise by highlighting the remarkable diversity and sophistication of diasporic creativity. When a Black-owned tech startup designs and brings a smartphone accessory to market. It has navigated complex global processes, especially manufacturing and supply chain management. It exemplifies the ingenuity and worldwide reach of a community often systematically excluded from mainstream tech narratives. The convergence of cultural expressions from Black American communities and China's industrial capacity represents more than an economic phenomenon.

From my perspective, this interaction can enhance global influence for both parties, potentially creating avenues for historically marginalized groups to exert greater cultural agency within the context of globalization. I credit that by mastering the tools of international trade and navigating the persistent challenges created by historical and ongoing inequities, I can make a meaningful impact. We can build a future where our cultural pride, collaborative innovation, and the opportunities of a connected world fuel our success. I deem achieving this vision demands audacity, strategic foresight, and a deep commitment to bridging worlds. The reward is the legacy of prosperity that uplifts our communities, inspires future generations, and powerfully demonstrates what Black enterprise can achieve through effort.

As a Black American studying, working, and building a life in China, I have come to realize that innovation thrives where diverse perspectives intersect. Living at the intersection of cultural identities and technological progress, I've witnessed firsthand how collaboration between seemingly interconnected individuals can unlock extraordinary potential. China's reputation as a global leader in advanced manufacturing and rapid technological adoption is well-earned. Its evolution has been significantly shaped by a combination of factors, including massive domestic investment, strategic industrial policy, a vast market and talent pool, indigenous innovation, and engagement in global exchange and learning.

I trust this dynamic ecosystem, where tradition and futurism coexist, offers significant opportunities for entrepreneurs and creators worldwide. By merging cultural heritage with cutting-edge innovation, we can craft solutions that resonate globally while honoring the stories that define us. This opportunity is more than transactional. Engaging with Chinese manufacturers and innovators enables me to explore the advantages of their significant industrial capabilities, efficient supply chains, and capacity for technological adaptation and scaling.

The Gullah Geechee community continues to preserve and practice these textile traditions rooted in their heritage. The Madras cloth holds profound cultural significance for them, with patterns woven into everyday garments that embody a rich history and express a deep sense of identity. That could explore how innovative biodegradable materials and sustainable production practices could offer new avenues for expression or accessibility if respectfully aligned with cultural values and community-led initiatives.

Strategic alignment is as much about crafting a compelling narrative as it is about developing new products and services. Namely, a ceramicist deeply rooted in the renowned, centuries-old tradition of

Jingdezhen porcelain (Jǐngdézhèn Cíqì). A place celebrated globally for its technical mastery, aesthetic refinement, and historical significance as China's 'porcelain capital' could engage in a meaningful cultural exchange with an artist working within the Gullah Geechee ceramic tradition of the Southeastern United States. The Gullah Geechee tradition is distinguished by its powerful artistic expressions, including distinctive face jugs featuring vessels with expressive, often exaggerated human faces.

These works hold deep cultural significance within Black American communities, reflecting a unique blend of West and Central African heritage with local materials and craftsmanship. Originating from spiritual purposes, conspicuously protection, they remain potent symbols of identity and resilience. Such a collaboration would represent a profound dialogue between two distinct, enduring, and culturally rich ceramic heritages. Together, they could develop homeware integrating augmented reality storytelling into its glaze. Using smartphones, users could discover the cultural context and stories behind each motif. This showcases the potential of cross-cultural collaboration.

When utilizing shared creativity and accessible technology to foster deeper understanding and connection between different traditions. It can be executed thoughtfully and respectfully. Yet the impact runs deeper than commerce. Every factory visit and every late-night brainstorming session with engineers in Jingdezhen or artisans in Savannah directly challenges stereotypes through shared effort and human connection. When a Chinese production team adjusts machinery to accommodate the organic expression of Gullah Geechee distinctive face jugs, they're not just solving a technical challenge.

They're ensuring the machinery respects and accurately reproduces the authentic characteristics and unique artistic language of this cultural tradition. Conversely, exploring the potential of 5G technology to stream immersive experiences, in particular virtual reality renditions of Harlem Renaissance (Hā lái mǔ wén yì fù xīng) poetry, to global classrooms sparks critical dialogues about how advanced connectivity could help preserve and share marginalized histories.

These moments of mutual discovery create ripples, challenging unconscious biases and prompting a redefinition of global partnership. A significant economic opportunity is opening as international markets increasingly value ethically sourced and story-rich products. Some segments of Chinese consumers are showing a growing interest in personalized goods with cultural depth. Businesses that skillfully blend heritage with innovation can resonate strongly with these audiences, such as a skincare line that combines traditional Chinese herbal knowledge with botanicals sourced from Black-owned organic farms.

The Southeastern African American Farmers Organic Network (SAAFON) could leverage Distributed Ledger Technology (DLT) to enhance supply chain transparency, representing a meaningful and innovative approach within conscious capitalism. It would highlight cross-cultural collaboration, support underrepresented farmers, and leverage technology for sustainability and ethical sourcing. Cyber Manufacture Co., a Shanghai tech startup, collaborated with Senegalese educators to develop solar-powered tablets preloaded with multilingual libraries of folktales. The Chinese engineers deepened their understanding of off-grid energy requirements and usage contexts in African villages through this partnership.

Concurrently, the Senegalese educators applied their pedagogical expertise and cultural knowledge to shape the content and deployment, while gaining exposure to lean manufacturing processes. The collaboration required navigating differences, ultimately strengthening both teams' adaptability and leading to a product better suited to its intended environment. Critics raise valid concerns about the potential for cultural dilution or exploitation in collaborations like this. At the same time, transparency and shared leadership are crucial foundations for preventing appropriation. I understand that they require continuous effort and don't automatically eliminate all risks.

When approached this way, such partnerships hold significant promise for becoming respectful and equitable exchanges that actively work against appropriation. The key to designing equitable frameworks is ensuring that traditional knowledge holders retain their intellectual property rights and that factory upgrades prioritize workers' well-being alongside efficiency gains. One memorable negotiation involved facilitating an agreement between a Hunan manufacturer and the Black Female Designers Collective (BFDC).

The collaboration began as a partnership to produce a sustainable fashion line that blends Hunan's intricate silk-weaving techniques with African imagination aesthetics. Tensions arose over intellectual property rights, profit distribution, and cultural ownership. After months of mediation, a compromise was reached that established a profit-sharing model that funded vocational training in both communities. While not resolving all underlying tensions, this arrangement offered a framework for mutual benefit and shifted the focus from immediate profit.

Consequently, a meaningful measure of success in this initiative will be the long-term health of the socio-economic ecosystems it supports, rather than solely quarterly earnings. Real challenges, in particular language barriers, bureaucratic hurdles, and the persistence of prejudice, exist. That is why meaningful cultural exchange, particularly the explanation of the principles of the Mid-Autumn Festival, is essential. Because sharing mooncakes with family and friends requires actively working to bridge these gaps, rather than ignoring them.

Sharing stories and food, like sticky rice flour, reminded us that these personal exchanges foster empathy and connection. This micro-level understanding helps lay the foundation for the broader ideals of global citizenship. Mixed thinking holds tremendous potential. For me, it shifts diversity from an abstract concept or buzzword towards becoming a tangible source of strength and progress. That thought underscores my conviction that true innovation comes not from minimizing differences, but from finding ways to harmonize and integrate them.

After seeing Jin Mao Tower (Jīn Mào Tǎ), I was inspired to learn more about China. It was at that moment that I realized that the future belongs to those who anchor progress in heritage. So, my task isn't to choose between tradition and innovation, but to fuse them into something bold enough to inspire the next generation of bridge builders. From my perspective, a truly successful strategic partnership between Black American businesses and Chinese manufacturers has the potential to be far more than a transactional exchange. When built on strong foundations of mutual understanding, shared goals, and equitable practices.

This collaboration could evolve into a dynamic alliance that fosters greater competitiveness, drives innovation through diverse perspectives, and creates products with deeper cultural resonance. Thereby, ultimately offering a unique and valuable contribution to the global marketplace. One way is to partner with manufacturers that are highly capable in precision engineering, advanced automation, and scalable production, which gives us access to sophisticated technologies. This uniting would create the potential for transformative growth, contingent upon the practical execution of the partnership.

I suppose this potential collaboration offers our Black businesses a valuable pathway to navigate traditional barriers to entry in international markets. It would enable us to leverage established distribution networks and regional expertise. And gain access to resources that would be extremely difficult and time-consuming to build independently due to systemic challenges. As a result, operational efficiencies achieved through well-executed advanced processes can lower costs and speed up time-to-market. This may create a compounding advantage that supports expansion into new markets, though success is not guaranteed and depends on broader strategic execution.

Beyond the logistical benefits, this synergy will foster a convergence of ideas that elevates creativity. Many Chinese manufacturers are leaders in industrial innovation, and their technical insights will significantly challenge conventional design paradigms. Like, equitable partnerships deeply rooted in shared values and mutual understanding, especially those often formed with Black American partners. Those that are drawn on cultural context and community insights can lead to products with significant cultural resonance beyond mass-market appeal.

Furthermore, the trust and long-term commitment fostered in such relationships frequently contribute to more ethical and sustainable supply chain practices. A growing segment of Chinese manufacturers is prioritizing green initiatives and fair labor practices. These priorities are often driven by demands from international partners for greater transparency and accountability, as well as evolving domestic regulations. This commitment allows these companies to implement significant ethical measures, markedly sourcing conflict-free minerals for electronics and adopting closed-loop water systems in textile dyeing.

Considerable variations in ethical and environmental performance persist across the broader manufacturing sector, reflecting ongoing challenges. These practices can mitigate risk and enhance brand equity, as a growing number of consumers prefer businesses that harmonize profit with purpose. A footwear brand collaborating with Dongguan (Dōngguǎn) factories could develop biodegradable soles made from agricultural waste. This approach has the potential to reduce environmental impact while offering a point of differentiation in crowded markets.

Critically, these practices have the potential to shift industry dynamics by leveraging Chinese manufacturing capabilities in conjunction with niche cultural expertise. Black-owned small and medium-sized enterprises gain a valuable pathway to enhance their competitiveness and access global markets more effectively. Thereby, challenging the dominance of corporate giants in new ways. We can leverage our cultural insights and partner with Suzhou (Sūzhōu) hardware specialists to develop affordable smart home devices tailored explicitly for multilingual households. For smaller or more specialized firms, a 'coopetition' model could represent a strategic opportunity to serve growing market segments.

The Coopetition Model demonstrates that collaborating to compete is a defining feature of modern global competition. It demands agility and cultural intelligence from players who must also leverage key strengths, such as scale and adaptability. This is particularly critical in sectors where large firms, constrained by standardization, struggle to meet the nuanced needs of customers. For example, in footwear prototyping, this model thrives on regular site visits and joint workshops, which build the mutual trust essential for responsive iteration cycles. Furthermore, by breaking down barriers between design and production teams through shared workspaces, coopetition significantly reduces friction points.

This collaborative environment fosters real-time problem-solving, enabling accelerated prototyping and driving innovative developments, notably by integrating graphene textiles into footwear prototypes for novel functionalities such as thermal regulation. When collaborations are successful, innovations stemming from shared goals can lead to the creation of new product categories, potentially positioning the partners as market pioneers. Furthermore, effective data sharing within such partnerships can significantly enhance our market responsiveness.

Leveraging Chinese manufacturers' deep connections to Asia-Pacific consumers enables Black American partners to gain valuable market insights. Thereby, creating a feedback loop that anticipates demand shifts. A Black-owned kitchenware brand could collaborate with a Chinese manufacturer to fuse Scandinavian minimalism with Shanghai's space-saving innovations. So they can produce stackable cookware that thrives in urban centers from Germany to Jakarta. With the benefit of hindsight, this global-local approach aims for relevance across borders, seeking to transform cultural specificity into broader appeal.

Ultimately, these collaborations have the potential to be incubators for systemic change. They demonstrate that ethical globalization can be an achievable standard in which profit and principle can coexist. By modeling how diverse perspectives drive progress. These partnerships inspire industries to break down barriers and adopt integrated approaches that foster innovation and growth. This leads to tangible benefits for 21st-century commerce, including better products. Hence, effective collaboration across cultures and continents is key to building enduring success. Such efforts mean that jointly developed products are valued not only commercially but also as meaningful outcomes of diverse expertise and empathetic partnership.

These partnerships hold significant potential for Black American entrepreneurs. Collaboration with Chinese manufacturers offers a practical strategy for scaling production, enhancing competitiveness, and accessing global supply chains. When successful, such ventures can amplify cultural narratives through broader distribution, generating meaningful economic benefits and fostering greater entrepreneurial autonomy. Historically excluded from dominant supply chains, creators within these communities could leverage partnerships to reclaim space and express their cultural identity within global commerce.

A fashion label blending Harlem's (Hā lái mǔ) jazz-era aesthetics with Hangzhou's silk-weaving heritage could do more than create garments. I imagine these projects could reflect stories of resilience and foster cross-cultural kinship. Personally, I feel that they could challenge monolithic narratives about globalization, suggesting that marginalized voices have the capacity not just to conform to markets, but to shape them actively. This cultural-economic symbiosis can potentially contribute to greater resilience against market volatility. Some businesses seek to mitigate the impact of regional disruptions by diversifying their production hubs and consumer bases.

During the pandemic, Chinese manufacturers demonstrated remarkable agility in pivoting production, particularly rapidly scaling up face mask output. Companies with robust international partnerships, including Sino-Western collaborations, were often particularly well-positioned to identify and respond to diverse global market needs. Some manufacturers quickly incorporated region-specific designs and preferences into their products, helping meet surging demand effectively across different markets. This overall adaptability highlights how strong manufacturing capabilities, combined with global market awareness, can transform challenges into strategic opportunities.

Furthermore, the exchange of technical knowledge elevates both partners through reciprocal learning. Chinese manufacturers are enhancing their understanding of Western consumer psychology and branding nuances, thereby strengthening their capabilities for global markets. Simultaneously, Western partners gain crucial insights into advanced manufacturing processes, cost-effective production scaling, and supply chain management from their Chinese collaborators, thereby fostering innovation and efficiency for both parties. Conversely, Black American firms can actively learn from global manufacturing leaders by integrating advanced lean philosophies and cutting-edge digital infrastructure expertise to streamline their operations.

A Philadelphia-based clean energy startup can directly implement the sophisticated, AI-driven quality control systems pioneered by innovators in manufacturing hubs like Ningbo (Níngbō). This approach could significantly reduce defect rates while meeting stringent American regulatory standards. The bidirectional learning inherent in these partnerships fosters mutual growth and effectively challenges the outdated notion that innovation flows only from West to East. These partnerships could often serve as bridges for policy dialogue between the involved parties. Based on my experience navigating complex regulatory systems, both domestically and internationally. I've gained practical insights. When entrepreneurs like me share these perspectives, they are genuinely combined with those from governments, civil society, and other stakeholders. They hold significant potential to contribute valuable input to the development of more effective and equitable trade agreements and sustainability standards.

A coalition of Black-owned businesses and Chinese business partners could effectively target incentives designed to promote the production and import of ethically sourced goods, such as those that ensure fair labor practices or environmental sustainability. This effort could help reshape trade policies toward greater equity and fairness. Over time, grassroots diplomacy fostered through commerce can help mitigate geopolitical tensions. This effort demonstrates how mutual economic interests, alongside other factors, can sometimes serve as a stabilizing influence in international relations. The alliance between Black American entrepreneurs and Chinese manufacturers can represent the aspirational potential of globalization. It can be a model where diversity catalyzes innovation, ethical practices align with profitability, and collaboration complements competition.

Realizing this potential requires navigating complex challenges, including labor standards, cultural differences, and equitable power dynamics. By embracing this model, I aim to do more than survive globally. I strive to innovate responsibly, ensuring that my progress benefits the Black American community and the ecosystems with which I interact. This approach enables me to help build a future of commerce that values inclusivity, adaptability, and a strong commitment to human and environmental well-being. I credit a commitment to building a supply chain ecosystem that meaningfully supports and empowers the Black American product and service industry as both a moral imperative and a strategic business opportunity. Yet, this commitment faces significant challenges, rooted in systemic barriers within established manufacturing practices and persistent biases in market perceptions.

During my engagements with Chinese manufacturers, the toys and other goods they produced often featured predominantly fair-skinned figures. This resistance to incorporating designs that reflect Black communities in such products as dolls with textured hair stems not from malice, but from a manufacturing framework that is deeply optimized for efficiency and mass production. Proposing such new product lines is crucial, but their true impact signals the need for a fundamental rethinking of who is valued within the industry's core systems and decision-making processes.

Manufacturers often weigh the significant risks of new product development, including uncertainty about market demand and the potential costs of retooling production lines. Their concerns about alienating existing customer bases can also make companies cautious. They must also consider these factors. This could sometimes lead them to prioritize refining proven products over pursuing unproven innovations. This perspective overlooks a critical reality. And that reality is that the global marketplace is evolving, and consumers increasingly expect brands to reflect the diversity of the world they inhabit. Through my work, I've learned that bridging this gap starts with fostering education and empathy before setting expectations. I've found that open, ongoing dialogue is essential for dismantling misconceptions.

During one factory visit, I attended a workshop where designers presented documented evidence from decades of American toy advertisements. It demonstrated how historical exclusionary practices in advertising actively shaped patterns of brand loyalty or distrust experienced by many Black families across generations. This visual history prompted a nuanced discussion on moving beyond tokenism towards meaningful representation. So, as I reflect on this one meeting, a manager acknowledged, "We never considered how something as simple as a doll's hair texture could signal belonging." Such moments underscore the need to frame inclusivity not merely as a charitable obligation, but as a strategic response to demonstrable needs and a driver of shared value. I trust sharing data about Black consumers in America is crucial. Though we wield over $1.6 trillion in annual purchasing power, industries continue to underserve us.

Data alone isn't enough. Chinese manufacturers could greatly benefit from a deep and sustained engagement with diverse Black American communities and experts. This includes collaborating with cultural historians, partnering with Black designers and entrepreneurs, and fostering ongoing dialogue to genuinely understand the cultural context, nuances, and emotional significance that shape truly resonant and attuned products. Authentically achieving this goal requires prioritizing Black voices as central to the process. This process entails moving past assumptions and actively learn how we truly work best together by focusing not just on the results.

It is about building strong relationships and effective communication that make collaboration authentic. Unlike packaging or marketing narratives, cultural contexts are foundational realities that require deep understanding and respect to avoid misinterpretation and harm. During a project to develop baby gear for Black families, one manufacturer incorporated Afro-centric patterns into a stroller design. It was initially overlooked that ergonomic needs differ for textured hair. The community feedback later emphasized that features like adjustable headrests, which prevent hair compression, were equally essential as visual representation for genuine inclusivity. Such insights highlight the interplay between form and function. Partnerships with Black designers, parents, and cultural advocates bring imperative perspectives and lived experiences that are crucial to achieving a balanced, inclusive outcome.

Based on my understanding and observations, market research needs to move beyond relying solely on generic surveys. From where I stand now, traditional focus groups often fall short in capturing the complex, nuanced experiences of Black consumers. That is shaped by navigating a marketplace that frequently overlooks or ignores significant historical contexts and injustices. Forward-thinking manufacturers are increasingly centering Black voices through community-based participatory research. This includes partnering directly with organizations rooted in Black communities, like the National Black Child Development Institute (NBCDI), and collaborating with Black influencers on social media who authentically share community knowledge, priorities, and experiences.

One company, Brown Toy Box, utilized TikTok feedback to refine a line of STEM kits featuring Black scientists. They discovered that parents valued not only representation but also accompanying materials linking the inventions to African diasporic history. By incorporating this feedback, the company involved consumers in the development process, helping build trust and ensure the products resonate on multiple levels. I think inclusivity gains strength when manufacturers recognize that catering to Black audiences doesn't mean abandoning existing markets but rather expanding into underserved ones. In my opinion, redefining our approach to risk is crucial for progress. While pivoting production presents logistical challenges, I suppose stagnation ultimately carries greater risks, as Gen Z consumers, who statistically show strong preferences for diversity, social consciousness, and digital engagement, are increasingly influential. They are becoming the dominant buying force.

Brands that lag in authentic representation will struggle to maintain relevance. Manufacturers who genuinely invest in cultural competency position themselves as essential contributors to a more equitable economy. This requires patience and trust, built incrementally through direct human relationships, cultural exchange, and a shared creative process that prioritizes transparent supply chains and ethical labor practices. By doing so, manufacturers tap into a loyal and passionate consumer base, addressing a significant market opportunity.

While also potentially contributing to broader cultural representation, where more children can see themselves reflected in the products around them. A Black toddler hugging a doll with hair like hers or a teen finding skincare that celebrates their skin tone offer moments that transcend mere commerce. They profoundly affirm dignity and belonging. And while this alignment of profit and purpose is sound business for manufacturers, the true significance lies in the ethical act of recognizing and valuing every person.

7

Mastering Unspoken Business Rituals

Cultural competency thrives not in theory, but in the messy terrain of real-world relationships. In China, I learned that business is often conducted over meals and sealed through unspoken understandings. An invitation to such gatherings is a meaningful gesture of trust, offering a window into informal decision-making and industry dynamics seldom seen in formal settings. Where guanxi (guānxi) is central, success relies less on transactional efficiency and more on nurturing deep relationships built on mutual obligation and trust.

Contracts establish a foundational framework for partnerships. However, consistent, non-transactional actions such as attending shared meals are a powerful demonstration of commitment. This builds trust, a strategic advantage often underestimated in purely transactional environments. However, dining together extends beyond social formality to become a ritual rich with symbolism, a meaningful bridge between individuals, and a significant element in building professional rapport. Through my experiences, I've learned that each steamed dumpling, the clink of a teacup, and a burst of laughter over a boiling hot pot build a unique trust and a deeply personal connection. This open, shared dialogue nurtures mutual respect. To me, the hot pot embodies collaboration: a symphony of shared purpose.

Just as instruments harmonize in a melody, ideas and aspirations mingle like ingredients in a communal broth. A slow-cooked meal allows conversation to breathe, with voices rising and falling naturally, like notes finding their rhythm, without feeling rushed. During one such dinner in Suzhou (Sūzhōu), the informal setting helped bridge a gap with a manufacturer I'd previously struggled to connect with. In that relaxed atmosphere, he candidly shared his concerns about supply chain delays. The group formulated a solution to spread risk through regional diversification, a plan later adopted across its entire factory network.

Sharing a meal holds significant importance across a wide range of Chinese business contexts. It provides a setting highly conducive to building rapport and fostering a harmony that reflects core values such as balance, mutual respect, and patience, which are deeply embedded and highly regarded within many Chinese business traditions. I appreciate that this practice of cultivating connections over food is a well-established and valued cultural norm. Yet, such a connection demands more than physical presence. It requires deep respect for cultural nuance.

Early in my career, I risked a misunderstanding with a Suzhou (Sūzhōu) hat manufacturer by overlooking banquet etiquette. A mentor later explained the unspoken language of respect in these customs: the angle of your glass relative to elders, matching the host's pacing, and the symbolism of dishes like the fish facing the guest of honor. Learning these nuances demonstrated my respect for their culture, which strengthened our professional relationship and proved invaluable in navigating delicate discussions.

Extended shared meals provide a setting for indirect communication, facilitating sensitive negotiations and discussions. This approach enables delicate topics, such as contractual disagreements or logistical issues, to be addressed through contextual discussion rather than blunt confrontation, an approach I've found helps preserve everyone's face (miànzi). Customer feedback on specific attributes, like beef tenderness or tea aroma, is more than a single data point. It can reveal deeper issues, such as production quality, or suggest new opportunities, like market expansion. Consistently gathering and interpreting this feedback builds a valuable knowledge base for making better decisions over time.

My long-term Shanghai packaging supplier consistently prioritizes our orders. I credit the trust and mutual support that sustained our relationship during the pandemic for this. Despite halted shipments, I continued to manage their agreements. When severe material shortages arose in 2022, we fulfilled our commitments through proactive planning and strengthened partnerships. This demonstrates that for us, trust is not a buzzword but a currency earned through shared resilience. While some criticize these practices as time-intensive, the measurable return on investment is clear.

Through my experience in China, I've learned that partnerships nurtured over shared meals, like Peking Duck, develop stronger foundations than those relying solely on email. Similarly, resolving disputes in person over morning tea is less adversarial and reduces legal costs. Breaking bread fosters a personal connection, making it harder to view someone as a faceless entity. In our digitized age, where Zoom calls often supplant handshakes, this enduring importance of physical togetherness is a vital counterpoint. It reminds us that algorithms cannot replicate the subtle trust forged through shared presence and thoughtful gestures. Ultimately, working with manufacturers throughout China has taught me that long-term success requires a balance between operational excellence and authentic relationship-building.

While technical proficiency and formal agreements are essential, the deepest and most resilient partnerships are forged through genuine human connection. Few things build this trust more effectively than the timeless, cross-cultural practice of sharing a meal. Therefore, studying, working, and living in China has been a profound experience, fostering deep cultural humility within me and fundamentally reshaping how I conduct business and perceive human connection.
In parallel, while textbooks and language classes provided me with an essential foundation, the actual depth of China's rich linguistic tapestry unfolded in unscripted moments.

These included sharing laughter over a casual meal, observing the focused attention within a traditional ceremony, or noticing a partner's quiet consideration in keeping my cup of hot water filled. These experiences showed me the living culture woven into the language in a way that formal study alone couldn't capture. As such, a series of excursions with a Chinese manufacturer profoundly shaped my perspective. Our casual post-meeting outings evolved into a cultural dialogue, revealing that trust was built not through contracts, but through shared experiences, patience, and a commitment to something beyond immediate transactions.

While navigating the mist-draped gardens, I passed a lively karaoke session and felt a flicker of shared amusement at the off-key singing. Such moments often led me to reflect, and I noticed a pattern: partners who invested in these gatherings were frequently our most reliable collaborators. I recall one evening when a manufacturer's CEO refilled my teacup with a level of attentiveness that perfectly illustrated this. In Chinese business culture, partnerships are cultivated for sustained mutual benefit, prioritizing long-term gains over short-term benefits. This emphasis on long-term relationships infuses simple gestures with deeper meaning. For instance, the deliberate act of serving tea, pouring it with both hands while steadying the pot, becomes a symbol of deep respect and reciprocity. Such gestures reinforce the personal connection at the heart of these carefully built relationships.

With genuine curiosity, I attended gatherings where I learned toasting etiquette and admired regional cuisine. Through this, respect is communicated within the culture through a complex system of social exchange. I initially interpreted the hospitality as a complex system of social exchange, where following tradition built relational credit. I now see it as a simpler, more heartfelt expression of kindness and shared humanity. These experiences taught me that in China, professional and personal boundaries often overlap with a fluidity shaped by cultural expectations.

During a banquet in Hangzhou (Hángzhōu), a supplier hosted a lakeside dinner featuring West Lake Vinegar Fish (Xīhú cù yú), a local specialty. He explained the dish's heritage, describing how fresh grass carp is poached and served with a sweet-sour vinegar sauce, which showcases both hospitality and cultural pride. As we dined, our conversation moved naturally from supply chains to personal topics, and by the third course, we were discussing his daughter's aspirations to study abroad.

I saw how our genuine conversation served to build a picture of each other's character and values. In this case, sharing a time-honored recipe was a powerful bridge, transforming our formal discussions into personal ones and fostering a sense of shared humanity. This reinforced my belief that intentionally sharing meaningful food is a valuable tool for building the trust essential to strong relationships. My initial adherence to my own cultural assumptions was quickly challenged. After declining a post-meeting invitation to prepare for the next day, I realized my polite refusal could be misconstrued as a sign of disinterest. I learned to embrace every opportunity to connect, from accepting a business card with both hands to understanding the nuances of banquet seating.

Through these interactions, I gained a deeper understanding of how rituals foster guanxi (guānxi) a foundational Chinese concept that prioritizes long-term relationships sustained by mutual respect, trust, and balanced exchange. Many of these traditions are rooted in Confucian (Rújiā) principles of harmony and respect, which continue to influence modern commerce. Understanding these values helped build trust and facilitated smoother negotiations. Beyond business outcomes, this immersion provided a deeper understanding of the cultural context. For example, during a factory tour in Guangdong Province (Guǎngdōng Shěng), a manager paused our inspection to introduce me to their team's dedicated tea master.

For decades, she had crafted blends for the staff. As she performed the Gongfu Tea Ceremony (gōngfu chá), her movements flowed with a practiced, dance-like grace. She explained how this daily ritual was more than a break; it was a tradition that strengthened camaraderie and mindfulness. To me, it reflected a core Chinese philosophy: that mindfulness, craftsmanship, and collective well-being are vital to productivity. This experience reshaped my leadership, teaching me to lead with empathy and intentional connection. I also saw firsthand the limitations of cultural reductionism, as China's business environment is a complex tapestry of generational, regional, and evolving factors that defy simplistic portrayal.

A tech startup founder in Hangzhou may prioritize speed and efficiency, while a state-owned enterprise in Xi'an might place greater emphasis on tradition and protocol. To navigate these differences, I've found that cultural fluency is essential. It helps me respect long-standing customs while adapting to modern expectations. Success often depends on research, emotional agility, and a willingness to listen as much as to speak. Ultimately, this experience taught me that cultural competence isn't about memorizing etiquette rules, but about cultivating what the Chinese call (tǐtiē), which is often referred to as The Art of Thoughtful Consideration.

I learned to recognize that actions like a delayed contract sign-off might reflect unspoken priorities in a partner's decision-making process. Or that a seemingly simple gift could hold more profound meaning. It's about sensitivity to context, not assumptions. This awareness helps turn potential friction into collaboration by uncovering shared goals beneath surface-level differences. When I mentor teams on cross-cultural engagements, I encourage them to view every interaction as the beginning of a meaningful dialogue, not just a transactional exchange. The global marketplace thrives not on uniformity but on our ability to appreciate the quiet, profound ways people express value.

In bridging cultural divides, I've found that we do more than close deals when we expand our capacity for understanding, one shared meal, one story, one cup of tea at a time. I understand that navigating the balance between personal and professional interactions is a delicate dance that requires equal parts intuition, intention, and adaptability. Over time, I've come to cherish this not as a series of calculated maneuvers but as an organic discovery process. Each opportunity to step away from the structured formalities of office life has enriched my understanding of my colleagues, revealing the nuanced layers of our shared culture.

Whether sharing a casual lunch, attending an after-hours outing, or collaborating on a cross-departmental project. I've learned that these moments are more than mere social interludes. They are vital gestures in workplace relationships, merging camaraderie and professionalism in ways that transcend rigid hierarchies. In traditional work settings, I've noticed that titles and roles often act as invisible barriers, subtly shaping how we perceive one another. But I've also seen how something shifts when colleagues gather outside conference rooms and email chains. Conversations flow more freely, filled with laughter and personal stories, as we share weekend adventures, family traditions, or hobbies that ignite our passions.

These moments remind me that behind every job title is a person with unique experiences and interests. Such exchanges are potent tools for humanizing colleagues and breaking down preconceived notions. , discovering a reserved project manager's talent for stand-up comedy or a data-driven analyst's international childhood can profoundly reshape our understanding of their strengths and perspectives. I've found that these kinds of revelations foster empathy, helping me see coworkers not just as abstract roles but as multidimensional people.

For me, this empathy serves as the foundation for better collaboration. When I understand the values, challenges, and aspirations that drive my peers, I communicate with greater patience, brainstorm with a broader perspective, and approach conflicts with more profound compassion. The ripple effects of these connections can be profound. In some cases, I've seen teams transition from disjointed groups to more cohesive units after bonding over a shared volunteer experience. Of course, results vary depending on the team and context. Working toward a common goal, like serving others, often helps uncover strengths that might otherwise remain untapped.

During a team-building retreat, a spontaneous barbecue trip unexpectedly unlocked new perspectives on a stalled manufacturing project. The collaborative cooking challenge mirrored our professional hurdles, and the shared success eased lingering tensions. This experience highlights a powerful dynamic: while trust can certainly grow in formal settings, it can also be challenging to build in informal ones. It often deepens most quickly in unscripted moments when vulnerability and authenticity take center stage. I think a workplace that nurtures these opportunities doesn't just boost morale; it also fosters a culture of innovation. It cultivates a culture where innovation thrives because people feel safe taking risks, sharing ideas, and admitting gaps in knowledge without fear of judgment.

Meanwhile, informal interactions require a nuanced awareness of boundaries. While laughter and casual exchanges can fuel creativity, they can also become distractions if not balanced with focus and professionalism. Early in my work in China, I realized the importance of striking a balance between relationship-building and task efficiency. During one project deadline, a well-meaning conversation about a colleague's upcoming shipment unintentionally turned into an hour-long discussion.

That experience revealed my role in the detour. Since then, I've worked on gently redirecting conversations, showing genuine interest in personal updates while keeping focus on priorities. Now, I might say something like, "That shipment sounds incredible! Let's revisit it after we finalize the payment." This balance isn't about stifling connection, but about honoring the dual priorities of any workplace: achieving goals and nurturing relationships. It requires attentiveness to subtle cues. Whether a furrowed brow signals urgency or a closed laptop suggests the need for a break. Such signals vary across individuals and cultures.

Ultimately, it's the wisdom to discern when to offer empathy versus when to drive focus that fosters both productivity and trust. Critically, this discernment isn't one-size-fits-all. Individual comfort levels vary, shaped by cultural norms, personality types, and past experiences. An introverted engineer might find small talk exhausting, preferring to bond over collaborative problem-solving. A new employee might appreciate flexibility in after-hours events but prioritize punctual departures. Recognizing these differences is key to fostering inclusivity. I suppose in nurturing our workplace, we can conspicuously replace a happy hour with a midday team lunch or pair personal check-ins with project updates. We could help create spaces where more people feel included.

Since no single approach works for everyone, I will stay open to feedback and adjust to ensure these changes meet the team's needs. This mindfulness extends to communication styles where some thrive on directness, while others rely on diplomatic phrasing. The goal is not uniformity but mutual respect, ensuring that camaraderie enhances rather than eclipses professional objectives. When teams achieve this balance effectively, they often experience benefits, such as outstandingly increased job satisfaction, reduced turnover, and greater resilience in the face of challenges.

These outcomes depend on various factors, including organizational support, team dynamics, and individual circumstances. When conflicts arise, a foundation of trust allows disagreements to remain task-focused rather than personal. When deadlines emerge, the goodwill earned through shared laughter becomes a reservoir of patience. And when successes occur, they're celebrated not as isolated victories but as collective triumphs. This synergy between the personal and professional doesn't blur lines. It bridges them, creating a workplace where people don't just coexist but genuinely collaborate. Ultimately, I learned that the dance between connection and professionalism is ongoing, a dynamic interplay that evolves with each new team, project, or challenge.

It asks me to be fully present to listen actively, empathize deeply, and discern wisely. The best work happens when we move beyond tasks to tap into the unique potential of every team member, creating a richer and more human experience for everyone. I've found that sharing my experiences and lessons learned can be a meaningful way to support others as they navigate unfamiliar professional challenges. For me, this isn't just about giving advice. It's about engaging authentically, fostering collective growth, and helping others find their way as we learn together.

At its core, this ethos requires more than mere generosity. It calls for intentional action because, for me, respecting others' time isn't just about punctuality or sticking to schedules. It's about truly valuing their contributions, fostering spaces where every voice is heard, and ensuring that collaboration is both meaningful and inclusive. While creating a lighthearted atmosphere is essential, I imagine professionalism remains the anchor even in lighter interactions where laughter and camaraderie thrive. Striking this balance enables me to maintain productivity without compromising the human connections that drive innovation and trust.

Mastering this balance depends on emotional intelligence, like the ability to "read the room" and know when to shift from casual rapport to focused problem-solving. In team meetings, I've noticed that off-topic banter can lighten the mood and strengthen bonds, but if it lingers too long, it risks slowing our momentum. I try to gently steer conversations back on track without dismissing the positive energy.

By saying something like, "Let's capture that energy for our next brainstorming session. For now, let's revisit the timeline." This way, I acknowledge the camaraderie while keeping us focused on our goals. To me, this approach transforms potential distractions into moments that reinforce mutual respect, thereby maintaining a productive and uplifting collaboration. When I share my own stories of struggle and triumph, I'm not just passing along experiences. I'm trying to break down the walls of isolation. My vulnerability becomes a bridge, allowing others to see their challenges reflected in what I've been through.

When I talk about how I navigated a cultural misunderstanding in a foreign office, I'm not just offering a possible solution. I'm showing that setbacks don't have to define us. They can be survived, even learned from. Personally, I've found that these stories help cultivate psychological safety, empowering individuals to take calculated risks, ask questions, and innovate without fear of judgment. I've observed that, over time, this kind of openness can become self-reinforcing. As more people share their experiences to strengthen the group's collective resilience, fostering a culture that values adaptability and trust, at least when the conditions are right.

For Black Americans working in complex professional environments, China's industrial sector stands out. Navigating cultural and systemic barriers can present unique challenges. In these contexts, shared knowledge and mutual support become especially valuable in overcoming unfamiliar obstacles. Navigating obstacles as a Black professional often meant visibility was a double-edged sword. A double-edged sword here, meant standing out in spaces where few looked like me brought both scrutiny and unexpected opportunities. I struggled with the pressure to conform to narrow expectations, sometimes minimizing my identity to fit in.

Over time, I realized that my unique perspective, forged by my community's resilience and the depth of my heritage, was not a weakness but a strength. It allowed me to see solutions and opportunities others might miss. This insight is not mine alone because it's echoed in the experiences of countless innovators. Take Pamela, a Detroit (Dǐtèlǜ) native who launched a sustainable textile startup in Shanghai. Initially, it met with skepticism from local manufacturers. She drew on her background in community organizing, turning her outsider perspective into a bridge rather than a barrier. By sharing Detroit's (Dǐtèlǜ) stories of grassroots renewal, she found common ground with Chinese partners who appreciated her collaborative spirit. Or consider Lorenzo, an engineer who confronted subtle biases not with confrontation but with curiosity. He utilized humor and data to challenge assumptions during product demos.

Their journeys, like so many others, reveal a nuanced truth. A truth that while marginalization imposes real barriers, it can also cultivate resilience and creative problem-solving. These are qualities often overlooked in conventional success narratives. Mainly, when systemic barriers constrain opportunities, creativity opens new paths. Yet individual success alone is not enough. There must be lasting change that allows collective action, where these stories are amplified to reveal systemic patterns and inspire broader change through more effective strategies.

Many professionals from marginalized or underrepresented backgrounds, including Black professionals working abroad, develop cultural code-switching techniques. This skill extends beyond linguistic adjustments to include nuanced adaptations in communication styles, negotiation tactics, and body language. These adaptations help bridge cultural gaps and foster rapport across differences. When shared openly, they become a valuable toolkit for others navigating similar challenges.

A casual conversation about interpreting indirect feedback in high-context cultures or a workshop on navigating guanxi (guānxi) networks in China can help outsiders better understand these complex social dynamics. This can make seemingly daunting environments more approachable. This is not about assimilation, but about empowering individuals to navigate systems without compromising their authenticity. It's about fostering resilience and mutual support within communities. From my experience, mentorship circles can be incredibly valuable. When I've seen young professionals hesitate to negotiate a contract or address a microaggression, hearing a peer's story of navigating a similar situation has sometimes helped turn anxiety into action.

Not every mentorship circle works the same way. Their impact depends on the participants' openness, the group's dynamics, and the guidance provided. Some digital platforms facilitate real-time knowledge sharing, as exemplified by WeChat. There are groups where Black expats exchange advice on topics ranging from navigating visa requirements and managing hair care in humid climates to discussing industry-specific challenges. This platform not only addresses practical concerns but also fosters a sense of community, reinforcing the idea that individuals are not alone in their experiences. I've come to believe that the ripple effects of setbacks in knowledge sharing are from rejected proposals, cultural misunderstandings, or moments of self-doubt. The ripple effects are significant and can extend beyond immediate losses.

When we openly discuss these challenges alongside our successes, we can create a more comprehensive picture of what it means to be a Black American in China. That one encompasses both our struggles and growth. We can provide environments where individuals, whether a Black American tourist seeking clarification without fear of seeming 'unprepared' or a mid-career manager requesting flexible work arrangements to honor family obligations, can thrive. Feel empowered to voice their needs without their competence being unfairly questioned. This could foster inclusivity by recognizing diverse experiences while ensuring equitable support for all. I credit cultural shifts that happen not through top-down mandates but through the collective power of everyday courage, vulnerability, and reciprocity.

When I share knowledge, I do so with faith, trusting that what I offer might ease others' way. For many Black Americans, storytelling carries deep historical and cultural significance. Rooted in traditions like those of West African griots and sustained through oral histories during enslavement and the Civil Rights Movement. Narration has often served as a means of resilience and community building. Today, that legacy manifests in diverse ways, particularly in global professional spaces, creative arts, or everyday life. So, every lesson I've shared, every challenge I've worked through, and every victory I've celebrated have strengthened not just me but the people around me. I've come to realize that the real power lies not in any single success story, but in how these shared experiences weave together.

My struggles and ours aren't just barriers to push past. They're what shape and strengthen us as a community. Navigating China's complex market requires more than ambition. It demands careful preparation. A key factor in any successful venture is thorough research. Research that goes beyond surface-level analysis to understand the economic, cultural, and regulatory dynamics at play. Western markets operate within well-established frameworks but are also dynamic, driven by technological advancements and shifting consumer demands. China's ecosystem is highly adaptive, shaped by rapid urbanization, a diverse consumer base, and evolving regulatory policies. Both countries have their complexities.

Western markets strike a balance between stability and innovation, while China's landscape combines rapid change with long-term strategic planning. I suppose ignoring this complexity could lead to missteps that might derail even the most promising endeavors. That's why I would start by carefully analyzing the local market. In my opinion, China's consumer behavior is deeply rooted in centuries of tradition, while also embracing modern digital innovations. In 2018, a European luxury brand faced backlash after its handling of a customer complaint highlighted the risks of overlooking cultural sensitivities. When a dissatisfied client raised concerns about a product defect. The brand's response, perceived as dismissive and confrontational, escalated the situation and drew public criticism. The incident highlighted the detrimental impact of inadequate customer service, particularly in cross-cultural contexts, on both sales and brand reputation. In China, where the concept of "face" holds cultural significance, the brand's misstep sparked widespread backlash.

The customer shared their experience on social media platforms, particularly Weibo, where the incident quickly gained traction. Many consumers expressed frustration, feeling the brand had overlooked local sensitivities. While some called for boycotts, the broader reaction was mixed, with both criticism and debate. That highlighted how cultural expectations and digital amplification can escalate a single complaint into a significant PR challenge. Meanwhile, a savvy competitor ingrained professionalism and a strong customer service philosophy into its operations (Zhèyàng zuò huì diū miànzi). Complaints were often addressed in private VIP lounges to maintain discretion, with resolutions including apologies, complimentary repairs, or exclusive gifts. These measures aimed to resolve issues respectfully while minimizing public attention and disruption. Staff underwent training in cultural empathy and were encouraged to prioritize humility and indirect communication.

The effectiveness of these methods may have varied depending on individual circumstances, and not all grievances may have been resolved to the satisfaction of those involved. From my vantage point, many loyal customers have come to appreciate the brand's alignment with their values and have become vocal advocates, helping to generate positive word of mouth. Another brand struggled with market share and trust, while this one thrived due to its emphasis on cultural sensitivity. This story bears direct parallels to real-world scandals, such as Dolce & Gabbana's 2018 ad controversy in China.

Simultaneously, brands, conspicuously Hermès, have succeeded by carefully adapting to local cultural norms. In luxury markets, where perception is everything, I trust understanding concepts like showing respect (gěi miànzi) isn't just about courtesy. It's a crucial, billion-dollar lesson in humility and strategic respect. Similarly, rapid urbanization has contributed to the growth of megacities with diverse consumer profiles. Tech-savvy millennials in Hangzhou often prioritize convenience and innovation. Concurrently, affordability and trust may be more influential for many consumers in tier-3 cities. These trends are not absolute, as preferences can vary within regions and across demographics. Effective market research should account for these regional nuances while recognizing the complexity of consumer behavior.

Equally critical is understanding the role of digital platforms. WeChat (Wēixìn) and Douyin (Dǒuyīn) are not merely social media apps, but ecosystems that shape commerce, communication, and culture. Perfect Diary, a relatively new cosmetics brand, gained rapid popularity in China's competitive beauty market by leveraging short-form video platforms, especially Douyin (TikTok). Instead of relying solely on traditional celebrity endorsements or high-budget advertising, the brand focused on user-generated content. They showcase everyday people applying lipstick or blending eyeshadows in 15-second clips.

This strategy helped Perfect Diary connect with Gen Z consumers by emphasizing relatability and turning customers into grassroots influencers. Rather than relying on traditional advertising campaigns, Perfect Diary embraced a dynamic, user-driven approach. They encouraged college students to create authentic content, with students sharing "get ready with me" tutorials or beginners showcasing their makeup transformations using the brand's popular Animal Eyeshadow Palettes. Their strategy leveraged relatable micro-influencers and tapped into viral trends, including hashtag challenges like #PerfectLook.

From my angle, their success stems from a combination of grassroots engagement, strategic partnerships, and products that generate organic buzz. A buzz that highlights Douyin's emphasis on authenticity has led brands like Perfect Diary to adopt a more relatable approach. Instead of polished perfection, they showcased raw, unfiltered content to better connect with audiences. The brand's clever use of limited-time releases, including zodiac-themed collections, created strong demand among beauty enthusiasts. This strategy, combined with engaged fans who eagerly commented and made purchases, contributed to the company's rapid growth, enabling it to achieve a $1 billion valuation in just three years.

From my viewpoint, Perfect Diary's success wasn't just about selling makeup. It was about fostering a sense of co-creation with their customers. Their strategy highlighted how, in China's competitive digital landscape, emotional connection and user-generated content can be as impactful as the product itself. Their approach suggests that brands looking to go viral might benefit from empowering their audience to shape the brand's story. I recall how Burberry's 2019 Chinese New Year campaign, which extended its signature monochrome aesthetic to WeChat, drew significant criticism in China. While the brand may have intended to maintain its luxury image, many consumers found the approach mismatched with the holiday's festive, vibrant spirit. When I think of Lunar New Year, I envision vibrant reds, golden dragons, and joyful family gatherings with symbols deeply rooted in the celebration. Burberry's campaign took a different approach, featuring stern-faced models in moody grayscale scenes.

While I understand that artistic choices are subjective, I found the contrast with traditional Lunar New Year imagery particularly striking. It has also sparked discussion online. Some Chinese netizens humorously compared Burberry's campaign to "haunted house chic" or "funeral vibes," noting a contrast with the Lunar New Year's traditional emphasis on vibrancy, luck, and warmth. Additionally, the brand's static, muted social media posts did not align with the interactive nature of the engagement.

Posts featuring red envelope giveaways, games, or festive filters were what many WeChat users expected during the holiday. While the campaign sparked discussion, it also highlighted the challenges global brands face in balancing their aesthetic with local celebratory customs. I think that Burberry's 2019 campaign underscores the significance of cultural intelligence in international marketing. This suggests that applying Western strategies to other markets without consideration can have unintended consequences.

I also recognize that navigating local values, aesthetics, and platform dynamics is complex. While not every adaptation will succeed, the key takeaway is that brands should enter new markets with cultural sensitivity, humility, and a genuine commitment to learning and growth. These examples highlight the importance of studying platform-specific behaviors rather than assuming strategies from other contexts will automatically apply. Regulatory adaptability plays a significant role in China's policy landscape, where adjustments are often made to align with domestic priorities and global dynamics.

The 2021 Data Security Law and the Common Prosperity initiatives have introduced substantial changes across various sectors, including technology and education. This change reflects both proactive governance and responses to emerging challenges. Regulatory changes in China's tutoring sector, aimed at reducing academic pressure and inequality, significantly disrupted the industry. While these reforms aligned with long-term social goals, their swift implementation contributed to the contraction of a once $100 billion market.

Some foreign investors, along with domestic stakeholders, were unprepared for the scale and pace of these changes, leading to financial losses. I believe that proactively monitoring legislative updates through government white papers, legal advisories, and industry bulletins is essential, although not the only factor in staying compliant. While partnerships with local consultancies can offer early warnings, regulations are just one part of the challenge. I've found that building relationships with regional stakeholders such as suppliers, distributors, and officials can also be critical for navigating barriers that might otherwise hinder progress.

When I arrived in Shanghai in 2002, I found that building a strong support network as an international student wasn't always easy. While some students had connections or institutional help, many of us often had to rely on our resourcefulness to navigate challenges. Recognizing this gap, I engaged in conversations with peers and educators both inside and outside the classroom. Through these discussions, shared challenges emerged, particularly educational hurdles, cultural misunderstandings, and feelings of isolation, highlighting areas where support was needed.

Through these discussions, we formed a group for international students, where more experienced members helped newcomers navigate both academic challenges and cultural adjustments. Off-campus activities also played a key role in deepening our understanding of life abroad. During my PhD candidacy, I participated in an activity related to Tongji University's (Tóngjì Dàxué) urban planning work. In 2003, Tongji University, a leading institution in architecture and urban design, contributed to major Shanghai projects, including the revitalization of the Huangpu Riverbanks and the conversion of industrial zones into mixed-use public spaces.

This involved designing pedestrian-friendly spaces, preserving historical architecture, and upgrading infrastructure. These efforts supported the city's broader urban development goals and its preparations for major international events, including the 2010 World Expo. Beyond this activity, I fostered relationships through dinners and academic support groups. These connections became essential to me, offering emotional support during challenging times and creating bonds that went beyond purely academic goals.

While I valued these experiences, others likely perceived them differently. Studying China without thorough preparation feels like navigating a complex experience without careful guidance. I've found that successful academic work here requires deep research, going far beyond surface-level data. The educational landscape is shaped by a combination of state policies, cultural traditions, and rapid technological integration, resulting in a system with distinct characteristics.

Likewise, to succeed in China's market, it's essential to carefully analyze its unique characteristics, as strategies or assumptions from other markets may not always be applicable. Immersing oneself in local markets can reveal significant regional disparities in consumer preferences, highlighting the need for tailored approaches. A product that succeeds in Shanghai's cosmopolitan hubs might require adaptation to resonate in Chengdu (Chéngdū). Since consumer preferences often emphasize localized flavors and cultural traditions.

This dynamic is evident in the rise of (Guóchǎo), a national trend in which younger consumers increasingly favor domestic brands that creatively integrate cultural heritage. Based on my observations, rapid urbanization in China, with over 65% of the population now residing in cities, has driven demand for convenience-driven services and premium goods.

I've noticed that price sensitivity remains a significant factor, especially in lower-tier cities. Understanding these nuances requires granular data, including demographic studies, purchasing patterns, and regional economic reports. Equally important is navigating China's regulatory environment, which demands agility and adaptability. In the meantime, policies may evolve rapidly in alignment with broader socio-economic objectives. Cultural fluency requires more than an understanding of regulations or data.

In China, consumer behavior is deeply embedded in digital ecosystems that often differ significantly from those in other markets. This poses a unique challenge for outsiders. Platforms like WeChat and Douyin are more than just social networks. They combine commerce, entertainment, and social interaction into integrated digital ecosystems. Live-streaming sales have significantly reshaped retail by merging entertainment with impulse buying.

While this model thrives on emotional engagement and identity-driven purchases (Qínggǎn jīngjì de juéqǐ), it also raises questions about sustainability, overconsumption, and the authenticity of influencer-driven marketing. For this reason, brands should adapt their storytelling to this emotional economy, but they must also consider their ethical responsibility and the long-term trust of their consumers. Even the most thorough data can't fully replace human insights. A lesson I learned when I arrived in Shanghai in 2002.

At the time, I found that many expatriates, including myself, were still figuring out how to navigate bureaucratic processes and local networks, and guanxi (guānxi). While some shared knowledge existed, it wasn't always cohesive or easily accessible, which taught me the importance of firsthand experience and personal connections alongside data. At first, I didn't fully grasp the gap between textbook theories and grassroots realities, partly because I lacked mentorship. Recognizing this, I made a conscious effort to bridge the divide by immersing myself in grassroots activities. Activities include attending English corners, participating in sporting events, and volunteering at cultural festivals. These experiences helped me gain a deeper, more practical understanding of what it's like to be in China. Over time, these fledgling activities evolved into a robust support system.

It's 2003. The digital landscape is still taking shape, communities are beginning to connect online, and early efforts in peer support are laying the groundwork for what would become a vital network. Based on my observations, the monthly roundtables held in those smoky conference rooms felt different from today's Zoom calls. Veteran business owners would share stories over bitter Longjing tea. I often noticed that many of them emphasized the importance of long-term relationships and trust with local distributors over quick profits.

Municipal officials, armed with Nokia phones, subtly favor companies that contribute to local initiatives, especially those that plant trees in parks or fund school uniforms. This struck me as an early, grassroots form of corporate social responsibility (CSR). CSR efforts at the grassroots level were only part of the story. During the SARS outbreak, when supply chains froze, I witnessed municipal officials relying on landlines, paper maps, and personal connections to reroute shipments.

Meanwhile, others closely analyzed official publications like the People's Daily, reading between the lines of phrases that marked "opening wider to the outside world" to anticipate policy changes. From my own encounters, trust wasn't just about digital outreach back then. It often depended on face-to-face relationships and demonstrable commitment. To me, sharing mooncakes during the Mid-Autumn Festival has always held a special significance. I remember sticky-fingered laughter under paper lanterns. Back then, relying on your community felt less like 'networking' and more like a natural part of life.

Today, even as technology shapes how we connect, the heart of the festival remains the same: gratitude, togetherness, and joy. In my dealings, building strong relationships with Chinese manufacturers is like a slow-cooked hotpot. It requires patience, trust, and mutual respect. While negotiating pricing, I discovered that the process involves more than just numbers. It includes a cultural understanding, long-term commitment, and clear communication, all of which play crucial roles in the process. Among these, the language barrier emerged as a persistent and multifaceted challenge.

Early in my dealings with suppliers, I discovered that communication was not merely about translating words but also about decoding layers of cultural nuance, unspoken expectations, and contextual subtleties. I've noticed that a phrase like 'we'll consider it' can sometimes mask hesitation, uncertainty, or even a polite refusal. This, of course, depends on tone, timing, or the maturity of the relationship. At the same time, it could also genuinely signal openness to discussion. Because of this, what appeared to be straightforward conversations often revealed deeper layers of nuance, requiring patience and careful interpretation.

Over time, I learned that effective negotiation extended beyond linguistic competence. It demanded attentiveness to the unspoken connotations of discussion. A conversation where meaning is shaped not only by what is said but also by what remains unspoken. For me, the actual resolution often emerged through this deeper understanding rather than through words alone. This verbal balancing act was further complicated by cultural differences in negotiation styles, particularly the Chinese emphasis on building long-term relationships based on mutual trust.

Initially, my approach was shaped by Western contexts where negotiations often prioritize efficiency and short-term outcomes, which didn't always align with this emphasis on relationship-building. I recall a tense discussion where I pushed hard for a lower unit cost, expecting a direct negotiation. Instead, I was met with prolonged silence followed by a vague commitment to 'explore options.' Later, a local colleague explained that my approach had come across as disrespectful because the supplier valued gradual rapport-building over aggressive tactics. I hadn't fully considered these cultural expectations at the time, and in hindsight, my initial plan was flawed. This realization changed my approach.

I started making time for informal conversations, shared meals, and small acts of goodwill, conspicuously acknowledging holidays or inquiring about a partner's family. Initially, I worried that these efforts were secondary to business results, but over time, they helped build trust and reduce resistance. Suppliers became more flexible, offering insights into cost-saving adjustments or production workarounds that hadn't surfaced in formal talks. The experience highlighted how building trust through negotiation can unlock collaborative solutions in specific business contexts in China.

As my relationships with manufacturers grew stronger, I also encountered the complexities of the production landscape. I found that timelines were often affected by unpredictable factors, such as regional power shortages or sudden changes in material availability. At times, minimum order quantities (MOQs) seemed inconsistent, with quotes varying depending on a factory's workload or shifting policies. Maintaining consistent quality standards also proved challenging, as expectations sometimes shifted without a clear explanation. In one order, a sample that had been meticulously approved arrived with inconsistent needlework. The supplier dismissed the issue as 'within tolerance,' but I knew it didn't meet our standards.

Resolving this required a careful balance, involving neither pushing too hard, which might damage the partnership, nor accepting it, which would hurt our quality and profitability. I learned to approach such situations collaboratively, framing concerns as shared problems to solve. Instead of issuing ultimatums, I asked, "How can we adjust the process to meet these specifications?" This approach preserved the relationship while upholding our standards. It transformed conflicts into joint problem-solving sessions. Demonstrating that many demands initially deemed 'unworkable' can be addressed through creative compromises, such as phased deliveries or modified designs. Differences in legal terminology and syntax between English and Mandarin sometimes introduce ambiguities during translation, creating additional challenges.

In one instance, 'flexible payment terms' was initially misunderstood as allowing all payments to be deferred until after delivery. This potential cash flow issue was resolved by clarifying the clause with a bilingual legal advisor, ensuring that both parties had a clear, mutual understanding of the terms. These near-misses taught me to treat language as a dynamic, living entity that will be put to the test across cultural and legal contexts. To bridge gaps in understanding, I sometimes integrated visual aids, particularly annotated diagrams and video walkthroughs, alongside textual descriptions.

Additionally, I found it helpful to use a glossary of high-stakes terms, such as "defect" and "urgency," with clear, mutually agreed-upon definitions to minimize misinterpretation and its potential costs. These experiences highlighted an important lesson. While negotiation can sometimes feel like a zero-sum game, the most successful outcomes often arise from a communal alignment, where mutual benefit is possible. By emphasizing collaboration over adversarial negotiation, I worked to align language, culture, and logistics in supplier relationships. This approach led to earlier communication about potential disruptions and more joint problem-solving efforts.

This experience allowed me to negotiate more favorable terms, as I had demonstrated both my commitment to their success and my own. It also reshaped my understanding of price. Open dialogue helped uncover key considerations, allowing us to negotiate terms more effectively. Agreeing to a modest increase in per-unit costs in exchange for modular design inputs resulted in significant savings in downstream engineering costs. In retrospect, these barriers were not merely obstacles but opportunities to deepen engagement.

They taught me that the most fruitful deals often arise from patience, empathy, and the willingness to adapt. Also, to recognize that collaboration succeeds where inflexibility fails. While spreadsheets quantify outcomes, the art of negotiation also lies in observing the unspoken, particularly in the form of pauses, smiles, and shared frustrations. When aligned with clear goals and mutual respect, these subtleties can forge partnerships stronger than any contract. Yet, I also learned that not every barrier yields to goodwill because discernment is just as vital as openness.

Over time, I came to realize that building solid relationships is not merely a transactional tactic but the bedrock for navigating the labyrinthine world of international trade and negotiation. I discovered that trust is not an abstract ideal, but a tangible currency that anchors interactions, dissolves barriers, and creates a shared purpose, even when priorities diverge. I underestimated the profound impact of cultural nuance and unspoken expectations on a deal. A pivotal moment occurred during a tense negotiation with a supplier in Guangdong Province

(Guǎngdōng Shěng), where a misinterpretation of contractual terms nearly brought months of planning to a halt.

It was my Chinese counterpart, fluent in both Mandarin and English, who intervened. With a diplomat's finesse, she helped bridge the communication gap by clarifying linguistic nuances and highlighting differing priorities, thereby ensuring mutual understanding. Her ability to bridge these gaps did more than salvage the deal. It illuminated how cultural and linguistic fluency transforms communication from a functional exchange into a foundation for mutual respect. This lesson became a cornerstone of my approach to investing more in relationships.

I found it invaluable as I navigated the challenges of running a midsize operation. Unlike multinational corporations, which benefit from bulk ordering power, my customers typically deal in midsize quantities. This sometimes puts me at a disadvantage in price negotiations, but it also allows me to offer more personalized service and flexibility. Manufacturers often reserve their most competitive rates for clients who order containers rather than cartons. While this could be seen as a limitation, I chose to view it as an opportunity to innovate. Instead of approaching suppliers as a vendor seeking discounts, I positioned myself as a partner offering value beyond order volume.

During a sourcing trip to Ningbo, I suggested a staggered order plan to a textile supplier. They start with smaller initial batches and scale up production gradually if they meet our quality and delivery standards. To strengthen our partnership, we exchanged market insights on trending designs in North America, ensuring both sides had a clear understanding of the landscape. This helped shift our discussions toward shared success rather than a purely transactional relationship. By prioritizing transparency and flexibility, we negotiated mutually beneficial terms to balance cost efficiency with feasibility.

Ultimately, it wasn't just economies of scale that secured our agreement, but a foundation of trust and aligned goals. Of course, trust alone doesn't erase the realities of a competitive global market. Early setbacks taught me the importance of resourcefulness. I recall a disheartening episode with a ceramics factory in Jingdezhen (Jǐngdézhèn), where a sudden tax shift wiped out my slim profit margin. The manufacturer, while understanding our concerns, explained that financial constraints initially made renegotiation difficult.

Rather than ending discussions, I focused on strengthening our relationship. Through ongoing dialogue, including numerous tea conversations, I gained insight into their challenges. Challenges include rising labor costs and a declining interest in traditional craftsmanship among younger workers. After discussing their priorities, I adjusted my request by reducing the order size while shifting focus to their higher-end product line.

This request is better aligned with their commitment to artisanal craftsmanship. Because this compromise not only strengthened our partnership but also opened a premium market opportunity for my business. Through this experience, I've learned that perseverance isn't just persistence. It's the willingness to listen, adapt, and find alignment, even when it appears unlikely. I've also come to appreciate the importance of reputation in China, where trust and relationships often play a key role alongside formal agreements.

On another occasion, a shipment of handcrafted furniture arrived with minor veneer cracks that were not visible in the pre-shipment photos. Instead of escalating the issue, I worked with the supplier to identify the cause. Due to improper humidity control during transit, we agreed to share the cost of replacements. That decision, while costly upfront, ultimately helped build trust. Over time, it led to connections with a network of specialty workshops, expanding my access to unique products. While not every choice yields immediate returns, this experience suggested that integrity, when aligned with partners who share similar values, can also offer strategic benefits.

Each challenge taught me something new about problem-solving. That challenge was whether to refine quality control metrics, navigate payment structures, or learn when to compromise. Over time, I came to see negotiation less as a clash of opinions and more as a process of finding common ground. The complexities of international trade, which include taxes, logistics, and cultural divides, are inevitable. All at once, trust and strong relationships are essential for navigating these challenges. They must be paired with adaptability, expertise, and collaboration to turn obstacles into opportunities.

I deem there's a profound humility in recognizing that my success is never solitary. It's intertwined through the insights of a bilingual colleague, the flexibility of a supplier, and our shared commitment to rise above the transactional. This experience has shown me that global commerce isn't just about high-stakes deals but also about the steady, often unnoticed work of building trust. I'm referring to trust that consistently shows up, acts with respect, and finds ways to transform opposition into collaboration.

As someone deeply immersed in the complexities of importing goods from China, I've come to recognize that the process from factory to final delivery is far more intricate than most newcomers anticipate. While securing a reliable manufacturer is undeniably critical, it represents only the first step in a process riddled with hidden variables that quietly and sometimes disastrously inflate costs. While supplier negotiations play a key role in pricing, they are just one part of a complex equation. The realities of global trade include currency fluctuations, supply chain disruptions, regulatory changes, and shifting market demands. This can also heavily influence costs.

Succeeding in international business, particularly with Chinese suppliers, requires not only strong negotiation skills but also adaptability, strategic planning, and a deep understanding of these external factors. The primary driver of pricing unpredictability is the mercurial nature of raw material costs. I've observed that commodities like steel, plastics, and textiles are heavily influenced by global market forces, fluctuations in oil prices, trade embargoes, and even weather-related disruptions in key producing regions.

A manufacturer's initial quote, often presented as fixed during early negotiations, is a snapshot of material costs at a single moment in time.

By the time production commences weeks or months later, a surge in copper prices is due to mining strikes in Chile. Or a spike in polyester demand from fast-fashion brands can render that original estimate obsolete. From my personal experience, profit margins can shrink unexpectedly when suppliers, many of whom operate on thin margins, are forced to raise their prices. I've often seen them renegotiate terms mid-production due to rising costs, which are driven by market volatility and global factors, such as China's environmental regulations. In parallel, it has been seen that these regulations are necessary for sustainability. They've contributed to a decline in small-scale material processors since 2017. Thereby, tighten supply in some sectors.

Raw materials are just one aspect of the financial challenges associated with importing. Even when material costs stabilize, production timelines can still be delayed by logistical bottlenecks. Consider the ripple effects of a single delayed component. A factory in Shenzhen (Shēnzhèn) is experiencing delays due to a shortage of specialty semiconductors sourced internationally. This disrupts production timelines, causing finished goods to arrive at the port close to the Lunar New Year shutdown. This is a period when logistics operations across China slow significantly. As a result, products may face extended storage times, increased freight costs due to congestion, and potential penalty fees from retail partners if delivery deadlines are missed. Such disruptions highlight how dependencies on global supply chains and seasonal logistical challenges can compound delays and added costs. Based on my experience, initial cost analyses often overlook these disruptive effects, which can increase total expenses by 15–20% due to demurrage charges, expedited shipping fees, and lost sales.

Navigating China's regulatory environment can pose unique challenges, particularly in terms of compliance and logistics. One area that requires careful attention is the correct application of Incoterms. Misunderstanding these standardized shipping terms can lead to unintended risks or costs during transit. As an importer, if I accept "EXW" (Ex-Works) terms without fully understanding the implications. I might later realize that my initial $10/unit price ends up costing significantly more. Perhaps $18/unit after factoring in inland freight, customs brokerage, and unexpected port fees.

My experience has taught me to look beyond EXW's attractive initial price and carefully assess all downstream logistics expenses. This knowledge gap becomes especially significant when tariffs are introduced. An America-China trade war demonstrated how sudden tariff changes, especially Section 301 duties, could dramatically impact landed cost calculations. Even outside periods of heightened trade tensions, anti-dumping and countervailing duties can pose unexpected challenges for importers who lack awareness of these risks.

Cultural differences in business practices can sometimes create challenges in pricing transparency. Western companies often prefer fixed-price contracts for predictability. I've also learned that Chinese businesses may value flexibility (línghuóxìng) in negotiations. They see adjustments as a practical way to adapt to changing circumstances rather than a breach of contract. A supplier might initially agree to absorb a 10% increase in raw material costs during negotiations but later request price adjustments due to sustained cost pressures. They might justify this as necessary to maintain quality standards, acknowledging the genuine difficulties of managing unexpected costs in the supply chain.

Negotiations often involve nuanced communication and relationship dynamics that a strictly data-driven approach could overlook. Misinterpretations can sometimes lead to financial inefficiencies or strained partnerships, underscoring the importance of striking a balance between analytical and interpersonal skills in international trade. Looking back, I recall a situation where a client almost lost a $2M order by refusing a 3% price adjustment. At the time, we didn't realize the supplier's reference to "production difficulties" was a way to address unprecedented PVC cost hikes without directly stating it. The misunderstanding led to weeks of strained communication until the underlying issue was identified.

This was a situation where more transparent communication and greater flexibility on all sides could have resolved the problem earlier. It revealed that beneath these visible challenges lies the undercurrent of financial risk management. This is where Letters of Credit (LC) offer payment security. It also introduces cost considerations, conspicuous bank fees, and stringent documentation requirements. However, discrepancies in paperwork, such as a misspelled product code or a mismatched HS classification, can delay customs clearance and tie up funds, potentially leaving importers with difficult choices. Choices remarkably include accepting imperfect goods or losing deposits due to prolonged disputes. Fintech solutions, such as Alibaba's Trade Assurance (Ā lǐ Mào yì Bǎo zhàng), have significantly reduced transaction risks for buyers by offering automated escrow services and dispute resolution.

They are not without limitations, as illustrated by a 2022 case in which a buyer faced challenges despite the platform's safeguards. The supplier subcontracted production to an unapproved factory, resulting in non-compliant products and significant losses in EU markets. While the buyer recovered $50,000 through escrow protections, they still incurred $300,000 in losses due to unsellable inventory and legal fees. This case highlights that while fintech tools offer valuable risk mitigation, they should be complemented by thorough supplier due diligence and proactive supply chain oversight. It is a false economy to cut corners on quality assurance, particularly when bypassing third-party inspections in favor of trusted suppliers. While many suppliers maintain consistent quality, over-reliance without verification can lead to costly failures.

One importer faced a $120,000 loss when a shipment of supposedly stainless-steel kitchenware began rusting within weeks. Later, it was traced back to the factory, where cheaper alloys were substituted during a surge in nickel prices. This underscores the importance of balancing trust with verification because short-term savings can sometimes lead to far greater long-term costs. I'd say that these scenarios challenge the assumption that quality control is merely an optional cost rather than a necessary investment.

They also highlight how quality control in supply chains can be critical, especially for importers who managed COVID-era disruptions. It appeared they were more effective because they had already diversified their supplier networks across multiple regions. This diversification enabled them to address raw material shortages through strategic quality control measures. Leading importers today increasingly treat pricing as a dynamic equation rather than a fixed target. Many now incorporate real-time commodity indices, freight rate analytics, and geopolitical risk assessments into their pricing strategies to stay competitive and adaptive.

They build strong relationships with freight forwarders to access real-time port congestion data and engage bilingual legal advisors familiar with China's Contract Law. And to allocate contingency budgets to account for unexpected costs. Their approach to cost control relies on meticulous scenario planning, cultural understanding, and detailed mapping of the supply chain. While the visible aspects of global trade, specific negotiations, and logistics execution are critical. The long-term success often hinges on anticipating and preparing for the less obvious challenges beneath the surface.

8

Art as Cross-Cultural Catalyst

Meaningful connections across cultures require a deep understanding of history, values, and shared goals. This philosophical foundation finds its practical expression in a commitment to a specific, transformative partnership. I am committed to fostering a relationship between Black America and China that transcends transactional exchanges to become mutually beneficial, sustainable, and grounded in genuine respect. In our interconnected world, we must prioritize dialogues that transcend geographical and cultural divides. These connections can fuel both economic growth and mutual understanding, anchored not only in pragmatism but also in equity and fairness. This is when benefits are shared justly, and where every community's stories and aspirations are valued. Achieving this vision, however, demands a clear-eyed view of what constitutes genuine progress.

Actual progress is not achieved through transactions that sideline one culture for the benefit of another, but through collaboration that actively uplifts all participants. This requires a careful balance that we must strike, seizing the potential for new opportunities while ensuring the integrity and preservation of each culture is honored. The successes we have already witnessed are a testament to the power of this collaborative approach. The successes of our past cultural exchanges are direct results of this principle being put into action. Principles grounded through genuine partnerships, built on a foundation of empathy, mutual respect, and a shared vision. When we consciously recognize and leverage the distinct strengths inherent in each community, we move beyond simple cooperation. We lay the foundation for sustainable, shared advancement where growth is not only economic or logistical, but also deeply human and cultural. This principle of leveraging distinct strengths is precisely what allows us to appreciate the unique heritages at play.

I hold a profound admiration for Black America's rich cultural heritage. A legacy forged through resilience and creativity in response to historical adversity. This tradition finds its powerful expression in a vibrant tapestry of art, music, literature, and social movements, each thread telling a story of survival and innovation. When these two distinct yet equally powerful traditions are placed in dialogue, the potential for mutual enrichment becomes immense. On the other side of the globe, China's monumental achievements in manufacturing, technological advancement, and long-term strategic planning present a formidable capacity for global-scale partnership. Yet, dialogues between our communities often linger at a transactional level, neglecting deeper, more meaningful historical resonances. There is a significant, frequently overlooked, parallel between Black America's enduring pursuit of civil rights and China's own century-long journey of national revitalization following colonial exploitation. Both narratives are testaments to an extraordinary tenacity in the face of profound challenges. By acknowledging this shared spirit, we can transcend the limitations of simple cooperation and advance toward a more ambitious and reciprocal model of co-creation. To unlock this potential, we must move from abstract parallels to concrete, actionable initiatives.

To bring this vision to life, we must champion concrete initiatives built on three pillars: sustained dialogue, reciprocal education, and entrepreneurial innovation. One promising avenue is the organization of targeted trade missions, designed not merely as observational tours but as catalysts for deep, operational partnerships. Imagine delegations of Black American tech founders immersed in Shenzhen's (Shēnzhèn) dynamic manufacturing ecosystem, while Chinese industrial leaders engage with the innovative business models of Atlanta's (Yàtèlán dà)

Black-owned startups. Such exchanges could directly lead to joint ventures, where design ingenuity and production prowess merge to create products for a global market. Parallel to this, forging formal educational alliances between Historically Black Colleges and Universities (HBCUs) and Chinese academic institutions could yield co-developed curricula in cross-cultural leadership. These programs would equip a new generation of students with the nuanced skills required to navigate and influence our interconnected world, turning cultural competence into a strategic asset. Beyond the realms of commerce and academia, art offers a uniquely powerful medium for this connection.

Artistic initiatives possess a unique power to humanize cross-cultural collaboration, moving it from the theoretical to the tangible. Envision an exhibition where the bold, narrative-driven canvases of Black American painters enter a visual dialogue with the minimalist, philosophically rich strokes of Chinese calligraphers. Consider a music festival where the improvisational spirit of jazz intertwines with the ancient, meditative melodies of the Guqin (gǔqín), creating a new sonic landscape. On a grander scale, a public mural that merges the vibrant social commentary of the Harlem Renaissance (Hā lái mǔ Wén yì fù xīng) with the iconic symbolism of the Shang Dynasty would not flatten their distinct histories. Instead, it would create a powerful visual metaphor for how artistic expression can transcend geographical and temporal boundaries while honoring the unique essence of each tradition. The actual objective of such projects is to foster a nuanced dialogue. One that acknowledges intertwined historical struggles and celebrates points of convergence yet does not shy away from the complex challenges and conflicts that persist. This approach frames art not as a tool for erasure but as a catalyst for a more profound and honest mutual understanding. Skeptics may question the feasibility of such collaborations, given very real obstacles.

Critics rightly observe that profound cultural and economic disparities, compounded by competition for finite resources, present significant hurdles to cross-cultural collaboration. These challenges, however,

ART AS CROSS-CULTURAL CATALYST — |227|

should not be seen as insurmountable barriers but as imperatives for a more deliberate, patient, and inclusive approach. Rather than being discouraged by these hurdles, we can view them as a catalyst for more innovative and equitable partnerships. Building trust is paramount and must be actively pursued through a commitment to equity and fairness. This involves implementing fair profit-sharing models in joint ventures, ensuring the voices of marginalized individuals are centered in cultural projects, and co-developing policies that dismantle systemic obstacles. Ultimately, meaningful success is not achieved by overlooking differences but by leveraging them as a powerful catalyst for joint innovation and shared growth. Consider, for instance, the groundbreaking innovation that could emerge from a thoughtfully constructed partnership.

Consider the potential of a partnership between a Black American tech startup, grounded in the principles of equity, and a Shenzhen-based AI firm, renowned for its engineering prowess. By integrating a deep understanding of social justice imperatives with advanced technical capabilities, such an alliance could pioneer algorithms specifically designed to identify and mitigate racial bias. This collaboration, sustained by mutual respect and a shared commitment to ethical innovation, would serve as a powerful testament to how diversity, when authentically leveraged, becomes a vital resource for solving complex global challenges. The ultimate goal of such partnerships is to foster a new generation of global citizens.

Aims to cultivate a balanced and reciprocal partnership, one where a young person in Guangzhou (Guǎngzhōu) and a teenager in Tarboro, Georgia (Zuǒzhìyà Zhōu Tǎ'ěrbólè), can perceive each other not as distant strangers, but as essential collaborators in building a mutually envisioned future. Recognizing this connection requires a dedicated, long-term strategy that focuses on empowering the next generation. Critical to this effort is mentoring youth ambassadors to develop cross-cultural leadership skills, robustly supporting dual-language immersion programs to dismantle communication barriers, and creating inclusive digital and physical platforms where emerging leaders can co-design projects that honor their distinct heritages while forging a common ground. It is through this sustained commitment that we can truly enable them to shape a world where cooperation is the cornerstone of progress. This long-term vision informs the personal philosophy I bring to this engagement.

My engagement with China, like any meaningful relationship, is an intentional practice rooted in humility, curiosity, and the discipline of active listening. This approach transcends the simple search for common ground, demanding an honest acknowledgment of our differences. It is through this clear-eyed recognition that genuine understanding can emerge. I am therefore committed to navigating this space with a balance of open-mindedness and critical discernment, confronting challenges not as obstacles but as necessary steps to be addressed with respect and a shared dedication to mutual progress.

An art exhibition serves as a perfect microcosm to explore this philosophy in practice. It is a curated space where dialogue, reflection, and participation converge. By presenting a diverse tapestry of artists and their works, we do more than display creativity; we create a vital context for communities to question their own narratives and forge new connections. In this process, shared experiences, common values, and collective aspirations are not just uncovered but collectively shaped, reinforcing the profound role of art as a catalyst for mutual understanding. Let us envision the specific, hybrid artworks that such an exhibition could inspire.

Envision an exhibition where Black American artists create new work inspired by dialogues with the Chinese community. This collaborative space would give rise to powerful hybrid artworks that bridge continents and histories, creating a unique blend of cultures. For instance, a narrative quilt might interweave iconic figures from the Harlem Renaissance (Hā lái mǔ Wén yì fù xīng) with the intricate blue-and-white patterns of Ming Dynasty (Míng cháo) porcelain, crafting a visual story of cultural resilience and creative reinvention across time and space. In another piece, the rhythmic cadence of spoken word poetry could merge with the melodic structures of Cantonese opera, creating a multimedia soundscape that evokes universal themes of migration, home, and belonging. These are not merely objects for passive viewing; they are dynamic conduits for cross-cultural conversation. By engaging with these layered perspectives, viewers are invited to reflect on their own identities, discovering points of connection and difference that challenge and enrich their understanding of the world. To make this vision interactive, the exhibition must extend beyond observation to participation.

To deepen engagement beyond passive observation, the exhibition could incorporate interactive workshops and seminars that transform visitors into active co-creators. These sessions would serve as dynamic forums for cross-cultural discovery, fostering direct and personal dialogue. For example, a calligraphy workshop might invite participants to blend the expressive forms of Chinese characters with the rhythm and resonance of regional Black vernacular. Such an exercise does more than teach technique; it frames language as a living vessel of identity, challenging attendees to experiment with how meaning is shaped and shared across cultural lines. This participatory spirit can be channeled into preserving and sharing living history.

Meaningful cross-cultural exchange flourishes in intentionally curated spaces where shared human experience becomes the primary language. Envision a storytelling circle where elders from Black American and Chinese communities offer their personal narratives. These are not merely isolated anecdotes, but living testimony, grounding abstract historical forces in the intimate reality of a single life. Their stories reveal how cultural memory, forged in the fires of systemic challenge and triumph, is actively woven into a resilient fabric of resilience. This deliberate act of sharing this oral tradition can transcend simple reminiscence to become a powerful, communal rite of preservation. It ensures that the wisdom of the past is not lost but is instead passed, with purpose, to the hands and hearts of subsequent generations, creating an unbroken chain of identity and strength. Culinary traditions offer another accessible yet profound avenue for this shared discovery.

Simultaneously, a collaborative cooking workshop could offer a tangible, sensory parallel to this narrative exchange. By pairing the hearty comfort of Southern soul food with the complex, piquant flavors of Sichuan (Sìchuān) cuisine, participants engage in a direct exploration of history on the plate. Both culinary traditions are profound products of migration, trade, and adaptation; each dish tells a story of available ingredients, cultural fusion, and the enduring human desire for flavor and nourishment. Such a workshop moves beyond taste to reveal how shared forces of history have distinctively, yet resonantly, shaped two seemingly distant culinary histories. When woven together, these diverse activities form a cohesive and robust framework for exchange.

This approach weaves together diverse activities into a single, unified narrative, ensuring that each element, whether an art exhibition, a workshop, or a trade mission, can contribute to a coherent and meaningful dialogue. By anchoring these initiatives within the shared purpose of cultural exchange, the framework creates thematic continuity and narrative coherence, allowing different forms of engagement to reinforce one another. This method not only strengthens the overall impact but also deepens the connection between participants, transforming isolated interactions into a sustained, mutually enriching conversation.

These initiatives are conceived not as isolated events, but as essential strands woven into the fabric of a continuous and evolving partnership. They move beyond a superficial exchange of ideas, inviting participants into a shared space of active co-creation. It is through this dynamic process that, working collectively to build something new, a deeper, more personal form of mutual understanding and enrichment naturally emerges and takes hold. The creative synergies born from such exchanges promise to resonate far beyond a single event.

The ripple effects of such collaboration promise to extend far beyond the gallery walls, forging new creative pathways. Imagine a dialogue where a Black American painter, steeped in narratives of social justice and abstraction, immerses themselves in the meditative discipline of traditional Chinese ink-wash techniques alongside a master in Shanghai. Their fusion could yield a revolutionary visual language where the fluid grace of ink captures the rhythmic intensity of the African diaspora. Similarly, when Chinese ceramicists, guardians of a millennia-old craft, engage deeply with the vibrant symbolism and Afrofuturist visions of Black visionary art, the results are transformative. They might re-envision classic porcelain vases with motifs drawn from the Gullah Geechee coast or incorporate forms that challenge conventional aesthetics. These are not mere stylistic borrowings, but profound, equitable exchanges where each tradition informs and elevates the other. When pursued with intentionality and mutual respect, such partnerships vividly demonstrate how global artistic dialogue serves as a vital catalyst, pushing creative practices into uncharted and enriching territory.

These cross-cultural exchanges are far more than symbolic gestures; they are the very catalysts for artistic and innovative evolution. The trust and mutual understanding forged through art provide a durable foundation for ventures that respectfully bridge heritage and progress. Imagine a generation of students, inspired by such an exhibition, who go on to launch a tech startup blending creative vision with Shenzhen's manufacturing prowess, or who produce a groundbreaking theatrical work that weaves the disciplined artistry of Beijing opera with the dynamic energy of hip-hop. Ultimately, the significance lies in this potent alchemy. This is where art serves as the essential groundwork for collaboration, enabling partners to honor their distinct traditions while co-creating a dynamic and inclusive future. Realizing this potential requires a dedicated ecosystem of collaborators.

This vision is brought to life through a collaborative ecosystem of diverse stakeholders, each contributing a vital perspective. Artists share personal and communal narratives, fostering empathy and a direct human connection. Curators design environments that are not merely for display but are dynamic platforms for critical dialogue and inquiry. Educators build essential bridges between artistic expression and its tangible social impact, framing art as a tool for understanding and change. Community leaders act as stewards, ensuring that local contexts and voices remain central to the project's development, grounding it in authenticity.

This active participation extends directly to the public through immersive, hands-on workshops. A visitor might find themselves grinding pigments alongside a muralist, discovering the cultural resonance of colors like ochre and indigo. In another session, participants could use generative coding to deconstruct and reinterpret the complex rhythms of jazz, translating musical heritage into a new digital language. These experiences intentionally blur the traditional line between creator and audience, transforming observation into a collaborative process. By demystifying the creative process, they empower every participant, demonstrating that cultural exchange is not a passive spectacle but a living dialogue to which everyone can contribute their unique voice. A key institution within this ecosystem has played a crucial role in providing authenticity and depth.

A pivotal force in this initiative is the National Alliance of Artists from Historically Black Colleges and Universities (NAAHBCU). Founded in 1999, the alliance has dedicated itself to elevating Black artistic excellence, acting as both a catalyst and a sustainer of creative expression across generations. The profound authenticity and contextual depth NAAHBCU bring were vividly illustrated in the 2023 Shanghai exhibition, "We Stand Together" (Wǒmen zài yīqǐ). Far more than a simple display, the event served as a dynamic forum for cross-cultural exchange, foregrounding the innovative visions and significant contributions of Black artists on a global stage. My role within this partnership involves intentional cultural translation.

My role as the inaugural international spokesperson in China for the NAAHBCU extends far beyond simply promoting artists; it is a mission of cultural translation and representation. I am tasked with thoughtfully contextualizing Black American art for Chinese audiences, a process that demands crafting new narratives to bridge profound cultural and historical divides. The exhibition itself is conceived not as a static display, but as a living, dynamic showcase. We treat each artwork as a platform for critical inquiry, inviting viewers to engage in a deeper dialogue. The aim is to significantly increase the visibility and understanding of Black American art within China, fostering a lasting appreciation that contributes to a more inclusive global artistic conversation. The 2023 exhibition provided a powerful case study of this approach in action.

The "We Stand Together" (Wǒmen zài yīqǐ) exhibition served as a dynamic crucible for cross-cultural dialogue, transforming the gallery into a space of active engagement rather than passive observation. Chinese visitors did not merely view the art; they immersed themselves in it, forming personal connections that bridged the continents of their experiences. In Hasaan A. Kirkland's "Natural American Spirit-Sawubona" (Zìrán Měiguó zhī líng Sàwū Bónà), they explored the layered symbolism of identity and communal recognition, finding points of convergence with their own cultural concepts of spirit and greeting. The portrait "Miss Doris" (Duǒ ruì sī xiǎo jiě) became a focal point for discussing the representation of womanhood, with visitors drawing nuanced parallels to the evolving roles and depictions of women in Chinese society across generations. Similarly, the introspective and spiritually charged "On My Celestial Journey" (Wǒ de tiānguó zhī lǚ) prompted deep reflection on universal questions of belief and the human search for meaning. These themes resonated with the personal philosophies of the Shanghai audience. This profound engagement demonstrated the exhibition's success in creating a shared space where art served as a conduit for mutual understanding and discovery. Importantly, the exhibition also created a space for confronting complex histories.

The exhibition did not shy away from presenting works of profound and challenging historical reckoning. Roymieco Carter's pieces, "White Lion" (bái shīzi) and "Clotilda" (Kè luò tí dá), serve as stark archaeological inquiries into the Atlantic slave trade, using their visual language to excavate layers of collective memory and folklore born from exploitation. In a powerful parallel, Dwight Smith's "Being Black in America Can Drive You Crazy" (zài měiguó dāng hēirén néng bǎ nǐ bīfēng) shifts the focus to the contemporary psychological landscape, using its visceral composition to articulate the enduring strains of Black American history and the complex journey toward liberation. Together, these artists moved beyond mere representation, engaging in a deep, critical dialogue with themes of culture, identity, and narrative itself. They compellingly challenged the conventional, often sanitized, historical accounts, insisting instead on a more truthful and unflinching examination. This exchange is never a one-way street, but a reciprocal process that enriches both sides.

This cultural exchange functions not as a simple transaction but as a symbiotic dialogue, where both communities contribute and gain a fresh perspective. A powerful illustration was the 2017 "Rhythms of America" tour, which brought an HBCU jazz ensemble to Beijing's concert halls. There, the syncopated rhythms of jazz improvisation meshed with the expressive fluidity of traditional Chinese opera, creating a new, hybrid sound that resonated with audiences. The reciprocal nature of this engagement was further revealed in the visual arts. One painter described her revelation when a Chinese viewer interpreted the bold strokes of her abstract work through the lens of Taoist balance. A perspective that, while unexpected, deepened her own appreciation for the piece's universal language. Similarly, Chinese participants found that engaging directly with the HBCU legacy enabled them to move beyond reductive Hollywood stereotypes, leading to a recognition of the rich intellectualism and profound depth inherent in Black artistic traditions. These moments of shared discovery demonstrate how genuine cultural exchange can challenge assumptions and foster a more nuanced, mutually understanding perspective, revealing the true, human-scale impact of cultural diplomacy.

True diplomacy transcends the formal arenas of state dinners and signed treaties. Its most profound work often unfolds in the quiet, unscripted moments of human connection. It is the shared understanding that passes between a Shanghai grandmother, unconsciously humming a spiritual she just heard from a visiting choir, and the musicians who recognize the universal language of solace in her voice. Simultaneously, it thrives in the studio of a young Atlanta artist, whose hands, guided by the forms of ancient Ming pottery, find a new visual language that crosses centuries and continents. These intimate exchanges, where culture is personally lived and remade, are the very bedrock upon which lasting mutual understanding is built. To build upon these intimate connections, we must commit to long-term, structural support.

The path forward demands a sustained and deliberate commitment. We must broaden the scope of cultural exchange programs, fortify institutional partnerships, and, most critically, create platforms where underrepresented voices are not only heard but are integral to the conversation. Throughout history, Black American art has served as a profound conduit for empathy, translating complex human experiences into a universal language that bridges profound divides. While the journey toward genuine inclusion is fraught with systemic barriers and inherent complexities, this artistic tradition offers a vital blueprint. It invites us to challenge ourselves to co-create a future where diversity is not merely acknowledged but actively celebrated as the very engine of our collective advancement. The exhibition in Shanghai stands as a powerful call to action, not just appreciation.

The NAAHBCU exhibition in Shanghai does more than display art; it ignites a future where empathy and equity can flourish. Realizing this vision, however, demands more than passive appreciation. It requires deliberate action, genuine accountability, and a sustained commitment to systemic change. Within the gallery, the artworks generate a dynamic space where ideas and emotions converge, fostering empathy and directly challenging entrenched biases. Each visitor encounter becomes part of an evolving dialogue, a reminder that art is not a static artifact but a living force, continually capable of reshaping perspectives and inspiring tangible transformation. This call to action is rooted in art's fundamental power to foster essential dialogue.

Art is fundamentally a dialogue through which a dynamic exchange of perspectives takes place, challenging assumptions and deepening our collective understanding. When the art world marginalizes Black American narratives, it forfeits critical insights, leaving audiences with an incomplete view of history and the human experience. This exclusion silences essential voices and narrows our cultural imagination. Consider the robust conversation that could unfold if Jacob Lawrence's Migration Series were exhibited alongside the work of Chinese artist Liu Xiaodong (Liú Xiǎodōng), who also depicts migrant laborers. Placed in dialogue, their art would reveal profound, shared themes of displacement, dignity, and resilience across disparate cultures. Such curatorial choices transcend mere representation, creating a space where universal struggles and aspirations resonate, thereby fostering a more nuanced and empathetic global discourse. The "We Stand Together" (Wǒmen zài yīqǐ) exhibition embraced this by rejecting marginalization.

The "We Stand Together" (Wǒmen zài yīqǐ) exhibition derives its power from a foundational refusal to compartmentalize. Instead of presenting Black American art as a niche or peripheral category, it positions this creative tradition as vital to the broader landscape of global artistic expression. This curatorial approach stands in contrast to the art world's frequently evolving, yet often inconsistent, relationship with diversity. While major institutions have made strides in acquiring more works by Black artists, that is usually in response to public demand, and accurate equity remains elusive. Token inclusion is not the same as meaningful integration. Achieving the latter demands a critical re-examination of the very foundations of art valuation: we must ask which works have been historically canonized, which narratives have been systematically preserved, and, most importantly, who has held the power to make these decisions. Accurate equity is not merely about adding diverse pieces to a collection; it is about transforming the criteria, context, and power structures that determine value itself. It is this very commitment to substantive partnership that made the exhibition possible and points the way forward.

The partnership behind the "We Stand Together" (Wǒmen zài yīqǐ) exhibition, which unites the National Alliance of Artists from Historically Black Colleges and Universities (NAAHBCU) with the Shanghai American Consulate, Shanghai People's Association for Friendship with Foreign Countries (SPAFFC), Jiaozhan, Harmony Arts Gallery, Shanghai Municipal Administration of Culture and Tourism, West Bund Fine Arts, and Shanghai-America Direct Import & Export Co., Ltd, marks a substantive evolution in cross-cultural engagement. This initiative moves beyond superficial representation, positioning Black artists as essential collaborators in the creation of cultural narratives rather than as subjects for interpretation. While the path toward full equity in the global art world remains a long one, this collaboration has successfully established a foundational framework for achieving this goal. It demonstrates a working model for dialogue that is both inclusive and empathetic, proving that shared creative endeavors can build bridges of genuine understanding and mutual respect.

9

Legacies of Interconnected Resilience

For Black American entrepreneurs, global trade is a landscape of unseen barriers. The challenge isn't just navigating supply chains. It's penetrating the complex systems of trust and coordination that sustain modern commerce. The "hidden costs" are more than just financial obligations. They are cultural and representational, eroding profitability and excluding us from the main stage of international exchange.

As a Black entrepreneur operating in competitive markets, I've learned that these costs, including customs delays, demurrage fees, and unpredictable tariffs, disproportionately impact those with the least capital and institutional support. But the exclusion runs deeper. It's about the absence of our voices in global dialogues and our products from the world's largest trade fairs. This raises a critical question in a world defined by the U.S.-China dynamic. How can Black America build direct, resilient pathways to economic and cultural self-determination?

The financial hidden costs act as a silent tax on ambition. A small business owner in Chicago might source a container of artisanal goods from China, calculating a profit margin based on a seemingly straightforward Free on Board (FOB) price. But this is where the illusion begins. The initial quote does not account for the labyrinth of subsequent expenses, including peak season surcharges that triple ocean freight rates overnight, customs brokerage fees that multiply when documentation is deemed non-compliant, or demurrage charges accrued when a shipment is held for a random inspection. These, of course, seem like a more frequent occurrence for lesser-known importers. For a large corporation, these are operational line items. For an entrepreneur operating on a razor-thin margin, each unforeseen fee is an existential threat. The lack of generational wealth or easy access to flexible lines of credit means there is no financial cushion to absorb these shocks. A single delayed shipment, accompanied by storage and penalty fees, can cripple a business for a quarter, force layoffs, or even lead to its closure. This financial precarity is the first and most immediate layer of exclusion, a filter that systematically weeds out those without deep-pocketed institutional backing.

However, to stop at the financial is to misunderstand the whole architecture of the barrier. The more insidious cost is the representational and cultural exclusion. This manifests in two critical ways: absence from the stages of global economic dialogue and distortion within the narratives that define cross-cultural exchange.

Consider the China International Import Expo (CIIE) (Zhōngguó Guójì Jìnkǒu Bólǎnhuì) in Shanghai, a colossal event designed to connect the world with Chinese buyers. As I walked the halls teeming with European luxury brands, Southeast Asian agro-exporters, and Latin American tech startups, the void was palpable. Where were the pavilions for Black American SMEs? Where were the delegations showcasing our innovations in green technology, healthcare, or consumer goods? This absence is not accidental. It is a symptom of a more profound disconnect. Black American trade and cultural organizations often lack established, funded liaison relationships with Chinese chambers of commerce and state-level trade bodies, which can facilitate participation in such events. Our business leaders are not embedded in the networks where invitations are extended and partnerships are seeded. Consequently, when Chinese buyers and officials survey the global market, the vibrant and innovative ecosystem of Black American enterprise is rendered invisible. This is a catastrophic hidden cost: the cost of missed opportunities, of relationships never formed, and of a multi-trillion-dollar market forming without our input or inclusion.

This representational void is compounded by a cultural narrative that flattens and misrepresents Black America in China. When a Shanghai student's understanding of America is forged through Hollywood blockbusters and Silicon Valley tech news, they receive a profoundly incomplete picture. The narrative centers on a white, mainstream America, inadvertently erasing the 40 million Black citizens whose contributions in policy, art, science, and social innovation are foundational to the modern American identity. Algorithms on platforms like TikTok, while popularizing Black dance trends, often fail to elevate Black thought leadership in fields such as economics, political theory, or entrepreneurship. The result is a distorted lens through which China views America. A lens that overlooks a natural partner in navigating issues of systemic inequity, community building, and resilient innovation.

This dynamic creates a vicious cycle. Without direct representation in trade, our cultural narrative is shaped by third-party intermediaries, often replicating the very stereotypes we seek to overcome. Without a nuanced cultural narrative that highlights our full humanity and capability, it becomes harder to be taken seriously as strategic economic partners. The hidden cost could give the appearance of the ability to define ourselves and our value proposition on the global stage, particularly in the world's second-largest economy.

This brings us to the central, daunting question: How can Black America build direct, resilient pathways in a world shaped by the U.S.-China dynamic? We cannot simply replicate the models of large, established corporations or rely on traditional American institutions that have historically underserved our communities. The solution requires a strategy of intentional circumvention and parallel institution-building.

First, we must leverage technology to create transparency and bypass informational gatekeepers. The traditional path to engaging with Chinese manufacturing involves layers of brokers and intermediaries, each adding cost and obscuring the ground truth. We can disrupt this by collectively investing in and utilizing digital platforms that offer direct, verified access to suppliers. Blockchain-enabled supply chain tracking can provide the transparency needed to build trust remotely, allowing a small business in Atlanta (Yàtèlándà) to monitor production in Shenzhen (Shēnzhèn) in real-time, verifying quality and timing without requiring a physical presence. Cooperative buying models, where several small Black-owned businesses pool their orders, can achieve the economies of scale necessary to be taken seriously by overseas manufacturers and secure better terms, effectively creating our own collective bargaining power.

Second, we must weaponize cultural exchange as a form of strategic economic diplomacy. The success of the NAAHBCU art exhibition in Shanghai was not merely an aesthetic victory; it was a proof of concept. It demonstrated that there is a Chinese appetite for authentic, nuanced engagement with Black American culture beyond commercialized hip-hop. We must build on this by fostering direct, institution-to-institution partnerships. Imagine a formal collaboration between the National Black Chamber of Commerce and its counterparts in Guangdong (Guǎngdōng) province. Or an annual "Black America-China Innovation Summit," rotating between cities like Atlanta (Yàtèlándà) and Hangzhou, focusing not on generalities but on specific sectors like fintech, sustainable agriculture, or creative industries. These are not mere cultural jaunts; they are the scaffolding upon which trust is built and deals are made. They are the forums where we can articulate our value proposition directly, unfiltered by the often-limiting narratives of the broader U.S.-China relationship.

Finally, we must adopt a posture of strategic agility within the U.S.-China rivalry. The constant tension and shifting tariff regimes between the two superpowers are typically framed as risks. For us, they can also be an opportunity. Our relative lack of entrenched interests can be a perverse advantage, allowing us to be more nimble. While large corporations are locked into complex, long-term supply chains in China, Black

American businesses can pioneer a model of multi-nodal sourcing. This means building relationships not only in China but simultaneously in alternative hubs like Vietnam, Mexico, and Eastern Europe, and even exploring reshoring opportunities to Black-majority cities in the American South. This diversified approach builds inherent resilience, ensuring that a geopolitical shock in one region does not spell our demise. It allows us to engage with China not from a position of dependency, but from a position of strategic choice.

Building these direct pathways is not about rejecting America, but about claiming our full agency within it and on the world stage. It is about recognizing that our community's survival has always depended on creating our own systems when those in power excluded us. The hidden costs of exclusion in global trade are immense, but they are not insurmountable. By building our own tables through technological empowerment, strategic cultural diplomacy, and agile, diversified economic models, we can transform the U.S.-China dynamic from a force that marginalizes us into an ecosystem where we can not only compete but thrive, writing ourselves into the next chapter of global exchange on our own terms.

On the surface, shipping appears to be a straightforward process. Goods leave a factory and arrive at their destination. Beneath this apparent simplicity lies a volatile and unforgiving labyrinth of hidden costs, regulatory pitfalls, and geopolitical gambits. Seemingly, a web of systemic risk that can devastate the undercapitalized. For Black American entrepreneurs, who often face systemic barriers to capital and generational wealth, this volatility isn't an abstract economic concept; it is a direct and immediate threat to their business's survival. The playing field is not level, and the labyrinth of global trade is riddled with traps that disproportionately ensnare those without the financial cushion to absorb unforeseen shocks.

Take tariffs, a tool of economic policy that becomes a weapon of uncertainty for small businesses. A product imported from China might face a manageable 25% duty today, only for that rate to double overnight during a trade dispute, as happened frequently during the America-China trade war in the late 2010s. For a large corporation with diversified supply chains and legal teams, this is a calculable risk. For a small, Black-owned business operating on razor-thin margins, such a sudden cost increase can erase profitability for an entire product line. There is no reserve fund to cover the gap; the choice becomes between absorbing a catastrophic loss and breaching contracts, which would result in losing customer trust. This volatility exposes a fundamental inequity: the systems designed to protect domestic industries or manage international relations often do so at the expense of the most vulnerable participants in the global marketplace. The uncertainty stifles long-term planning, discourages investment, and forces entrepreneurs into a reactive and defensive posture, from which it is difficult to build sustainable growth.

This systemic risk multiplies and compounds across the entire supply chain. The advertised freight charge is merely the entry fee, a baseline quickly inflated by a cascade of ancillary costs. Port fees, customs brokerage charges, and insurance premiums form a hidden tributary system that steadily erodes profit margins. Consider shipments delayed by the predictable yet disruptive Southeast Asian monsoon seasons. For the unprepared, these delays incur demurrage fees, which are charges for the prolonged use of port space, which can accumulate rapidly. Newer importers, often lacking the mentorship and institutional knowledge that comes with established networks, frequently overlook this cost in their pricing strategies. When unaccounted for, these fees can turn a profitable shipment into a significant loss.

Similarly, warehousing costs, a critical node in the logistics chain, are frequently underestimated in initial budgets and vary significantly by region. Renting storage space near the congested ports of Los Angeles commands a premium far above space in rural Texas. While proximity to key entry points can justify the higher cost by speeding up distribution, this calculation is far from foolproof. A shipment delayed by a random Customs inspection, a common hurdle particularly for goods from certain countries, can force a business to pay for weeks of unplanned storage. The popular "just-in-time" inventory model, while cost-efficient in stable conditions, crumbles under such disruptions. The 2021 Suez Canal blockage, which stranded an estimated $9 billion in daily trade, served as a stark reminder that a single point of failure in a highly interconnected system can have global repercussions. For a small business relying on timely deliveries, a week-long delay can mean missing a critical sales season, resulting in dead stock and a potentially irreparable blow to its reputation.

The ongoing Red Sea crisis, escalated in late 2023 and early 2024, is not a distant headline but a live demonstration of this geopolitical fragility. Attacks on commercial vessels in the Bab el-Mandeb Strait have significantly disrupted one of the world's most critical maritime trade routes. For large conglomerates, this might mean rerouting ships around the Cape of Good Hope, adding days and significant fuel costs to a journey becomes an inconvenience, but one that is manageable. For a small, Black-owned business, the implications are far graver. The resulting months-long delays ripple through their entire operation: pre-ordered stock sits unused, storage costs skyrocket, and customers become increasingly frustrated, potentially taking their business elsewhere. This is not merely a logistical problem; it is an existential threat. The entrepreneur, already facing systemic barriers to securing affordable financing, now must navigate a crisis that was entirely beyond their control or foresight, further straining their limited resources and threatening their hard-won market foothold.

The resilience required to survive and thrive in this environment, therefore, is not found in avoiding risk, which is an impossible feat, but in strategic adaptation and proactive risk management. This necessitates a fundamental shift from a reactive to a predictive and agile operational model. For the underserved entrepreneur, this strategic navigation is not merely a business tactic; it is a necessary form of self-preservation in a tumultuous global system.

The first pillar of this resilience is diversification. Reducing reliance on a single country or supplier is paramount. This involves actively cultivating partnerships with factories in alternative locations, such as Vietnam or Mexico, alongside existing Chinese suppliers. While the feasibility depends on company size and industry, even small businesses can begin this process by sourcing non-critical components or exploring small-batch production in new markets. This creates a buffer, ensuring that a sudden tariff change or regional disruption does not cripple the entire operation.

The second pillar is contractual and procedural clarity. Leveraging internationally recognized Incoterms (International Commercial Terms) is not just best practice; it is a shield. These standards explicitly outline the responsibilities of buyers and sellers for risks and costs, preventing costly misunderstandings with suppliers. Who is responsible for insurance when the goods are on the high seas? Who pays the port fees? Incoterms provide the answers. Furthermore, negotiating "all-in" contracts with logistics providers can consolidate a myriad of unpredictable fees into a more stable, predictable rate, providing crucial cost stability for businesses that cannot afford financial surprises.

The third pillar is technological empowerment. In today's tumultuous global markets, leveraging technology is no longer optional; it is a key differentiator that can level the playing field. Predictive analytics can enhance tariff forecasting and optimize shipping routes, enabling businesses to anticipate disruptions rather than merely react to them. Inventory management software helps reduce overstocking and lower exorbitant storage costs. Trust platform-enabled tracking systems provide real-time visibility into shipments, empowering businesses to respond proactively to delays and manage customer expectations effectively. For Black entrepreneurs, who may lack the extensive traditional networks of their counterparts, these digital tools can serve as a force multiplier, providing the data-driven insight and operational control needed to compete.

In conclusion, the labyrinth of global trade, with its tariffs, shipping volatility, and geopolitical crises, is a system inherently stacked against those with limited capital. For Black American entrepreneurs, these challenges are not isolated incidents but interconnected manifestations of systemic risk that compound historical inequities. However, within this reality lies a path forward. By embracing strategic adaptation through deliberate diversification, contractual clarity, and technological adoption, these entrepreneurs can transform vulnerability into resilience. This is more than a business strategy; it is an act of forging resilience in the face of systemic pressure, ensuring that their businesses not only survive the complexities of global commerce but also find a way to reshape their place within it.

My own understanding of this interconnected world began with a narrow, distinctly American perspective of China. It was a collage of media portrayals, fortune cookies, and symbols, such as the Great Wall. This was a monochrome sketch of a civilization built on centuries of rich history. My America was a place where China was often a headline, a rival, or a source of affordable goods, but rarely a complex tapestry of human stories. My perceptions were filtered through a lens polished by Hollywood narratives that oscillated between exotic mysticism and Red Scare anxieties, and by well-intentioned but shallow cultural festivals in my own city, where the entirety of Chinese philosophy was sometimes reduced to a paper lantern and a sugary cookie. I carried these mental shortcuts with me, unaware that they were not just incomplete but actively blocking the light of a deeper understanding. I saw the silhouette of a nation but knew nothing of the people living within its contours, their ambitions, their sorrows, or the weight of their history.

That sketch began to gain color in graduate school, through challenging courses and late-night debates that cracked the shell of my certainty. It was there that I first encountered theories that challenged the very notion of a single, linear path to modernity. But the most transformative influence was Dr. Hong Zhaohui, my faculty advisor from Hangzhou. He didn't just lecture. He painted living portraits of China on moonlit lakes where poets floated wine cups and of Shanghai's neon-lit ambition. In his office, surrounded by teetering stacks of books, he would shift seamlessly from dissecting the socioeconomic impacts of

Shenzhen's Special Economic Zone to recounting the Legend of the White Snake at West Lake (Xī Hú Báishé Zhuàn), her tragedy echoing across a thousand years of Chinese folklore. He possessed a scholar's mind and a storyteller's heart. "China," he told me one afternoon, the scent of oolong tea hanging in the air, "can't be understood through simplistic frameworks. Its depth comes from layers of history, culture, and a transformation so rapid it gives its people cultural whiplash. You must engage with it on its terms, not from the comfort of your own assumptions."

This was more than an academic advisory; it was an invitation to a different way of knowing. Dr. Hong's mentorship was the catalyst that led me to a study abroad program in the summer of 2000. Stepping off the plane in Shanghai was like walking into a future I hadn't been prepared for. The air itself felt different with a mixture of thick humidity, diesel, and a palpable, kinetic energy. The Pudong airport was a monument to aspiration, all soaring glass and steel, a stark contrast to the more familiar, utilitarian airports I was accustomed to. This was not the ancient, ossified China of my imagination. It was a nation in a ferocious hurry, and I was suddenly in its midst, my textbook Mandarin feeling stiff and artificial in my mouth.

The intellectual frameworks from my urban studies courses collided with the visceral reality of Beijing's hutongs. Walking through those narrow, winding alleys was a sensory overload in the best possible way. The air was a symphony of scents of cumin-spiced lamb skewers (yángròu chuàn) sizzling over open coals, the faint, sweet smell of rotting persimmons from a nearby courtyard, and the ever-present hint of coal dust. I heard the clatter of mahjong tiles from behind faded wooden doors, the laughter of children chasing a ball, and the rhythmic scraping of a shopkeeper sweeping his doorstep. Here, the contrast was not just visual but deeply human. These ancient lanes, the lifeblood of old Beijing, were nestled in the shadow of gleaming skyscrapers, like fragile roots being paved over by concrete. I saw an older woman meticulously tending to a pot of orchids on her windowsill, her world a quiet courtyard home that had housed her family for generations, while just beyond the alley's mouth, the city throbbed with the relentless beat of progress. It made me wonder about the invisible costs of this transformation, about the families and memories that were being displaced to make way for a new Chinese dream.

It was in this context that I met factory workers who had migrated from agrarian provinces like Anhui (Ānhuī) and Henan (Hénán). Their stories were not told in grand narratives but in quiet conversations and observed moments. A young man, no older than me, spoke of leaving his village's rice paddies for the deafening roar of a textile factory in Guangdong (Guǎngdōng), his hands now skilled at operating machinery his father could never have imagined. His search for opportunity, his endurance in the face of grueling work, and the loneliness of being far from home echoed with a haunting familiarity. It resonated with the resilience of my own ancestors, who fled the terror of the Jim Crow South during the Great Migration, trading the brutal certainty of sharecropping for the uncertain promise of Chicago's stockyards or Detroit's assembly lines. They, too, were internal migrants, driven by a similar, fundamental yearning for dignity and a better life.

This wasn't an academic parallel, but a profound connection that struck a chord deep within me. I began to see that both groups, Black Americans in the 20th century and Chinese migrant workers in the 21st century, were navigating systems not entirely designed for their success. They faced systemic marginalization, building thriving cultural and economic spaces in the face of immense obstacles. For Black communities, it was redlining and legalized segregation that confined them to specific neighborhoods, yet could not suppress the flowering of the Harlem Renaissance (Hāléi Wényì Fùxīng). For the Chinese workers, it was the hukou residency system that officially designated them as outsiders in the very cities they were building, restricting their access to healthcare and education for their children, creating a floating population of hundreds of millions. Their struggles were distinct, shaped by vastly different historical and political forces. Political forces where one is rooted in the legacy of chattel slavery and legalized racism, the other in the tumultuous transition from a socialist command economy to state-led capitalism. But their resilience was a shared language, a universal grammar of human endurance.

In that summer of 2000, surrounded by the dizzying contrasts of a China hurtling into the future, my perspective irrevocably shifted. I was no longer an outsider looking in, collecting data points on a foreign culture. The distance between my Black American experience and the lives I was witnessing collapsed into a profound sense of kinship. I was beginning to see myself as a bridge, not in an arrogant sense of having all the answers, but in a humble recognition that our stories, though separated by an ocean, were flowing into the same human delta. The narrow American sketch had been replaced by a living, breathing, and beautifully complex portrait, and I now felt a responsibility to myself, to my ancestors, and to my new friends to help others see beyond the monochrome.

In the 21st century, China has launched a series of spectacular events to showcase its rise, including the 2008 Beijing Olympics, the 2010 Shanghai World Expo, and the 2018 China International Import Expo (CIIE) (Zhōngguó Guójì Jìnkǒu Bólǎnhuì). Each was a masterclass in soft power, a narrative of global engagement and modernization.

And in each, I observed a conspicuous absence: Black America.

At the Olympics, the world marveled at the harmony of pagodas and skyscrapers. At the Expo, pavilions showcased global creativity, ranging from Nordic sustainability to African textiles. At the CIIE, one of the world's largest trade fairs, I scanned directories of 3,600 exhibitors and found a notable lack of representation from Black American SMEs, tech startups, and creatives.

This was more than a missed marketing opportunity. It was a failure of imagination. Where were the collaborations blending jazz with traditional Chinese music? The dialogues between Atlanta's (Yàtèlándà) tech pioneers and Shenzhen's (Shēnzhèn) manufacturing ecosystems? When a Shanghai student's view of America is shaped solely by Hollywood and Silicon Valley, the contributions of 40 million Black citizens are erased. This absence perpetuates cycles of marginalization, just as China's consumer class, which now numbers 700 million, becomes the world's most critical market.

The 2008 Beijing Olympics were not merely a sporting event; it was a meticulously choreographed argument for China's return to global centrality. The opening ceremony, a breathtaking symphony of synchronized human precision and ancient cultural symbolism, presented a nation seamlessly blending a 5,000-year-old civilization with hypermodern ambition. The narrative was one of harmonious synthesis: traditional calligraphy brushes gave way to futuristic LED scrolls, and the Bird's Nest stadium stood as a monument to this new era. The world was invited to witness a China that was both profoundly cultured and powerfully modern, a reliable and capable partner on the world stage. Yet, within this curated harmony, a specific dissonance resonated for me. As I watched the parade of nations and the celebration of global unity, I asked: Where is the Black American component in this dialogue? The cultural performances highlighted China's 56 ethnic groups, showcasing internal diversity, but the global Black diaspora, particularly the distinct cultural force of Black America, was a silent spectator. The athletic prowess of Black American Olympians was visible on the track and the court, but their cultural and economic narratives were absent from the broader story being told. This was a missed opportunity to connect the struggle and triumph embedded in Black American history with China's own narrative of overcoming a "century of humiliation." Imagine a performance segment featuring the Fisk Jubilee Singers alongside a Chinese folk orchestra, a fusion that would speak to the shared histories of perseverance through artistic expression. That symbolic partnership would have added a profound layer of depth to China's message of global inclusion.

This theme of selective inclusion continued at the 2010 Shanghai World Expo, an event that took the Olympics' narrative of engagement and expanded it into a six-month-long dialogue on humanity's future.

Under the theme "Better City, Better Life," (chéngshì, ràng shēnghuó gèng měihǎo), the Expo was a dazzling bazaar of global innovation and cultural heritage. I walked through Germany's floating orb, a testament to engineering and sustainability, and marveled at Saudi Arabia's mesmerizing lotus-shaped pavilion. The breadth of global creativity was on full display, from Nordic minimalism to the intricate artistry of African textiles. Yet, this expansive, cosmopolitan vision had a glaring blind spot. As I moved from pavilion to pavilion, I was struck by the absence of a curated, institutional presence that spoke to the Black American experience. Where was the pavilion exploring the Great Migration as a foundational urban narrative, one that could offer lessons on resilience and community building to a rapidly urbanizing China? Where were the exhibits on the technological innovations born from HBCUs, or the aesthetic revolutions of the Harlem Renaissance (Hāléi Wényì Fùxīng), presented in dialogue with China's own New Culture Movement? The Expo served as a platform for nations and corporations to position themselves within the narrative of "our shared future." The absence of Black America from this stage signaled that our contributions to this future were not considered essential to the narrative. We were consumers of this global vision, not co-authors. This exclusion is not merely symbolic; it has tangible economic consequences. The connections forged at the Expo, between European engineering firms and Chinese provincial governments, between Southeast Asian agricultural exporters and Chinese distributors, were the seeds of future trade partnerships. By not being at the table, Black American businesses were excluded from this network-generating event, reinforcing a cycle where they are perpetually playing catch-up in the U.S.-China economic relationship.

The culmination of this pattern was at the 2018 China International Import Expo (CIIE) (Zhōngguó Guójì Jìnkǒu Bólǎnhuì). If the Olympics were about culture and the Expo about ideas, the CIIE was unabashedly about commerce. China declared that it was not just a "world factory" but a "world market," open for business and eager to import. The scale was staggering: exhibition space equivalent to eight

Hangzhou Bay Bridges, teeming with Argentinian beef, German robotics, and Indonesian batik. The air buzzed with the palpable energy of deal-making, a symphony of negotiations in a dozen languages. It was here, in this temple of global capitalism, that the absence of Black America became most stark and economically consequential. Scouring the show directory, I found no dedicated pavilion for Black American small and medium enterprises (SMEs), no delegations from Black-majority districts advocating for their local tech startups or agribusinesses, no booths showcasing the burgeoning Black-owned ventures in green energy, fashion, or healthcare. This was not an issue of invitation; China was clear that it was open to all. This was a failure of internal organization and strategic vision on the part of American trade and cultural institutions, which were purportedly representative of diverse interests.

The implications are severe. As China's middle class expands to 700 million consumers, their tastes and brand loyalties are being formed now. If their exposure to American products is limited to established Fortune 500 companies and a Silicon Valley-centric tech narrative, the unique value propositions of Black American businesses often rely on community-specific insights, innovative problem-solving for underserved markets, and a rich aesthetic tradition. Therefore, they may never have the opportunity to compete. A Shanghai student's algorithmic feed, shaped by platforms like Douyin, might be filled with clips of Black cultural dance trends. Still, it remains silent on Black economic thought, policy innovation, or entrepreneurial models. This creates a dangerously incomplete and potentially caricatured understanding, reducing a vibrant and diverse community to a single, stereotyped dimension. The "bargain" of a $20 gadget from Shenzhen (Shēnzhèn), as I learned in my own business, often conceals a complex web of hidden costs. Similarly, the "bargain" of engaging with America without the complicating, enriching presence of Black America results in a relationship built on an incomplete picture, one that is inherently unstable and lacks the resilience that comes from true, multifaceted partnership.

This trilogy of absences across culture, ideas, and commerce points to a systemic gap. It is a gap in the strategic planning of Black American trade and cultural organizations, which have yet to marshal the resources and political will to engage with China's rise as a cohesive, ambitious force. It is also a gap in China's vision of global engagement, which, while expansive, has yet to fully integrate the distinct and powerful narrative of Black America into its understanding of what constitutes a "global" partner. Bridging this gap requires more than mere attendance; it demands a proactive, institutionalized effort. It involves the creation of a "Black America-China Trade & Culture Council" capable of curating a presence at future CIIEs, pitching collaborative exhibitions to the organizers of the next World Expo, and facilitating people-to-people exchanges that turn abstract opportunities into tangible partnerships. The podium China has built for itself on the world stage is immense. The silence from one of the most innovative and resilient segments of the American populace on that podium is a loss not just for Black America, but for the depth, authenticity, and ultimate success of the U.S.-China relationship itself. The potential for a partnership that blends the logistical prowess of Shenzhen (Shēnzhèn) with the fintech innovation of Atlanta (Yàtèlándà), or the traditional medicine of Hangzhou with the community health models of Baltimore, remains untapped, waiting for the moment when we finally, meaningfully, occupy the space that has been left empty.

The solution to this absence is not to wait for an invitation, but to build our own bridge. This was the vision behind the National Alliance of Artists from Historical Black Colleges and Universities (NAAH-BCU) art exhibition in Shanghai, titled "We Stand Together." This initiative was conceived as a direct and proactive response to the systemic gaps and missed opportunities outlined throughout this text. This is exemplified by the lack of Black American representation at the 2010 Shanghai Expo, the CIIE, and in the broader narrative of U.S.-China cultural exchange. If the global trade system is fraught with hidden costs and logistical hurdles for Black entrepreneurs, and if primary diplomatic stages overlook our contributions, then we must engineer our own platforms for engagement. The NAAHBCU exhibition was not merely an art show; it was a strategic intervention, a proof-of-concept that demonstrated how mutual engagement could be initiated from the ground up, bypassing traditional, often exclusionary, gatekeepers.

This was not merely about shipping artworks; it was an act of cultural diplomacy. The exhibition consciously centered on the underrepresented dimensions of American art, challenging both American and Chinese narratives. In the American context, it pushed back against a monolithic view of "American art" that is often synonymous with white, Eurocentric traditions, insisting on the centrality of the Black experience to the American story. For Chinese audiences, it challenged any simplistic or stereotypical understanding of America, and of Black America in particular, that might be filtered solely through Hollywood or news headlines. By placing these works in Shanghai, a global hub of forward-looking ambition, we made a declarative statement: Black American art is not a marginal subcategory; it is a vital, dynamic force in contemporary global art, offering profound insights into universal themes of identity, memory, struggle, and joy.

The exhibition's goal was to create a space where dialogue could replace monologue. "We Stand Together" was chosen as a title that both declared solidarity among the artists and served as a genuine invitation to the Shanghai community. We sought to move beyond the transactional nature of some cultural exchanges. A transaction where art is imported and displayed, and instead fosters a generative environment where new meanings can be created through encounter. The artworks were carefully curated to serve as catalysts for this conversation. A stunning mixed-media piece by a Morris Brown College graduate, for instance, wove together canvas, reclaimed wood, and sculptural elements to explore the intersection of femininity, fertility, and strength. The piece, rich with texture and symbolic depth, did not simply represent a figure but evoked an entire lineage of Black womanhood. A lineage that has its burdens, its beauty, and its unassailable power. Nearby, a

Tougaloo College alumnus's work, "Beautiful Black and Brown Butterflies," offered an abstract meditation on loss and transformation. Using layered paper, ink, and found materials, the piece visualized metamorphosis not as a gentle process, but as a turbulent and beautiful dismantling and reassembling of self. It spoke a silent, powerful language of resilience that needed no translation.

Perhaps one of the most politically resonant pieces was Rev. Dr. Clarence Talley, Sr.'s "Untitled #5." This mixed-media work employed a profile layout, rendered in acrylic paint. Still, its true power emanated from the intricate use of decorative beads in the red, black, and green colors of the Pan-African flag. That, of course, are the unambiguous colors of Black liberation. These were not subtle accents; they were the heart of the piece, a deliberate and proud invocation of a historical struggle for freedom and self-determination. In the context of Shanghai, these colors created a fascinating point of friction and connection. For an American viewer, they carried the weight of the civil rights and Black Power movements. For a Chinese viewer, the red of the national flag might resonate, symbolizing revolution and a distinct, yet powerful, history of liberation from colonial and feudal oppression. The artwork became a silent mediator, asking viewers from both cultures to reflect on their own histories of struggle and the symbols they hold sacred.

Logistically, mounting this exhibition was a masterclass in the very complexities of global trade and cultural exchange I had documented. It was a challenge that required navigating not just customs forms and shipping timelines, but also the more subtle negotiations of meaning across divergent historical and social contexts. Securing insurance for irreplaceable artworks for a trans-Pacific journey involved intricate valuations and fraught conversations about risk. Coordinating with shippers required a deep understanding of Incoterms to ensure clear responsibility for the pieces at every leg of the journey, from the studio door in the American South to the gallery wall in Shanghai. We had to account for climate-controlled storage, potential port delays, and the labyrinthine Chinese customs bureaucracy for cultural artifacts. Each crate was more than a container; it was a vessel carrying fragile pieces of soul and history, and the logistical process felt like a physical manifestation of the bridge we were trying to build.

The diplomatic challenges were equally profound. The hesitation we sometimes encounter from potential local partners is not a setback, but a revealing moment where an opportunity arises to ask the essential, often unvoiced question. How do Black America's cultural narratives resonate in China? This hesitation was rooted in a lack of familiarity, not outright rejection. It forced us to become not just curators, but educators and translators of our own experience. We had to articulate, with clarity and confidence, why this specific exhibition mattered. We had to explain the historical significance of HBCUs as pillars of Black intellectual and artistic life post-emancipation. We had to contextualize the art within the broader story of the Great Migration, the Harlem Renaissance (Hāléi Wényì Fùxīng), and the ongoing quest for racial and economic justice. This process of explanation was itself a form of diplomacy, building understanding one conversation at a time.

Our collaboration with New York University Shanghai (Niǔyuē Dàxué Shànghǎi) was pivotal in bringing this vision to life. Together, we co-developed an educational lecture series that ran parallel to the exhibition, creating an intellectual framework for the visual experience. This was where the gallery truly transformed from a passive viewing area into an environment of mutual learning and engagement. During interactive Q&A sessions, Chinese students asked probing questions about the symbolism in the artworks, drawing parallels to themes in their own cultural history. They wanted to know about the artists' inspirations, the techniques they used, and the socio-political context that shaped their work. In turn, the artists and curators gained invaluable insights into how their work was being perceived and interpreted across a vast cultural divide. These dialogues were often electric, filled with moments of surprise, recognition, and the thrilling discovery of shared human ground.

The exhibition became a living archive, a testament to what is possible when communities decide to engage on their own terms. It proved that true inclusion isn't about charity or tokenism, but about recognizing our interconnected futures and having the courage to create the spaces where that interconnection can be celebrated and explored. The artworks, in their vibrant, unflinching glory, were not simply objects to be observed; they were active participants in a cross-cultural dialogue, challenging assumptions, provoking thought, and forging empathy. The success of "We Stand Together" serves as a practical and replicable model. It demonstrates that before trade delegations and major policy initiatives can be truly inclusive, the foundational work of human understanding must be laid through cultural awareness and understanding. By building this bridge ourselves, we did not wait for a seat at the table; we built our own, and in doing so, created a new space where Black American and Chinese voices could finally, and powerfully, stand together.

Economic resilience is inextricably linked to cultural understanding and direct engagement. The hidden costs of exclusion are both in the tangible realm of trade and the intangible sphere of representation that can only be overcome by building proactive, non-transactional partnerships. This is not a theoretical ideal but a practical necessity, forged in the crucible of global supply chains and the silent gaps in international cultural forums. The journey detailed in these pages, from demurrage fees in congested ports to the curated silence in Shanghai's exhibition halls, converges on a singular truth. A truth that our systems are profoundly interconnected, yet our pathways to participation remain stubbornly segregated. Resilience, therefore, cannot be built in isolation. It must be co-authored through a deliberate and empathetic collaboration between communities that have historically navigated the peripheries of global power.

The relationship between Black America and China is ripe for a transformation that moves beyond the transactional and into the transformative, rooted in a mutual respect forged not from sameness but from a shared recognition of struggle, innovation, and the relentless pursuit of self-determination. We have seen how the Great Migration and China's internal migrations, though born of distinct historical pressures, both tell stories of human resilience in the face of systemic displacement. We have observed how the resourcefulness of a street vendor in Anhui mirrors the entrepreneurial hustle that built Bronzeville, and how the top-down poverty alleviation campaigns in China offer a provocative, if not directly transferable, counterpoint to the grassroots mutual aid societies of Black Chicago. These are not parallel histories, but intersecting ones, offering a rich, textured canvas for a new kind of dialogue.

To operationalize this vision, we must move from observation to architecture. Imagine a "Black America-China Innovation Fund," established not as a charitable grant but as a strategic partnership, perhaps in collaboration with initiatives like the China Africa Project. This fund would not simply finance trade; it would underwrite synergy. It could provide seed capital for Black-owned tech startups to develop solutions for Shenzhen's (Shēnzhèn) urban challenges, or for Chinese green energy firms to partner with Black communities in Arkansas to co-design and implement solar infrastructure. This would create a feedback loop of innovation where cultural intelligence becomes a market advantage, and where bonds of mutual interest and respect reinforce supply chains. The fund's board would comprise an equal number of visionary leaders from HBCUs, Black venture capital firms, and their Chinese counterparts in academia and state-owned enterprises, ensuring that the flow of ideas and capital is genuinely bidirectional.

Simultaneously, we must institutionalize the cultural bridgework that gives economic collaboration its soul and sustainability. A partnership between the National Museum of African American History and Culture (NMAAHC) and the National Museum of China, exploring the Harlem Renaissance (Hāléi Wényì Fùxīng) and the May Fourth Movement, would be a monumental start. Such an exhibition would not merely place artifacts side by side; it would stage a conversation between two revolutionary moments in which communities used culture as a weapon to redefine their identity and destiny against oppressive systems. It would ask visitors to consider how Langston Hughes's invocation of "I, too, am America" resonates with Lu Xun's critiques of a society in transition. This is the kind of deep, contextual understanding that prevents business partnerships from faltering on the rocks of unspoken cultural assumptions.

The human capital pipeline is equally critical. Envision a formalized pipeline for HBCU students to intern at Tencent (Téngxùn), Alibaba (Ā lǐ bā bā), or BYD (Bǐ Yà Dí), and for students from Peking University (Běijīng Dàxué) and Tsinghua (Qīnghuá) to apprentice at Black-owned financial firms or media companies in Atlanta (Yàtèlándà) or Charlotte (Xiàluòtè). These are not mere resume-building exercises; they are the incubators of a future leadership cohort that is fluent in the languages, business customs, and social nuances of both worlds. These future leaders would be the ones to re-draft the contracts, foresee the logistical snags, and build the trust that turns a one-time deal into a generational alliance. They would be the ones to ensure that the next China International Import Expo (CIIE) features a vibrant pavilion dedicated to Black American innovation in agritech, fintech, and the creative industries.

This blueprint culminates in the most powerful image of all: a Guangzhou (Guǎngzhōu) teenager appreciating James Baldwin alongside Confucius. In this vision, the teenager does not see a contradiction but a conversation. From Baldwin, they learn the searing, intimate cost of societal hypocrisy and the fiery demand for one's humanity to be recognized. From Confucius, they know the framework of ren (benevolence), li (ritual), and the responsibilities that bind a society together. This teenager would be equipped with a more complete toolkit for understanding the world. A world where Black Americans' struggles against systemic inequality are not isolated American phenomena, but part of a global dialectic on power and justice. Similarly, a Chicago activist could draw profound insights from studying both Dr. King's Poor People's Campaign and President Xi's targeted poverty alleviation campaigns, not to endorse one system over the other, but to understand the different mechanisms and metrics of societal uplift.

The NAAHBCU exhibition in Shanghai was one foundational step on this path. It demonstrated that our differences are not obstacles to overcome, but treasures to celebrate. The vibrant, unflinching artwork did not just hang on the walls; it posed questions, challenged narratives, and created a space where empathy could flourish. By amplifying these marginalized voices, we do not narrow the global dialogue; we radically enrich it for everyone. The act of inclusion is not a zero-sum game; it is an additive process that enhances our collective capacity for innovation and problem-solving.

The legacy we must now build for future generations is a world where borders become bridges, and where diverse communities see themselves not as guests or supplicants, but as essential authors of the global narrative. This requires a conscious departure from the old models of engagement, which were often mediated through a predominantly white American corporate and cultural lens. It demands that we build direct lines of communication, commerce, and creativity. The potential of this direct partnership is profound, offering a template for how other marginalized communities might engage with rising global powers not from a position of weakness, but from a position of unique cultural strength and strategic insight.

Now is the time to act. The volatility of global trade, the urgent challenges of climate change, and the disruptive power of technology are not waiting. Communities that have learned to be resilient out of necessity now can lead. By weaving together the threads of Black America's hard-won resilience and China's monumental transformative energy, we can create a fabric of interconnection that is more durable, more innovative, and more just than the systems that currently define our world. The blueprint is drawn. Let us begin the construction.

10

Bridging Cultures, Building Trust

The vision of a collaboration with and in China is not just an abstract ideal. It's a tangible outcome that manifests in the practical work of bridging cultures. As a Black American entrepreneur operating in China's rapidly evolving business environment, I've found that each success offers more profound lessons about cross-cultural exchange. Behind the scenes of closed deals and celebrated milestones, my experience has demanded persistence and dedication. Late nights were spent navigating cultural differences, building trust across language barriers, and occasionally feeling isolated even in busy rooms. But these challenges also reinforced my resilience and adaptability.

Resilience and adaptability aren't just buzzwords. They're the foundation of my ability to deliver tangible outcomes. Success requires more than ambition. It demands the courage to turn obstacles into opportunities, skepticism into collaboration, and to proactively align my vision of working in and with China with diverse industries. The challenges of communication often reveal themselves in unexpected ways. A misplaced phrase, an unspoken assumption, or even a well-intentioned gesture can lead to confusion when navigating cultural differences. Such moments seem to remind me that understanding is a shared effort. It requires openness and patience from all involved.

During my early days in Shanghai, I pitched a business idea to someone I hoped to work with. At the time, I didn't realize that my straightforward approach might have come across as pushy or abrupt in this context. When weeks passed without a response, I worried my ideas had been dismissed. Later, I understood that the silence wasn't rejection but a reflection of the importance of harmony and indirect communication in Chinese professional culture. It was a humbling lesson because succeeding here would require more than just learning the language and adapting to a new culture. It would mean adapting my approach in a way that aligns with others' expectations.

Hence, moments like these have enriched my journey as a Black American entrepreneur in China. At the same time, language barriers left me momentarily stranded in conversation, and cultural nuances made me pause, because each misunderstanding became an opportunity to learn and adapt. Over time, these experiences chiseled away my assumptions and refined my approach. They reminded me that growth often lies in the uncomfortable spaces, and China's vibrant, fast-paced environment has been both a teacher and a catalyst for my evolution. On one occasion, during a product launch, a miscommunication left me sitting in my office, questioning whether my background had prepared me for the challenges of this new environment.

But over time, I came to see these obstacles as valuable lessons. Each setback taught me to listen more carefully, observe more closely, and adapt my approach with patience and creativity. What strengthened me through these trials was the unwavering support of a community that believed in my value even when my faith wavered. My mentor, a veteran of domestic manufacturing, once shared a piece of wisdom over steaming cups of oolong tea that stayed with me. "In China, business grows at the dinner table, not the conference table." Up until that moment, I understood guanxi (guānxi) as just a necessary part of doing business. Still, her words reshaped my perspective, helping me see it as an art form built on trust and shared experiences rather than mere transactions.

Colleagues became allies, patiently teaching me how to decipher local customs throughout various provinces in China. Eventually, this gave me a sense of belonging that is not about erasing differences but embracing them as connective tissue. Their generosity taught me that success is never achieved alone. For me, every challenge I overcome is not just a personal achievement but also a reflection of the collective strength of those who have supported me. I feel that navigating China's entrepreneurial landscape as a cultural outsider has been both rewarding and challenging, and I'm grateful for the lessons I have learned along the way.

At trade show events, I've sometimes noticed curiosity or questions about how my Black American heritage intersects with my pragmatic approach, which reflects both my cultural identity and professional values. Yet, this connection soon revealed its power at the Shanghai International Hotel & Catering Expo (Hotelex Shanghai), (Shànghǎi Guójì Jiǔdiàn Jí Cānyǐnyè Bólǎnhuì). It was during the 2008 event that I became aware of a concept designed to create opportunities for Black Americans by connecting them with innovative products, potential partnerships, and industry insights. This opportunity aimed to support their growth in the hospitality sector while fostering cross-cultural collaboration that aligns with shared values of community and innovation.

I believe this opportunity could have secured a pivotal foothold in a key industry sector by showcasing the adaptability of Black American businesses through strategic integration. By specializing in bespoke products, tailored services, and cutting-edge innovations designed exclusively for hotels, restaurants, spas, and commercial spaces, we could have carved out a distinct and valuable niche. As I understand it, integrating heritage-inspired storytelling into dynamic marketing campaigns and reimagining traditional designs for modern contexts. From artisan-driven spa concepts to modular hospitality furnishings, we can create authentic, culturally meaningful experiences. This approach would bridge the gap between tradition and innovation, thereby enabling us to design spaces and brands that resonate with contemporary audiences.

This isn't a straightforward path, as I've encountered twists, turns, and unexpected roadblocks along the way. Sometimes I'll hit walls of red tape that slow me down like mud clogging up the flow. Other times, cultural misunderstandings, like things I didn't even see coming, will pop up like hidden rocks trying to throw me off course. There have been days when progress feels stuck, and frustration builds up like steam in a pressure cooker. But when I least expect it, things start moving fast. I'll find a breakthrough, a new angle, and suddenly everything falls into place. That's when I realized that persistence pays off. China's business landscape might seem harsh to crack, but like water, I adapt. I didn't smash through the obstacles; I learn to flow around them to find a new path forward. The key is to keep moving, stay patient, and trust that even when the journey feels slow or confusing, my persistence will ultimately lead to success.

Imagine a dynamic digital ecosystem where Black creators, tech innovators, and global buyers converge to shape the future of business. Although it may face initial skepticism, its goal is to celebrate, promote, and elevate Black-owned companies in the hotel supplies, FF&E, sustainable technology, textiles, and interior design industries. Entrepreneurs could merge cultural heritage, sustainability, and technology in exciting ways. Some can create sustainably dyed linens inspired by Gullah Geechee traditions, aiming to preserve history while meeting the demand for eco-conscious products.

On the other hand, others can identify Black-owned tech ventures that utilize AI to reduce energy waste and pair them with educational platforms to achieve a broader impact. I also think that cross-cultural collaborations, such as those between Savannah-based professors and Nanjing hotel owners, could redefine the hospitality experience by blending Black sci-fi Art, biophilic design, and solar-powered installations. In the meantime, Black-owned hotels can integrate IoT systems with Feng Shui (fēng shuǐ) principles to optimize room energy flow and enhance guest experience.

This innovative approach to sustainability and well-being could create opportunities for eco-conscious vendors, such as a Black-owned cleaning company specializing in non-toxic, plant-based disinfectants and eco-friendly products, to partner with hotels prioritizing green initiatives. If successful, such collaborations could expand to include Nairobi hotels sourcing cost-saving, modular furniture from Black designers, Dubai resorts integrating Gullah Geechee-inspired textiles into their luxury interiors, and AI tools optimizing linen cycles to reduce waste.

From this vantage point, the transition from Savannah to Nanjing presents an opportunity to explore how cultural heritage and innovation can intersect, leveraging diversity as a catalyst for reimagining the hospitality industry. At the same time, this shift has the potential to blend technology with human-centric values and tradition with modernity. It also requires navigating challenges such as differing cultural expectations and market dynamics. If approached with inclusive collaboration, sustainability, and adaptability, this evolution could challenge conventional industry norms. It would demonstrate that progress can balance local identity with a global vision, although not without thoughtful negotiation and mutual respect.

Amid these professional highs and lows, my personal growth has been equally transformative. Living abroad stripped me down to my core, confronting me with questions of identity that once seemed settled. I've learned to wear my heritage not as armor but as an invitation to build bridges for others to share their stories. I realized that vulnerability could dissolve barriers faster than any polished pitch. This journey has also demanded a reckoning with legacy. As a Black entrepreneur, I carry the weight of ancestors whose stories are often underrepresented in global narratives, including those in China.

Yet, this awareness fuels my commitment to fostering inclusion and bridging cultural divides. Collaborating with local designers on an outdoor equipment project while highlighting their company's untold stories has shown me how manufacturers that honor diverse histories can foster innovation. This experience has been multifaceted, with moments of excitement, such as securing a new contract, alongside challenges, like adjusting to life in a new city. As such, my emotions have ranged from the satisfaction of overcoming obstacles to the occasional thought of homesickness, but each step has helped me gain a deeper understanding of both my work and myself.

I've grown to expect situations like these, where even setbacks are aligned with possibilities. As I look ahead, I am convinced that the bridges we build today, whether through a shared meal, a collaborative project, or simply the courage to say "I don't understand, please explain" (Wǒ bù míngbái qǐng jiěshì yīxià), lay the groundwork for a more inclusive tomorrow. My story is one of many in China's ongoing development, where diverse voices contribute to its progress. In this interconnected world, I've found not only a career but also a sense of purpose. A purpose that demonstrates that meaningful contributions arise not from predefined roles but from dedication and resilience.

However, as I grappled with fear and moments of self-doubt, I recognized that these challenges, though difficult, were also shaping my resilience. The sleepless nights spent questioning my efforts didn't diminish my progress. Instead, they highlighted my determination to keep moving forward. Each obstacle, no matter how daunting, became a challenge to my ability to endure and adapt. A test that reveals the path ahead remains uncertain, but I could see how far I'd come and this quiet strength I am steadily building within myself. In doing so, have I come to understand that vulnerability is not a weakness but a bridge?

At first, admitting my fears felt like dismantling my armor, exposing the fragile core beneath. These questions make me reflect on my experiences. I learned that, sometimes surprisingly, allowing myself to be vulnerable strengthens my resilience. By sharing my struggles, I didn't just express my insecurities; I also found a way to connect with others. I create space for connection, where I find solidarity with other Black Americans in China who are navigating their challenges. Through these conversations, I realize how often hardship can bring people together by turning personal battles into shared strength.

Through late-night messages of encouragement, brainstorming sessions where we openly dissected failures, and the unspoken solidarity of knowing I wasn't alone. These moments teach me that obstacles are not roadblocks but opportunities to innovate. One individual's story of pivoting a failing business during a supply chain crisis shows me how setbacks can be reimagined. Another's candid account of burnout reinforced the importance of sustainability over speed. I've often found my footing by turning stumbling blocks into stepping stones. And not just through my resilience, but by drawing on the collective strength of shared stories, wisdom, and support. This experience, which includes moments of mutual courage where giving and receiving encouragement have made all the difference, led me to a pivotal revelation. The true power of synergy lies not just in pooling resources but in blending diverse perspectives toward a shared goal. My work with local counterparts taught me this. It wasn't always smooth at first because we faced missteps, including cultural misunderstandings, differing approaches to deadlines, and unspoken assumptions about hierarchy. But through persistence and open dialogue, we began to bridge those gaps.

What started as friction gradually transforms into a collaboration where our differences strengthen the outcome. And not hindering it. During an early meeting, I presented a marketing strategy I'd spent weeks refining, only to be met with polite silence. Later, a colleague kindly pointed out that my direct approach had unintentionally overlooked the team's preference for collaborative decision-making. At first, it was discouraging, but it became a turning point. I realize that to succeed, I needed to adapt not just by hearing others' words, but by truly understanding the unspoken dynamics of teamwork. This turning point proves impactful by combining my focus on rapid adaptation with their emphasis on long-term relationship-building. I begin by developing projects that could achieve meaningful cross-border reach.

One such development is an eye-hand coordination sports training device designed as a personal-use catching practice tool. The device is ideal for amateur athletes looking to improve their reaction time and basic catching mechanics. While it primarily targets beginners and intermediate players, seasoned athletes can also use it for precision drills and to refine their technique. The training device addresses common athletic challenges, such as reaction-time deficits and hand-eye coordination, making it a versatile training aid for athletes at all skill levels. Its goal is to measure the device's impact by tracking the percentage increase in user engagement and conversion rates among amateur athletes, then comparing these to a defined baseline or control group over a specified period.

The success will depend on incorporating local insights and avoiding reliance on external assumptions. Thereby, ensuring the solution is tailored to the target audience's needs. Progress is not a solo race. It relies on each participant contributing their unique strengths to move forward together. This insight informs my approach to partnerships and engagement with China. As I see it, entering this dynamic country as a Black American entrepreneur requires not only ambition but also qualities such as humility, adaptability, and a commitment to mutual learning. In this context, immersion became my strategy. I attended industry meetups in Shanghai, prioritizing observation over participation to gain a deeper understanding of negotiation dynamics and unspoken norms.

Additionally, joining trade groups for foreign entrepreneurs helps uncover practical insights that are often absent in textbooks. These networks, cultivated over time, became essential supports, demonstrating that resources are not merely material but also relational. Through these experiences, I've come to see how vulnerability, collaboration, and resourcefulness are deeply connected. Each time I face fear, work with others, or learn from a new challenge, I feel less isolated and more part of something bigger. A single connection, even one initiated by a seemingly small or kind gesture, could potentially lead to a partnership with a manufacturer. As such, over time, a manufacturer might even become a key advisor on innovation.

Innovation thrives in the dynamic interplay of diverse perspectives and shared humanity. As I navigate life, I strive to cultivate virtue (dé) through continuous self-reflection and learning, guided by the wisdom of Confucius. "When you encounter excellence, learn from it. When you witness fault, reflect on your own." Because each stumble can become a lesson in humility and an opportunity to reflect and refine one's conduct (xiū shēn), where actual growth lies not in perfection but in the sincere pursuit of (qiú rén) benevolence that connects us all.

Yet, this journey is intensely personal. Some may find wisdom in adversity, while others may need compassion and support to rise again. In Confucian (Rújiā) thought, harmony (hé) is often understood as emerging from the Five Relationships, in which mutual respect and duty form the foundation of a well-ordered society. Other Chinese philosophical traditions may interpret harmony differently, emphasizing natural balance, spontaneity, or universal cohesion beyond hierarchical roles. To "dare to walk together" (Gǎn yú tóng xíng) reflects a spirit of mutual commitment and shared purpose. While not a direct Confucian term, it aligns with the principle of (shù, reciprocity/forbearance) in cultivating harmonious relationships.

The phrase also resonates with the classical ideal of tiānxià ("all under Heaven"), which emphasizes collective moral responsibility in Confucian thought. Like the Mandate of Heaven, the future belongs not to the solitary seeker but to those who tread the moral and ethical path (dào) collectively, nurturing community as a gardener tends a grove. As I'm reminded, a more effective and sustainable way to build alignment is often to foster shared purpose rather than rely solely on individual self-interest. In unity, we find the accurate measure of righteousness (yi), and the legacy of sagely wisdom endures in shared progress.

That said, the global marketplace is dynamic, and success rarely follows a straight path. For entrepreneurs seeking to tap into China's vast potential, ambition alone is insufficient. It requires a strategic blend of cultural understanding, operational adaptability, and resilience. While local government trade organizations and eager investors create openings for foreign ventures, I recognize that these opportunities come with both advantages and complexities, particularly in Chinese agencies. A provincial agency may often sponsor free exhibition booths and offer tax incentives to industries aligned with national priorities, such as tech innovation or renewable energy. Navigating these opportunities requires careful understanding of local regulations and market dynamics.

In 2022, Shenzhen's municipal government launched the "Shenzhen International Innovation and Entrepreneurship Program" to attract foreign ventures aligned with its strategic tech sectors, including AI and green energy. One notable case is CarbonX, a German startup specializing in AI-driven carbon capture solutions. The company secured a municipal grant covering 30% of its research and development (R&D) costs, approximately $450,000. As a result of the program, they can pilot its technology in Shenzhen's industrial parks. Such programs aren't handed out merely. They're earned through proposals that strike a balance between bold vision and cultural fluency.

Investors, too, seek more than profit potential. Why does this matter? It matters because Shenzhen's grants reflect China's broader strategy to lead in global tech innovation while addressing sustainability challenges. For Black American startups, such incentives could reduce financial risk and provide access to China's vast manufacturing and testing ecosystem. They can explore funding opportunities and strategic partnerships by aligning with Shenzhen's key initiatives, such as AI applications for carbon neutrality. Engaging with organizations like the Shenzhen Foreign Investment Association or participating in events like the China Hi-Tech Fair may facilitate connections. Since municipal agencies and industry stakeholders often seek international collaborations in these forums. From my research and observations, I've noticed that China's business landscape typically reflects a mix of opportunities and cultural nuances.

Coastal provinces like Guangdong Province (Guǎngdōng Shěng) tend to emphasize speed and experimentation in business practices, which may stem from their historical openness to trade and foreign influence. However, inland regions like Sichuan (Sìchuān) often prioritize methodical consensus-building, possibly due to their distinct economic and cultural traditions. I recognize these are broad trends, and individual businesses or local contexts may vary significantly. These insights reshaped my approach in Shanghai, where I prioritized scalability, while in Chengdu (Chéngdū), I focused on long-term stability. As a Black American entrepreneur, such cultural immersion proved invaluable.

At a trade fair in Guangzhou (Guǎngzhōu), a vendor hesitated to work with me, seemingly unfamiliar with Black-owned businesses in America. Rather than confronting the bias directly, I connected with him through our shared respect for family legacy. Therefore, we present our potential collaboration as an extension of a generational supply chain ecosystem. I turned initial distrust into a collaborative partnership, knowing that cultural competence is only part of the battle. To truly navigate China's supply chain ecosystem, this is dynamic and influenced by geopolitics, technological changes, and seasonal traditions; I needed a deep operational understanding.

The annual migration of China's migrant workforce, comprising over 290 million people returning to their hometowns for the Lunar New Year celebration, created a critical vulnerability in global supply chains, which was starkly highlighted during the 2022 shutdown. It is a significant phenomenon. This large-scale migration contributed to labor shortages in ports, factories, and logistics hubs. And the pandemic-era backlogs and broader economic disruptions further delayed an industry already under significant strain.

During the holiday period, the Port of Shanghai, which handles approximately 20% of China's cargo, experienced a temporary decline in productivity of around 30%. This disruption caused delays in container processing, with some shipments experiencing extended wait times. As such, the overall impact varied depending on industry sector and individual company contingency plans. Most businesses that rely heavily on "just-in-time" manufacturing, particularly in the electronics and automotive sectors, faced significant disruptions due to delayed components. These delays sometimes led to production stoppages, particularly in overseas operations.

As a result, the impact could vary depending on inventory reserves, supply chain diversification, and their contingency strategies. While I recognize that one factory may offer attractively low per-unit costs as part of its contingency plan, I've found that hidden logistics fees can sometimes erode profit margins. Another manufacturer might provide transparent pricing and greater flexibility to adjust orders during disruptions, such as a major lockdown. These situations show how adaptability can strengthen partnerships, especially when both parties approach challenges with mutual respect and understanding.

Consequently, in my experience, some conventional American business practices didn't work as well for me, and letting go of them felt like shedding armor I'd mistaken for skin. Over time, I adopted the Confucian principle of continuous learning (xuéxí), which helped me reframe mistakes as opportunities for growth. When a negotiation stalls, I ask, "What haven't I understood?" rather than "What's wrong with them?" For me, the lesson is clear after entering China. Success hinges on viewing obstacles as diagnostic tools. Each logistical delay, communication misfire, or bureaucratic tangle reveals systemic patterns that can be decoded.

Local provincial incentives and Black American investors could uncover new opportunities together. I also think sustained growth for Black America might depend on curiosity and a willingness to ask why some provinces hesitate to collaborate. By exploring these dynamics, we could reshape trade corridors or even rethink how we communicate. Cultural communication styles can vary between individuals and communities. Some Black Americans may value directness and expressiveness in communication, while some Chinese individuals may prioritize subtlety, respect, and harmony because these tendencies are not universal.

Recognizing these differences can help foster a deeper understanding of cross-cultural relationships. Adapting communication methods, such as supplementing digital messages with handwritten notes, can be seen as a thoughtful gesture, depending on the context and relationship.

As such, I recognize this is a complex challenge, but through deliberate steps, these efforts could contribute to a stronger, more resilient relationship between Black communities in America and China. And in that space lies the potential for collaboration and mutual understanding, where shared ambition could help bridge cultures and foster meaningful connections with a growth-oriented mindset.

A growth-oriented mindset has shown me that innovation often stems not from chance but from a willingness to adapt. Early in my career, I relied heavily on familiar strategies, assuming consistency alone would lead to success. Yet over time, I realized that stagnation could arise from resisting change. When I began embracing challenges as opportunities to learn rather than obstacles, I discovered a greater capacity for creativity. A creativity that has proven invaluable in my development. While everyone's path is different, this perspective has been transformative for me. This shift from rigidity to flexibility transformed my approach. I learned that progress often demands the courage to question old patterns. And experimenting with the unknown could lead to rebuilding with newfound insight. In a world where industries and markets evolve rapidly, excessive reliance on the status quo can hinder growth and innovation. Yet, discernment is the key because not all change is progress, and not all traditions are obsolete.

Adopting a growth-oriented mindset became my compass. I used it as a tool that steadied me in times of uncertainty and helped me thrive in a country that many in the West view as volatile. While the challenges were real, I learned to see them not just as obstacles but as opportunities to adapt and innovate. Every setback became an opportunity to refine my strategies, and every pivot strengthened my confidence in my ability to navigate change. What others saw as chaos, I began to see as clay, something I could shape with persistence and flexibility. During a sudden change, I've come to understand that growth isn't about avoiding challenges but learning to navigate them with resilience.

When the mind is nurtured with intention, it can unlock remarkable potential. This is the belief I share with those seeking their path, for our minds are more than just liabilities. It's a powerful force that, when fueled by curiosity, can overcome obstacles. When cultivated with care, it can thrive even under challenging circumstances. And when it embraces reinvention, it may discover that what once seemed like barriers were, in fact, opportunities in disguise. I've found that a growth mindset not only fuels personal development but also serves as a powerful catalyst for effective collaboration. While it requires a safe and trusting environment to flourish, this approach encourages teams to tackle complex challenges, view criticism constructively, and ultimately achieve more innovative results together than they could individually.

Strategic partnerships, I've found, are the lifeblood of innovation. When I first started in China, I partnered with a family-owned food packaging manufacturer that was hesitant to delay equipment upgrades or adopt advanced technologies through automation due to high upfront costs and an uncertain return on investment (ROI). We supported their transition from a local operation to a global brand through incremental, cost-effective upgrades, including modernizing production lines in phases rather than disruptive overhauls. This collaboration reinforced a key insight: strong partnerships thrive when treated as ecosystems of mutual growth rather than just transactional exchanges.

Collaboration among individuals with diverse skills, cultural perspectives, and problem-solving approaches can lead to outcomes that surpass what any one person could achieve alone. This dynamic is especially valuable in a developing country like China. A developing economy where rapid modernization intersects with deep-rooted traditions, creating a unique opportunity for innovation. Based on my observation, this manufacturer navigated the crisis effectively while laying the groundwork for a recovery. After 2010, as markets stabilized, they strategically reinvested in automation, sustainability initiatives, and global expansion to strengthen their position. Lightweighting and the use of recycled materials have become industry standards, while partnerships with startups have led to innovations such as compostable packaging for international clients. These adaptations reveal a resilient and forward-thinking approach among businesses in China.

I've found navigating this terrain to be both challenging and enlightening. I initially struggled with cultural barriers, including miscommunications around business etiquette, differing negotiation styles, and even confronting assumptions rooted in stereotypes. These experiences, while difficult, have also been revealing and formative in my journey. A journey that offered more profound learning experiences well beyond formal business settings. I've gained valuable insights by participating in local festivals, mentorship programs, and grassroots initiatives. Ironically, I am referring to experiences that cannot be fully captured in a textbook. In this case, China's vast and complex market has taught me more than I could have imagined, shaping my understanding in ways I hadn't anticipated. "Here, I've noticed an interesting dynamic where some of the most impactful innovations arise when traditional practices are combined with modern advancements.

Integrating e-commerce platforms like Alibaba (Ā Lǐ Bā Bā) and JD.com (Jīng Dōng Shāng Chéng) enables small and medium-sized enterprises (SMEs) to access global markets directly, bypassing intermediaries and expanding their reach. Through this integration, I've learned that these digital platforms allow SMEs to engage directly with international users and offer complementary products and services, without the added complexity of establishing overseas subsidiaries. These platforms are particularly invaluable because they streamline global outreach while minimizing operational overhead.

Accessing global markets directly through e-commerce platforms like Alibaba and JD.com could offer significant economic empowerment for Black America by expanding revenue streams and reducing reliance on domestic intermediaries. These platforms provide access to over a billion consumers worldwide, helping Black-owned businesses scale more efficiently and compete internationally. If leveraged successfully, they could diversify customer bases, increase brand visibility, and support long-term financial growth.

Success would depend on overcoming challenges like competition, logistics, and digital accessibility. Still, I see potential in these global marketplaces to help bridge economic disparities by creating new opportunities for wealth generation and community upliftment through trade. These platforms have profoundly impacted my life by offering opportunities where economic diversity and collaboration thrive for Black Americans, like myself, who have felt hesitant to step into new spaces. My experience has shown me that embracing change is not a threat but an opportunity, which has led me to possibilities I once thought were out of reach. By investing in myself, seeking collaboration, and staying open to learning from different cultures, I've been able to reshape my path. For me, innovation isn't about chasing trends. It's about building resilience to adapt and grow, even in the face of uncertainty. My journey is teaching me that when I stay curious, barriers soften, opportunities expand, and what once seemed impossible starts to feel within reach.

While I've experienced personal growth from embracing change, I've found that the most meaningful shifts often happen when I move beyond my efforts and join with others. It took me time to fully appreciate collaboration, not just as a catchphrase tied to school projects or work meetings, but as something more profound. For me, real collaboration means listening, adapting, and sometimes setting aside ideas to foster regional stability, drive economic integration, and address shared challenges like climate change and maritime security.

It's easy to treat partnerships as mere afterthoughts when ideas that sound good in theory but lack real-world impact. This is based on my experience navigating international markets, particularly through engagements such as the Association of Southeast Asian Nations (ASEAN) beauty trade event. I've seen firsthand how vital strong partnerships are for driving growth, sparking innovation, and deepening mutual understanding in ways that go beyond clichés.

When I attended Beauty Expo Malaysia (BEM) at the Kuala Lumpur Convention Centre in August 2018, the atmosphere was electric. And not just because of the newly launched products on display, but because of the sense that the beauty industry was evolving. The event, held from August 17-19 and organized by Informa Markets, brought together a diverse mix of professionals, including cosmetic chemists, digital-savvy marketers, and halal certification specialists. It serves as an essential meeting point for Southeast Asia's beauty industry.

As I navigate aisles filled with chrome packaging and live demonstrations of AI skin diagnostics, what stands out isn't just the sheer scale of over 500 exhibitors from 35 countries, but the intriguing blend of tradition and futurism on display. While the event retains the core features of a trade show, it also serves as a showcase for how the beauty industry is evolving, merging Malaysian heritage with global innovation. Mosque-certified lotions sat alongside augmented reality makeup mirrors, highlighting a unique crossroads of cultural specificity and borderless tech trends.

Yet beneath the spectacle, the industry's commercial ambitions and competitive dynamics remained unmistakable during my participation in their business-matching meeting program. I was struck by how the expo's design reflected Malaysia's unique duality. A Muslim-majority nation with deep-rooted herbal traditions is leading the $30 billion global halal beauty industry. Their embrace of East-West innovation also helps them appeal to non-Muslim markets seeking ethical, science-backed beauty solutions.

The BEM 2018 highlights a dynamic interplay of tradition and innovation in beauty and wellness. Deliberate collaborations and spontaneous exchanges alike create a vibrant showcase. At the same time, attendees explore striking contrasts, such as K-beauty's elaborate routines alongside Western minimalist trends. As well as creative fusions, such as a third-generation spice trader adapting heritage rempah recipes for modern halal skincare. Meanwhile, at Booth C12, I notice a bomoh, known as a traditional healer. This individual demonstrates the application of kelulut honey masks by connecting historical Malay healing practices with contemporary beauty rituals. These interactions, whether planned or emergent, underscore the event's role as a crossroads for diverse beauty philosophies.

What I see now is that halal certification has evolved from a niche requirement to a significant global standard, although its impact varies across different industries and regions. Malaysia's 200+ halal-certified exhibitors attracted international attention, alongside offerings like French vegan brands and Korean beauty products. At the same time, halal certification ensures compliance with specific religious guidelines, such as the use of alcohol-free formulations or pork-free alternatives. I see it also reflecting a broader interest in ethical consumption. And not the only driver of this trend.

I wonder if some Black American dermatologists who support the principles of the global clean beauty movement might also be interested in Malaysia's halal beauty products, given their avoidance of alcohol, non-halal animal derivatives, and harmful chemicals. This direct access could align with their preference for specific consumers who prioritize ethical and clean beauty standards. This should resonate with dermatologists seeking gentle, inclusive skincare solutions for diverse skin conditions, including those familiar among Black communities, such as hyperpigmentation and eczema.

In my experience, some clients, regardless of religious or cultural background, are drawn to products featuring the crescent logo because they associate it with cruelty-free practices and ethical supply chain integrity. This shift from religious obligation to a broader symbol of trust may reflect a strategic adaptation. An adaptation that trusts in cultural heritage to influence global beauty standards rather than simply adhering to existing ones. Yet, what I experienced at the expo's true strength was in its refusal to isolate innovations. Instead, it encouraged deliberate connections with its open-floor design.

It places perfume houses next to herbalists, which possibly fosters unexpected collaborations. Another standout example is the tech pavilion's startup battlefield. In this area, AI tools are addressing diverse needs, such as predicting hijab-friendly hair-fall solutions and translating ingredient lists into multiple ASEAN languages. This highlighted how cross-industry interaction can drive creative solutions by bringing together perfume houses, herbalists, and tech founders. The expo showcases Malaysia's dynamic blend of tradition and innovation, highlighting its ability to bridge heritage and modernity. With the benefit of hindsight, the expo reflects Malaysia's dynamic halal ecosystem. A framework where tradition isn't just preserved but actively adapted, proving that the country's blend of heritage and innovation isn't a contradiction, but a strength.

Amid the buzz of 3D-printed perfume samplers, I observed a developer developing an algorithm to match skin types with halal-certified products across 18 global markets. This isn't just progress. Its progress is rooted in real needs. The samples are inspired by a grandmother's experience with allergic reactions to imported creams, reflecting the expo's commitment to solving everyday challenges. I see that Malaysia's multicultural and multigenerational society offers unique perspectives that drive inclusive innovation. Issues like sensitive skin, humidity, and diverse skincare needs are increasingly universal concerns, and having seen it firsthand, I believe these solutions can benefit people everywhere.

Hence, the economic impact was swift. Following the expo, Malaysia's beauty exports rose by 23%, driven in part by halal skincare's growing influence in ASEAN's $4.8 billion expansion into the Middle East and North Africa. The broader significance extends beyond trade figures. The event highlighted Malaysia's unique position in the global beauty industry, blending tradition with innovation. This suggests a growing cultural and economic influence rather than mere trend-following. As the convention center's final day ends, I'm reflecting on the expo's key takeaway.

In a divided world, the future favors those who can balance innovation with tradition, turning unique cultural insights into ideas that resonate widely. I believe this represents Malaysia's meaningful contribution to the beauty world. An influence not just through its products, but by offering Black America a way to engage with areas within the industry that are often treated as opposing forces. It bridges faith and science, heritage and innovation, local traditions and the global search for meaning. The next big thing won't emerge from just one place.

I trust it will come from the unexpected intersections of tradition and modernity, where a Black American grandmother's beauty recipe meets a coder's vision, and where the world's oldest wisdom fuels its newest innovations. Of course, black-owned labs and universities will contribute, but so will kitchens, street vendors, and community centers, because transformative ideas flourish where diverse perspectives meet.

My purpose, which has been growing in me for some time, felt clearer than ever as I faced a room full of collaborators. Their eager eyes seem to mirror the challenge ahead, like honoring the past while embracing something new. "It's a pleasure to see everybody," I said, my voice steady despite the weight of the moment. The air buzzed with unspoken questions. How could we respect tradition without stifling innovation? Was there a way for both to strengthen each other rather than compete? I believed the answer wasn't in avoiding that tension but in harnessing it.

That energy, that push-and-pull, is precisely what would drive us forward. Imagine a partnership where ancestral wisdom informs supply chain decisions, and storytelling is woven into the measurable outcomes of logistics. This is not just collaboration but real-world execution. When milestones like increased order volumes are achieved and future growth is anticipated, the numbers reflect more than performance metrics. They demonstrate that when different cultures collaborate effectively, commerce can go beyond mere transactions and foster meaningful connections.

This experience is no longer just theoretical; it has become a reality. It is the tangible outcomes of Black America's economic potential. Malaysia's example stays with me, like a quiet mentor demonstrating how trade and cultural exchange could work. It shows me that progress isn't about abandoning our roots but adapting them for the future. And it's those adaptations that could be where our first real successes emerge. Successes that result from the merging of heritage and strategy to redefine our cross-cultural collaboration.

Our path forward in cross-cultural collaboration should begin with a straightforward, detailed approach that centers on two key priorities. First, let's commit to a thorough analysis of our foreign trade history to inform future targets. This review shouldn't focus on just one country, because each past shipment offers valuable insights into three critical areas. These areas are cultural preferences that shape product designs, seasonal trends tied to Black American celebrations, and logistical challenges that highlight opportunities for stronger cross-cultural collaboration. By analyzing these patterns, we can identify strengths to amplify our ability to customize shipments from niche countries and weaknesses to address, including our over-reliance on single suppliers.

Moving forward, we'll need not just an agreement but a strategy that ensures Black America's economic aspirations are fully integrated into and supported by the realities of global trade. Second, I recognize the importance of strengthening our partnerships with factory networks across ASEAN, with a particular focus on exploring opportunities in Malaysia as a strategic gateway. The region presents a compelling mix of rapid industrialization and skilled craftsmanship, offering value beyond just cost efficiency. Many factories there have effectively integrated handcrafted precision with advanced automation.

Replicating this success requires thoughtful collaboration, respect for local expertise, and a willingness to adapt to each market's specific conditions. Imagine a Black-owned business that combines sustainable practices with artisanal craftsmanship, using modern technology to minimize waste, including turning fabric scraps into stylish accessories. Or consider a Black-owned startup leveraging a track-and-trace system to enhance transparency in energy-efficient home upgrades for underserved neighborhoods. I believe partnerships like these could not only drive operational improvements but also help connect the innovation and entrepreneurial spirit within Black communities with ASEAN's manufacturing expertise. I am mindful that technology and systems alone aren't enough. This success depends on the people driving these initiatives, fostering collaboration, and building meaningful relationships across cultures.

To successfully transition to the next phase of our global strategy, collaboration with ASEAN member countries is essential for fostering business, trade, and investment opportunities. This approach could offer significant benefits, making it a compelling consideration for key stakeholders. I now understand that this move represents more than just geographical expansion. It's a strategic response to the evolving dynamics of global trade, where ASEAN members are becoming increasingly attractive due to their favorable tariff structures, streamlined import processes, and participation in regional trade agreements. I also recognize that operating in these markets presents challenges, including regulatory complexity, political risks, and competition.

A successful strategy must account for both the opportunities and the obstacles. Aligning operations with those of ASEAN countries, which have distinct cultural norms, business practices, and consumer behaviors, can pose a challenge for businesses. At the same time, it offers significant growth potential due to the region's dynamic markets, economic integration, and increasing consumer demand. One challenge is integrating into a dynamic regional market that offers competitive advantages, particularly for businesses seeking alternatives to higher-cost regions.

Consequently, key benefits include access to a fast-growing market and strategic trade and investment opportunities. It seems that success will depend on how well local regulations are navigated, supply chain complexities, and varying infrastructure development across member countries. This realization could enable us to better serve diverse industries by leveraging the strategic advantages of key markets. Markets are characterized by economic dynamism, regional connectivity, and opportunities for trade, investment, and business expansion. And which are experiencing significant growth across various markets.

Vietnam's manufacturing and tech sector, Indonesia's consumer goods and digital economy, Thailand's tourism and wellness industries, Malaysia's halal market and fintech, and the Philippines' BPO and entertainment sectors. Engaging with the diverse and dynamic economies of ASEAN could open up new opportunities for Black American businesses to connect with these rapidly growing, interconnected markets. This partnership could foster mutually beneficial economic growth and collaboration. By leveraging this partnership and forming strategic alliances with suppliers in ASEAN countries, I believe we can strengthen relationships and foster an innovation ecosystem.

This approach aligns with our commitment to adaptive growth, where proximity to resources and markets may help us refine product design and improve production efficiency. At the same time, I recognize that success isn't guaranteed. This accomplishment would depend on how effectively Black American businesses integrate these partnerships and remain flexible in addressing logistical or collaborative challenges that may arise.

While I'm optimistic about ASEAN's potential, I also recognize the logistical and collaborative challenges that come with ambitious ventures. Cost savings and logistical advantages are compelling, but they lose their appeal if product quality doesn't meet expectations. I believe the stakes are high because maintaining trust is critical in business, and setbacks can have lasting effects. That's why I emphasize that Black American companies should not only meet but also strive to exceed clients' expectations for established suppliers. To do this, we must go beyond simply following existing models. We need to innovate and improve them. While I acknowledge that competing factories across ASEAN countries meet ISO 9001 standards, many also implement advanced quality assurance systems capable of detecting micron-level defects in parts, ensuring they meet global benchmarks. Quality assurance is just one aspect of the broader challenges in manufacturing competitiveness.

Yet, another major challenge we must address is the logistical and cultural complexities of cross-border collaboration. Time zone differences, language barriers, and differing business practices can turn routine communication into a source of misunderstandings. While a delayed email or a mistranslated specification might seem minor on its own, these small frictions can add up, potentially leading to production delays or misaligned outcomes.

To address this, a dual approach could help. First, we should implement standardized communication tools, such as daily briefings on a unified platform, real-time project dashboards, and bilingual documentation. These communication tools are necessary to ensure that everyone has access to consistent information. Second, I'd recommend cultural competency training to improve collaboration, but with a focus on individual and team dynamics rather than broad stereotypes. While some team members may prefer direct feedback, others might emphasize harmony. So, in essence, we should adapt our communication styles to open dialogue and mutual understanding, not to assumptions about cultural norms. For these reasons, I am confident that this dual approach promotes efficiency and mutual respect by providing teams with essential insights.

These insights are not roadblocks but opportunities to understand how regional diversity may complicate communication and enrich our problem-solving capabilities. I believe local partners' familiarity with the ASEAN market is valuable because they can help drive innovation, leverage regional resources, and apply lean manufacturing techniques effectively. Their expertise in optimizing operations under resource constraints and navigating regional challenges could be key to overcoming strategic investment barriers. I understand that strategic investments require a careful balance of ambition and execution.

By establishing a strong presence in ASEAN, Black America could secure not only cost advantages but also a foothold in a rapidly growing region poised to play a significant role in 21st-century trade. With ASEAN's nominal GDP projected to reach $4.5–5 trillion and sustained annual growth of 4–5%, the region's economic influence is undeniable. Consequently, I believe success depends on combining big-picture vision with careful attention to detail, a commitment to quality, cultural awareness, and the ability to adapt to changing markets. For me, this opportunity isn't just about keeping up with competitors.

It's about redefining the game altogether. My experiences in China have shown me that engaging with the Southeast Asian global trade network can further expand my purpose. Moving forward with purpose, I aim to demonstrate that adaptability, when paired with strategic intent, can become the ultimate competitive advantage. The ideal of a Black American Trade and Cultural Organization competitive advantage initiative represents more than just a concept. It reflects a commitment to fostering economic empowerment, innovation, and cultural resilience. This commitment depends not only on vision and determination but also on collaboration, equitable access to resources, and systemic support. Once implemented, it serves as a powerful platform for marginalized communities to leverage collective strength and thrive in a complex global economy.

During this experience, I frequently reflected on past challenges, whether logistical setbacks, cultural misunderstandings, or shifting market demands. Rather than seeing them as mere obstacles, I recognize them as formative moments that deepen my understanding of what sustains meaningful partnerships. It is through these partnerships that I've come to value resilience and collaboration even more. One of my key realizations is that trust is the currency of progress. I've learned that it's built over time through consistent actions and open communication, and once established, it enables risk-taking and innovation. This principle resonates deeply with me as I reflect on my own experiences.

I've seen how rebuilding trust after moments of friction requires more than just formal assurances. It demands vulnerability, a willingness to acknowledge mistakes, and a shared commitment to realigning priorities. A delayed shipment risked damaging a key client relationship the previous year. While the logistical recovery is significant, it is the transparency of daily updates, accountability for the error, and collaborative problem-solving that ultimately repaired trust. This experience reinforces my belief that trust is not static but an ongoing practice.

It guides how I approach both challenges and opportunities. These lessons now shape my approach to new ventures. When discussing future strategies, I often reflect on the relationship between trust and ambition. While my partnership's strength comes from facing challenges rather than avoiding them, I recognize that setbacks aren't always easy to handle. They often test resilience as much as they spark innovation. For me, responding with adaptability rather than defensiveness, I've found that obstacles can reveal unexpected opportunities.

Take, for example, a failed product launch years ago, which led our team to conduct a cross-departmental audit of our design process. This assessment ultimately introduced a more agile prototyping model that reduces development timelines by 30%. For me, this experience reshapes how I approach obstacles. I approach them not as setbacks, but as diagnostic tools. Now, when challenges arise, I try to start conversations with curiosity rather than blame. I ask myself, "What does this reveal about my blind spots?" and "How can we adapt together?" This shift in perspective helps me cultivate a culture where transparency isn't just surface-level but a strategic strength.

Within this context, I believe there is significant potential for a Black American Trade and Cultural Organization to build meaningful partnerships with ASEAN member countries. While differences in markets, regulations, and business practices exist, shared interests in innovation and entrepreneurship create opportunities for collaboration. ASEAN's dynamic economies, with a combined GDP of $3.6 trillion and a rapidly expanding middle class, present significant opportunities for innovation and market growth.

Countries like Vietnam and Indonesia, with their fast-growing, price-sensitive consumer bases, are emerging as opportunities for Black American businesses that can align with local preferences and affordability. I contend that there are strong opportunities for collaboration between Black American farmers and agribusinesses in food exports to Thailand and Malaysia, where demand for diverse, high-quality products is growing. I see potential in linking Black-owned entertainment and creative startups with Filipino audiences, who have a deep appreciation for Black American music and style, as well as with Malaysian audiences. I do not doubt that this multicultural society will embrace our global influence. These connections could facilitate meaningful economic and cultural exchange. Beyond transactional trade, such collaborations encourage co-creation.

A partnership between the Gullah Geechee fashion collective and Indonesian textile artisans could explore blending traditional prints and patterns. The resulting designs appeal to markets such as Singapore, given its high-income consumer base and strong logistics infrastructure. These successful collaborations are built on mutual respect, iterative learning, and the courage to push boundaries, especially beyond traditional industries. In the ASEAN market, there's a growing demand for culturally resonant products that reflect local heritage, creating new opportunities for Black American innovation. ASEAN's diverse craftsmanship, from Filipino sustainable furniture design to Malaysian halal-certified gourmet foods, has strong potential to meet this demand.

Their success depends not just on product alignment but on fostering ecosystems of trust. Such systems enable suppliers and buyers to exchange more than catalogs. They would be able to share stories, challenges, and aspirations, thereby fostering deeper and more sustainable partnerships. Let's say a skincare brand owned by a Black entrepreneur in Atlanta (Yàtèlándà) discovers that a family-owned essential oil distillery in rural Vietnam shares similar values in community-focused sourcing. If both parties commit to transparent communication and equitable terms, their collaboration could pave the way for a joint line that balances ethical practices with profitability. Such partnerships require careful navigation of cultural, logistical, and economic differences. Successful ones can transform supply chains into value chains, where transactions support equity, sustainability, and innovation.

Consequently, the geopolitical complexities and logistical barriers could pose significant challenges to these ambitions. My past experiences include overcoming skepticism about cross-functional teams and addressing intellectual property concerns. A proactive engagement can mitigate these risks. In the past, strategies such as joint workshops, third-party mediation, and incremental pilot projects have helped us navigate uncertainties and build trust. While the challenges ahead may differ, I'm confident that a similar approach, one of careful planning and collaboration, can help us succeed. When I consider the ASEAN initiative through a skeptical lens, I see an opportunity to turn perceived vulnerabilities into strengths, fostering goodwill and momentum.

Standing at this crossroads, the question is not whether such partnerships are possible, but how boldly we choose to pursue them. A Black American Trade and Cultural Organization would represent more than just an economic opportunity; it would also symbolize a sense of community and cultural identity. It's an opportunity to break down barriers to global collaboration through conviction and shared purpose. As such, by building on the principles of hope, flexibility, and collective problem-solving, we can foster partnerships that prioritize both global impact and shared value.

Imagine a Black-owned toy company partnering with Filipino engineers to co-create STEM kits that highlight the contributions of African diaspora inventors and ASEAN innovators. These kits could be distributed worldwide, with packaging that educates children on the interconnected histories and achievements of these communities. Such collaborations would not only bridge cultural and economic divides but also inspire future generations through inclusive storytelling and innovation. For me, this is the power of intentional collaboration that drives not only results but also cultural change.

I've learned that the strongest partnerships acknowledge their humanity, whether through the messy, imperfect, yet intensely creative process of building something meaningful together. Thereby, I'm guided by the belief that trust, built through both challenges and successes, is one of the most potent forces when approaching new challenges. Clear communication plays a vital role in fostering successful collaboration and innovation. As organizations navigate the complexities of foreign trade, streamlining processes and reducing ambiguity can significantly enhance efficiency.

A key step in this effort is identifying contacts within each team. These are those individuals who facilitate smooth coordination across departments, particularly for inquiries related to design, product development, and supply chain management. These designated points of contact serve a crucial role beyond simply relaying information. They help maintain efficiency by preventing bottlenecks that could slow progress. Additionally, they establish clear, direct communication channels, enabling teams to respond more quickly to opportunities and challenges. This, in turn, supports an environment where decisions can be made in a timely, informed, and collaborative manner.

An effective organizational structure should prioritize clear communication with stakeholders to foster trust, especially in partnerships where transparency and responsiveness are critical. I witness that to ensure diverse perspectives are considered and concerns are actively addressed. An organization should align individual efforts toward a shared vision to enhance collaboration and achieve a greater collective impact. This alignment occurs before addressing any pressing questions that may arise. It is essential to structure these communication channels to reflect the values and strengths of the diverse cultures we serve.

A community that has long relied on mutual support and shared knowledge to overcome systemic barriers deserves particular attention in efforts to foster resilience and growth, as seen within the Black American business community. It is in this optimism that this collaboration has strong potential to embody the principles of unity and collective advancement. By fostering a culture of open information sharing and valuing mentorship, we can honor this opportunity with ASEAN while working together to strengthen it. I acknowledge that achieving this vision won't be easy. It requires deliberate effort to overcome barriers like competition, trust gaps, and differing priorities.

If we are to succeed, Black America should build a robust network in which experienced entrepreneurs guide emerging ventures, and supply chain experts collaborate with creatives on solutions that extend beyond America. These successes are a celebration of shared victories. However, for this to work, our trade and cultural organizations must commit to unlearning their American indoctrination and relearning strategies that foster connection, transparency, patience, and genuine partnership in the global marketplace outside America at every step.

A strong network of solidarity can draw strength from shared cultural heritage, offering Black American businesses a potential competitive advantage in global markets. When built on trust and transparency, such partnerships foster collaboration, allowing diverse perspectives to drive innovative solutions that exceed what any single entity could achieve alone. Consequently, effective communication within these networks goes beyond mere data exchange. It helps to align goals, strengthen relationships, and contribute to shared success to bring this vision into reality.

It's essential to develop communication strategies that are as nuanced as the stakeholders they serve. In contrast, generic approaches may not always address the unique cultural, operational, and aspirational differences within each partnership. Strategies such as regular strategy sessions, digital collaboration tools, and feedback loops grounded in active listening can help ensure that all participants, from various suppliers to executives, can feel heard and valued. In my experience, different businesses thrive under different communication styles.

A Black-owned agriculture supplier in rural Georgia might prefer structured weekly check-ins, while a tech startup may opt for agile, app-based communication. Consequently, adapting to these preferences isn't just about efficiency. It's about respecting diverse work cultures, which leads to a more meaningful and productive engagement. For this reason, I believe that when Black American businesses feel their perspectives have a meaningful influence on global trade discussions, they are more likely to invest in collaborative efforts with partners like ASEAN countries. This engagement leads to mutually beneficial innovations that blend cultural insight with strategic business approaches.

While the potential is substantial, success would depend on sustained dialogue and equitable partnerships, not just goodwill. If done effectively, this collaboration highlights Black American businesses as key contributors to inclusive economic growth. I believe that alliances rooted in clarity and trust unlock new possibilities by amplifying local ingenuity. For me, this isn't just about efficiency. It's about fostering communication that is both inclusive and precise, thereby creating opportunities for meaningful collaboration. Collaboration that involves Black America engaging with China to gain direct access to global trade draws parallels to historical narratives of persistence, strengthening our collective voice.

At the same time, I recognize that global influence and success in international trade are aspirational goals that demand sustained effort, systemic support, and broader alliances. That's why we need to revolutionize a more sustainable future for the Black American community in America. And that starts with establishing a cultural and trade organization outside America in countries like China, where access to a diverse global market is more practical.

Conclusion

Over the past two decades, my journey from a curious student to an entrepreneur and cultural bridge-builder in China has been nothing short of transformative. I arrived in Shanghai in 2002, awestruck and filled with questions, and immediately felt the vibrant pulse of this city caught in a whirlwind of transformation. The towering cranes and neon lights painted a picture of relentless growth, yet I couldn't help but wonder. Where were the voices of Black America in this narrative? This realization ignited a fire within me, sparking a determination to carve out a space for Black Americans in China's dynamic economy and cultural landscape.

Living in China has taught me that borders are not just lines on a map but also the boundaries of perception and understanding. For too long, Black Americans have been consumers rather than collaborators in global trade. This book is my response to that dissonance, and a call to action for Black America to reclaim its seat at the global commerce table, starting with China.

China's rapid economic rise and technological advancements present unparalleled opportunities for Black entrepreneurs. From its manufacturing prowess to its vast consumer market, China offers fertile ground for innovation and collaboration. Yet, these opportunities are not without challenges. Navigating the complexities of Chinese business culture, language barriers, and systemic biases requires resilience, adaptability, and a deep understanding of both worlds.

My experiences in China have taught me that building bridges between Black America and China is not just about profit margins or market share. It is about creating a legacy by ensuring that future generations of Black Americans can not only navigate the global economy but also shape it. This journey demands audacity, education, and a willingness to rewrite the rules of engagement. It requires recognizing that our liberation is bound to the liberation of others and that our collective strength lies in our interconnectedness.

Guangzhou's (Guǎngzhōu) factories, Yiwu's (Yìwū) markets, and Shenzhen's tech hubs have become battlegrounds for my dreams and challenges. In these spaces, I have witnessed the power of collaboration and its transformative potential. I have learned that in China, business is not just about transactions but about relationships, trust, and mutual respect. By immersing myself in Mandarin classes, negotiating with vendors, and navigating the intricacies of guanxi, I have come to understand that success in China demands patience and cultural fluency.

The story of Black American entrepreneurs in China is one of perseverance and ingenuity. It is a story of individuals like me who have dared to step into the unknown, armed with little more than hope and determination. It is a story of businesses that have overcome insurmountable odds to establish a foothold in one of the world's most dynamic economies. And it is a narrative that is far from over.

As I reflect on my journey, I am reminded of the words of the late John Lewis. "The only way to bring about change is to get in the way." This book is my way of getting around the systemic barriers that have long marginalized Black Americans in global trade. I attempt to disrupt the narrative and to embody the change I wish to see.

The road ahead is uncertain, but I remain steadfast in my belief that Black America's future is intertwined with China's. By leveraging China's manufacturing might and global influence, Black American entrepreneurs can create products and services that not only meet the needs of their communities but also resonate across cultures. By sharing our stories and cultural heritage, we can build bridges of understanding and forge alliances rooted in mutual respect.

I envision a future where Black American businesses are not just participants but leaders in the international marketplace. A future where our voices are heard, our stories are told, and our contributions are recognized. This future is not a distant dream but a tangible reality. It can be achieved through strategic collaboration, relentless innovation, and an unwavering commitment to equity.

As I continue this journey, I carry with me the lessons of the past and the hopes of the future. I am reminded that progress is not made by those who wait for change but by those who dare to create it. And I am confident that together, we can build a more inclusive and equitable world. One where the narrative of Black America is not just a footnote but a vibrant chapter in the story of global commerce.

With gratitude and determination,

William D. Frazier

AUTHOR'S BIOGRAPHY

For over 25 years, William D. Frazier has been the trusted advisor companies turn to when navigating China's most complex trade deals and regulatory challenges. As a key figure behind Shanghai-America Direct Import & Export Co. Ltd (Shànghǎi Xiàngměifēi Jìnchūkǒu Yǒuxiàngōngsī), he has managed supply chains with tens of thousands of SKUs and built a trade portfolio worth over millions of dollars, turning regulatory complexity into a competitive advantage.

Yet, William's identity is far more layered than that of a business consultant. His academic roots in Urban Planning at Tongji University provided a deep theoretical understanding of China's development, which he applied practically in the boardroom and on the factory floor. He is a sought-after keynote speaker, a published author, and has been featured in documentaries chronicling China's transformation.

His life in Shanghai is a testament to complete cultural immersion. He has acted as a government minister in the Chinese TV series "Welcome to Meili Village" (Huānyíng láidào Màilè Cūn), co-curated art exhibitions, and co-organized the city's inaugural Juneteenth celebrations. An avid salsa dancer and American football sports official in China, his personal journey is as dynamic as his professional one.

William's memoir is the compelling, behind-the-scenes account of an entrepreneur who didn't just do business in China. He built a life there. It's a story of resilience, commerce, and liberation, offering readers an invaluable guide and an inspiring portrait of what's possible at the intersection of two superpowers.

www.ingramcontent.com/pod-product-compliance
Lightning Source LLC
Chambersburg PA
CBHW061744070526
44585CB00025B/2799